ISLAM BELIEFS AND OBSERVANCES

by Caesar E. Farah, Ph.D.

UNIVERSITY OF MINNESOTA

BARRON'S Educational Series, Inc.

Woodbury, New York • London • Toronto • Sydney

All inquiries should be addressed to:
Barron's Educational Series, Inc.
113 Crossways Park Drive
Woodbury, New York 11797

Library of Congress Catalog Card No. 72-135505

Printed in the United States of America

345 510 16 15 14 13 12 11

TO MY PARENTS

"Say (O Muslims): We believe in Allah
and that which is revealed unto us and that
which was revealed unto Abraham,
and Ishmael, and Isaac, and Jacob,
and the tribes, and that which Moses
and Jesus received, and that which
the Prophets received from their Lord.
We make no distinction between any of them,
and unto Him we have surrendered."

QUR'ĀN 2:136

Preface

IN THE INTEREST of making the precepts and motivation in the religion of Islam better appreciated by a larger segment of the reading public this presentation has been limited specifically to the religious aspect of Islam. The socio-political and cultural aspects have been treated only to the extent that they materially influenced the fundamentals and observances of the faith.

It is the author's wish that the reader will acquire a more accurate perspective of what Islam stands for today as a mainspring of human action for hundreds of millions in a large segment of the world. To help him towards that end, a conscious attempt has been made to simplify as much as is reasonable the most important ingredients of the Islamic religion and to show the range of their impact on the lives of its adherents.

In citing translations of the Qur'ānic verses used herein, I have depended very frequently on the versions of authors whose rendition has been deemed expressive not only of the word but also of the spirit of the Arabic original. M. M. Pickthall's THE MEANING OF THE GLORIOUS KORAN is most useful in this regard.

Transliterations from the Arabic follow the linguistically preferred method with slight modifications introduced where called for. A full listing of the terms used in the body of the text can be found in the Glossary with explanations oriented towards the context wherein they were cited. The list of recommended reading is designed to help the reader pursue his study of Islam in still broader detail than afforded in the presentation herein made.

I should like to express my appreciation to my wife for her encouragement, assistance, and forbearance.

Bloomington, Indiana Caesar E. Farah

Table of Contents

—— Medieval Land Trade Routes	Sunnites Majority
------ Medieval Sea Trade Routes	Sunnites Important Minority
△ Islamic Universities	• Sunnites Scattered Minorities
☐ Holy Places of Islam	Shiites Majority
+ Holy Places of Shiites	
○ Principal Medieval Trade Centers	

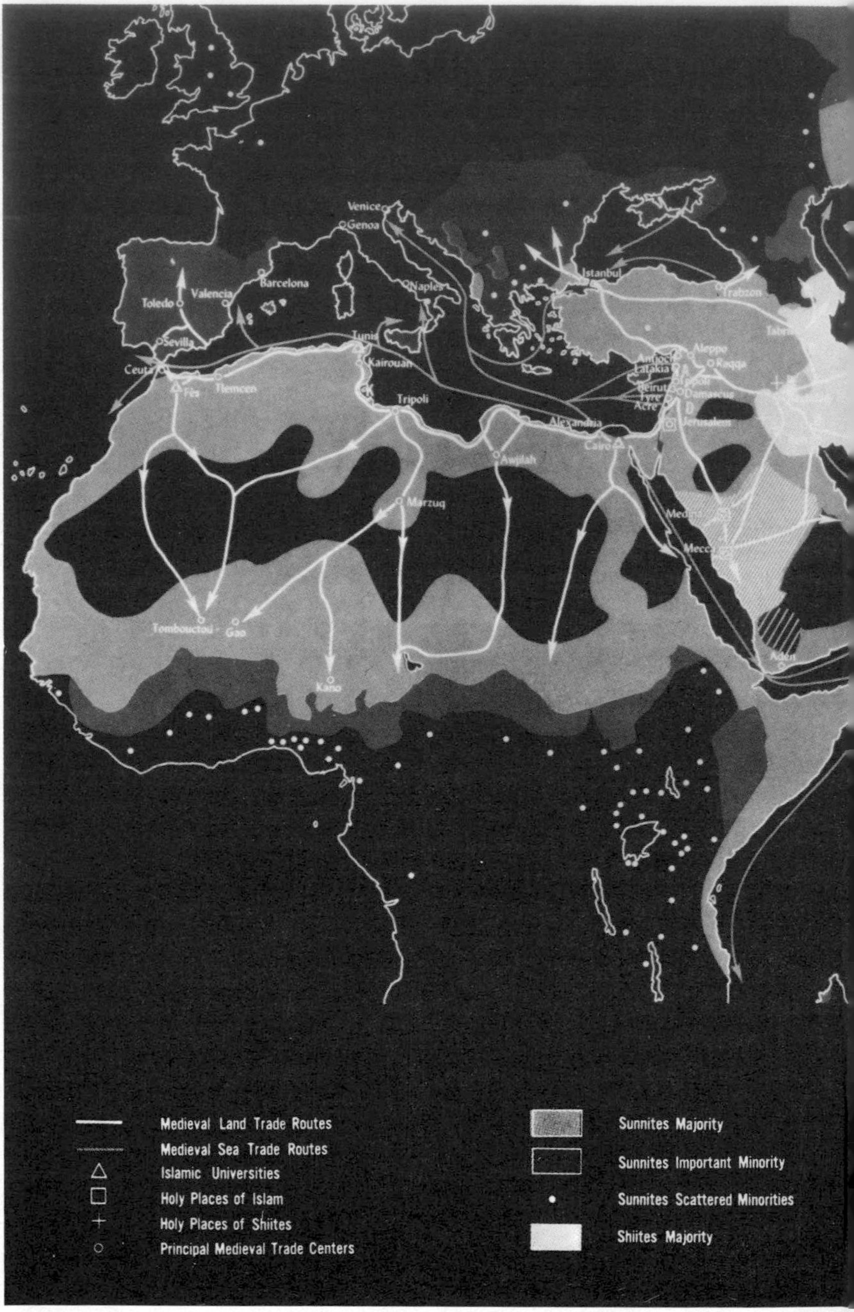

Venice
Genoa
Barcelona
Naples
Istanbul
Trabzon
Toledo Valencia
Sevilla
Tunis
Ceuta
Fès Tlemcen
Kairouan
Aleppo
Tabriz
Antioch
Latakia
Tripoli
Beirut
Tyre
Acre
Jerusalem
Tripoli
Alexandria
Cairo
Awjlah
Medina
Marzuq
Mecca
Tombouctou Gao
Kano

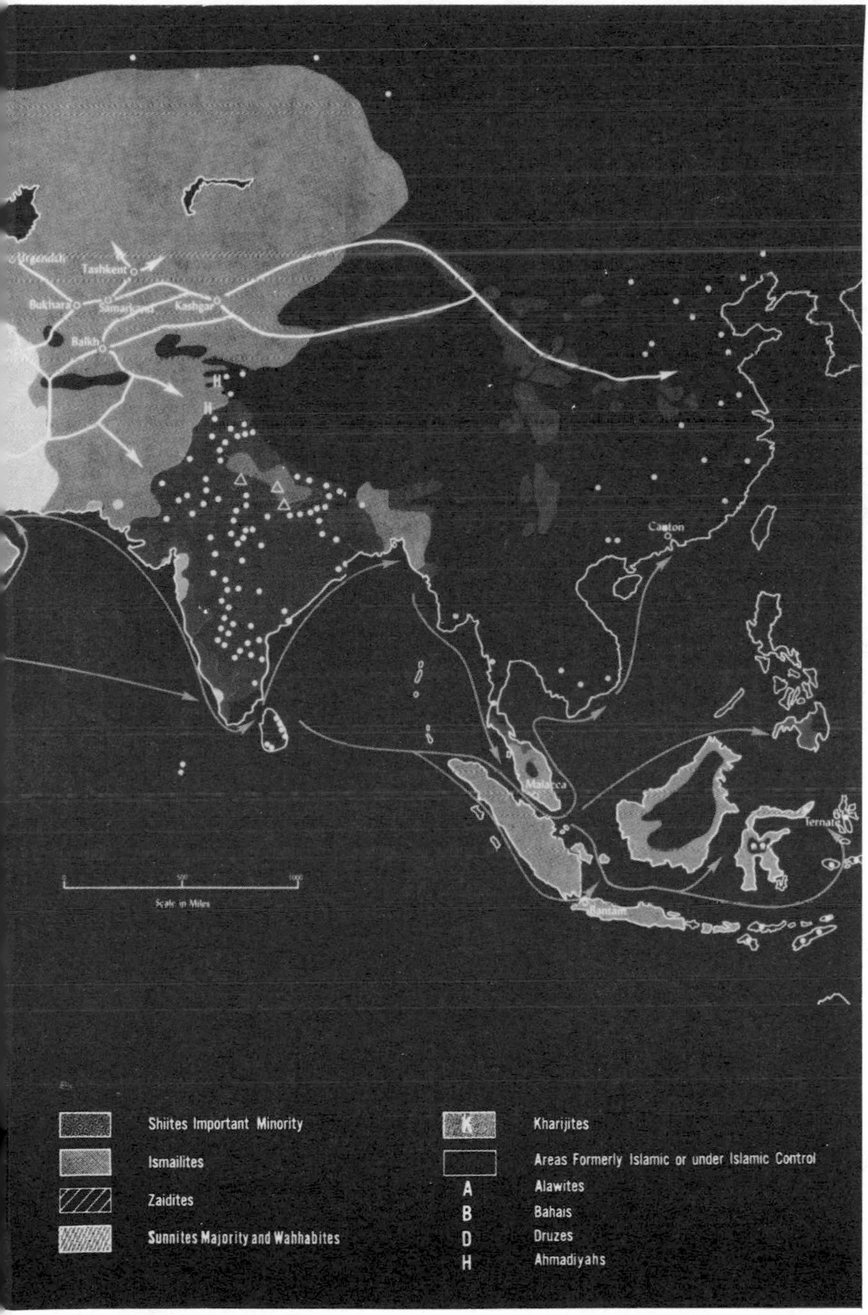
Tashkent
Bukhara
Samarkand
Kashgar
Balkh
Canton
Malacca
Ternate
Bantam
Scale in Miles
Shiites Important Minority
Ismailites
Zaidites
Sunnites Majority and Wahhabites
K
Kharijites
Areas Formerly Islamic or under Islamic Control
A
Alawites
B
Bahais
D
Druzes
H
Ahmadiyahs

CHAPTER 1

An Introduction to Islam

WHEN WE SPEAK of Islam we are concerned not only with a religion akin to the other monotheistic religions, Judaism and Christianity, but with a way of life, a system that encompasses the relationships of the adherents to each other and to their society from birth until death.

The religion of Islam provides a strong bond that brings together Muslims regardless of race or nationality in a fellowship constructed upon faith in the one God. When considered in this context, Islam has much in common with both Christianity and Judaism. To the extent, however, that Islam stresses communal solidarity, as measured in terms of successes encountered in this area, it has more in common with Judaism than with Christianity.

In the thirteen and a half centuries of its existence, Islam the religion fostered the growth of a political commonwealth and of a distinct culture. At one time it commanded the allegiance and following of diverse peoples incorporated into a vast fraternity which stretched from the Pyrenees in Western Europe to the Philippines in the Western Pacific. Within such wide territorial reaches Muslims, formerly of varying creeds and cultural backgrounds, forged a common culture drawing on the precepts of their religion and expressing itself through the medium of the

Arabic language. Muslims evolved basic philosophical and religious concepts that shaped the fundamentals of Islam and added luster and richness to their way of life. Unrestrained by dogmatism, Muslims readily engaged themselves in the pursuits of philosophy, literature, science, mathematics, and astronomy, converting their chief cities from Spain to Central Asia into the foci of a brilliant civilization when Europe for the most part was experiencing a period of cultural arrestation.

Hence in projecting our study of Islam we can not achieve a meaningful understanding of the religion without giving some consideration to its institutional and cultural facets. All three aspects of Islam shaped what may be termed "the system of Islam" and assured the triumph and efflorescence of the faith. The study also requires relating the forces which for centuries had a molding effect on the religion as it evolved from a simple set of elementary beliefs to an all-encompassing complex framework of theological reference. It is equally necessary for us to draw attention to powerful forces of attraction which enabled Islamic society to cohere and withstand disruption under strong pressure. Pride in belonging to a unifying faith coupled with the spirit engendered thereby contributed to the social solidarity and cultural development of the believers in Islam.

But this commonly shared pride did not always succeed in safeguarding the socio-religious solidarity of the Muslims. Such breaches as disrupted the cohesiveness of Islam will be given due consideration as we follow the fluctuations in its historical career through alternating phases of accomplishment and decline.

For a number of centuries the Muslim East and the Christian West confronted each other across the length and breadth of the Mediterranean basin. Sometimes their relations were characterized by peaceful and fruitful exchanges; quite often both sides viewed each other with antipathy and indifference punctured by frequent conflicts. Generally, neither the Muslim nor the Christian world appeared to be aware of the fundamental religious precepts they shared in common, derived as they were from the common fount of Judaic and Hellenic beliefs. Not many Christians today, for instance, are aware of the fact that Muḥammad, the messenger of

Islam, believed Jesus and Moses to be the most important bearers of God's one hallowed message to His people as enshrined in the Testaments and the Torah. Indeed, to millions of Christians for hundreds of years Muḥammad was an object of contempt; certainly in no way did he command the respect which his followers accorded Jesus, whose position of deference in the holy book of Islam is permanently assured.

Until recent scholarship began to strip Islam of the prejudicial views surrounding it, the Western world, at the very best, had contented itself with a distorted understanding of one of mankind's significant living religions. Geographical proximity and frequent exchanges notwithstanding, the Christian accused the Muslim of worshiping a "false prophet." To the follower of Christ the follower of Muḥammad was a blasphemer who would not figure in God's great design, or in the salvation reserved for the faithful believers in Jesus. Indeed, in the eyes of the Christians Islam was synonymous with "Mohammedanism," with its false implication of being a system of belief founded upon the worship of the person "Mohammed" (Muḥammad). Yet nothing is more repugnant to the devout Muslim than to be called a "Mohammedan"; from the point of view of his religion, to accord devotional respect to any being other than Allah, God of the Worlds, of Christians and Jews, is to commit the major unpardonable sin.

The term *Islam* in the lexicon of the Arabs means "Submission" to God. The religion of Islam is the religion of submission to the will of the omnipotent and omniscient Creator, the only God, who admits of no associates in the worship of Him. In the eyes of the believers, Muḥammad, like Abraham, Moses, and Jesus, is a prophet of God. But unlike the Christian conception of Jesus, Muḥammad is not regarded as divine; to the believers in him he is a mortal who was called upon by God to deliver His eternal message to the unbelieving Arabs, as Moses had delivered it to the Hebrews and Jesus to the rest of mankind.

Muḥammad lived, preached, and died in the full light of history. Countless millions since the time of his death in 632 have paid homage to him as they journey far and wide to reach his burial place in Medina.

Distortions prejudicing the Western conceptions of Islam may be dated to the earliest centuries, but particularly from the period of the Crusades, when Christian Europe's hostility for the people and their religion crystallized. The church fathers treated Islam as a heresy; Muslims were infidels; Muḥammad a "renegade bishop," an "impostor," who rebelled against the central mission of Christ. Dante ranked the prophet of Islam low among the ill-fated occupants of the Inferno. Christian authors in subsequent times held him in no better regard. In his *Vie de Mahomet* (Life of Muḥammad), published at the end of the seventeenth century, the French writer Prideaux held Muḥammad up as a mirror to "unbelievers, atheists, deists and libertines." To the irreligiously inclined Voltaire, the prophet of Deism, Muḥammad was the fount of fanaticism. The more generous Abbé Maracci regarded Islam as a distorted extension of Christianity while he begrudgingly conceded in his Latin translation of the Qur'ān (Koran), the sacred book of Islam, that "this religion contains many elements of natural truth evidently borrowed from the Christian religion, which seems to be in accordance with the law and light of nature." [1]

Early attempts to place Islam and its messenger in a more objective framework of reference were few and far between. Late in the eighteenth century, a Dutch professor of theology at the University of Utrecht came to the conclusion that "no religion has been more calumniated than Islam." The noted English scholar George Sale spent long arduous hours translating the Qur'ān into English, seeking to obtain a deeper insight into the real meaning of the message of Islam. In the preliminary discourse he brought out the point that "there is no false doctrine that does not contain some truth."

With such scholars paving the way, systematic attempts aimed at casting light upon the falsities surrounding the Christian view of Islam were in full evidence by the 1830's. Henceforth scholars, mostly German Orientalists, began to examine Islam from a detached point of view shorn of preconceived notions and assumptions.

That these scholars were inclined to view Islam in a more favorable light is evident in the testimony of Professor Weil: "In so far as he brought the most beautiful teachings of the Old and New Testament to a people which was not illuminated by one ray of faith, he may be regarded, even by those who are not Mohammedans, as a messenger of God." [2] Other reputable Orientalists—de Perçeval, Lammens, Caetani, Muir, Nöldeke—pioneered works on Muḥammad and Islam that have since their time become classical for their authoritativeness. It was largely through their efforts that we witness the gradual lifting of the veil of tendentious fiction and emotional bias that had blurred the European's vision of Islam. This trend towards an objective understanding of Islam in its multiple facets has persisted, both in Europe and the United States, up to the present time.

Major breakthroughs in the area of communications have drawn the peoples of the world into closer contacts. There is more interest, and a greater awareness, in the cultural values and institutional beliefs of non-Westerners. To be sure a great deal of this interest derives from a superficial observation, largely through sightseeing tours of the exotic cities of Islam—Cairo, Tangier, Baghdad, Damascus, Istanbul; but a lot of it is engendered also by need. The oil of Arabia is as alluring to the Western companies that exploit and market it as the bazaars of Cairo to the American tourist. The entire history of the post-World War II era is replete with incidents that have focused attention on the strategic importance of the Muslim world, particularly in the East-West struggle. Scholars, technicians, diplomats, and the average citizens of the Western world, all from their varying points of interest, have demonstrated the need for a more positive understanding of the vital significance of the Islamic world, its peoples, institutions, and beliefs.

As curiosity arouses interest and interest leads to inquiry, and as the scholar begins to examine more closely the whole posture of Islam in its historical and environmental contexts, the Western reader begins to appreciate the reasons for a systematic study of Islam.

In the first place there are over five hundred million people today who adhere to the religion of Islam. Not only do they represent all the known races of mankind, but they inhabit a nearly contiguous stretch of land from the shores of the Atlantic in the West to the confines of China and Malaysia in the East. Geographically, the followers of Muḥammad are concentrated in North Africa, the regions of the Near and Middle East, Soviet Central Asia, western China, the Malayan peninsula, northern and central India, Indonesia, and the Philippines. In more recent decades the Muslims have gained a wide following south of the Sahara in the very heart of Negro Africa. One out of every seven human beings today subscribes to the faith of Islam; he lives within a social structure largely the product of Islam, and he is guided in his daily life by norms and precepts forged in the caldron of Islam.

Secondly, the role of Islam in regulating the affairs of the believer can not be overlooked. On an average the Muslim invokes the name of Allah (God) no less than twenty times a day. No other known prophet of a monotheistic religion receives as much mention in prayer as the Prophet of Islam. More children bear Muḥammad's name than any other name popular to mankind. No known body of sacred literature is as thoroughly and systematically committed to memory, or is recited as frequently, as the holy book of Islam. At certain prescribed times of the day from atop a minaret in the towns, hamlets, and cities of Islam, the voice of the muezzin rings out in clear melodious Arabic the call to prayer. Spontaneously, devotees everywhere turn in the direction of Mecca, birthplace of Islam and its perpetual shrine, to perform the ritual prayer as established in the days of Muḥammad. If by some magical flight an outsider could transplant himself into the midst of the faithful during the noon-hour prayer on the day of congregation in any given mosque, he would behold lines upon lines of Muslims representing the major races of mankind performing in unison, and according to prescribed form, the same prostrations and genuflections and uttering the same prayer to Allah, in Arabic, regardless of their native tongues.

Thirdly, it would be difficult to observe a more thorough manifestation of devotion to God than is evinced by the followers of Islam. No other religion appears to inculcate as much dependence on God in the trivia of daily life; nor does God figure so centrally among other religious groups in the ups and downs of ordinary living. Indeed, no task, commitment, performance, journey, or repose, however minute or momentous, pleasurable or unpleasurable, is undertaken without the involvement of Allah. No blessing or bounty of any sort is received except through the grace of Allah. Misfortunes are endured with passivity and resignation, but faith in Allah remains unwavering as it is His sole prerogative to bestow or withhold as He sees fit. From early dawn until sunset in the month of fasting which according to the lunar calendar observed can be unusually lengthy—the devotee consumes no food or drink and indulges in no carnal acts which may constitute ritual defilement of the body.

When thousands of pilgrims continuously stream to Arabia on the annual pilgrimage, they observe for themselves the strong bonds at work in gathering them together from all parts of the world. These are the bonds of Islam, equating all Muslims regardless of race or nationality, economic or social status. As a symbol of their equality in Islam, the believers shed the attire of daily life for a plain white linen cloth worn by all preparatory to entering the sanctuary of Islam in a state of ritual purity. This manifestation of egalitarianism can be attributed to the sense of unity in faith for which the religion of Islam is directly responsible. The leveling force of Islam has not ceased to attract to the faith the downtrodden of humanity with the same power of appeal that gained it the loyalty of Arabians and non-Arabians in earlier centuries. Through conversion abetted by the expansion of the polity, Islam grew steadily in stature until it came to enjoy the rank of a major world religion that still attracts converts to its fold.

Unity in belief accounts for the unusual display of solidarity in Islamic society and for the dynamism which propelled the faith forward. Pride in faith explains the accomplishments of the believers not only in religion, but in the areas of political and cultural endeavors as well. The historical development of Islam in all of its facets reflects its power of appeal; this appeal has been decisive in winning over to the religion the inhabitants of Africa in the face of strong competition from Christianity.

The growth from modest and obscure beginnings in an unheralded corner of Arabia to the status of a great world empire is the historical testimony to the zeal with which Islam infused its believers. This growth was occasioned less by a conscious effort to spread the faith than by the exemplary conduct of the conquerors as manifested in their personal lives. Military conquest, to be sure, created the polity, but the society molded by the polity was buttressed by values imparted to it by the Islamic faith. The bonds which caused Islamic society to cohere reposed in the tenets of the faith. These in turn nurtured the forces that made for the unity of Arab, Persian, Turk, Indian, Berber, and Spaniard on the basis of adherence to a common religion, not nationality.

Molded into a coherent community by the tenets of Islam, Muslim society succeeded in weathering the political disintegration of the polity when localized dynasties inherited the great Islamic empires. Although Islam the religion and Islam the polity have not been coterminous since the first Muslim century, it is noteworthy to remark that with the exception of the Iberian peninsula, Islam the religion has remained firmly implanted in the soil that once gave it political sanctity.

The triumph of the principle of nationality and the concomitant growth of nationalism in certain parts of the Muslim world resulted in the supplanting of the theocracy by political entities presently enjoying the ramifications of sovereign rule. Among them may be listed such national states as Turkey, Iran, Pakistan, Indonesia, Syria, Iraq, the United Arab Republic, the Kingdom of Jordan, Saudi Arabia, Libya, Sudan, Tunisia, Algeria, Morocco, and a number of independent states and sheikhdoms on the periphery of the Arabian peninsula. In addition, there are autonomous Muslim republics in the Union of Soviet Socialist Republics and strong enclaves of Muslims in China, Burma, Malaya, India, the Philippines—not to mention such African states as Nigeria, Tanzanya, Somalia, Chad, etc.

One discerns lately in the Muslim world increasing victories for secularism achieved at the expense of Islamic solidarity. Secularism to be sure has imposed a rival claim for the allegiance of Muslims. But the ties based on religion, which continue to transcend national boundary lines, have not been seriously impaired. Indeed, the Western observer becomes aware of a pattern of challenge and response within the fragmented polity of Islam that is strikingly Muslim. Unifying institutions, such as those centered on mosque or bazaar, persist in Islamic countries in spite of their ethnical heterogeneity and continue to be reflected in the practices which they still share in common.

While focusing attention on the historical forces that enhanced the religion when the polity had disappeared, one can not ignore the role of philosophical ideals attending the evolution of Islam and contributing both to orthodoxy and heterodoxy in the shaping of an Islamic identity. Cultural trends, like social trends in general, were shaped by the precepts of Islam and, in turn, played a constructive part in the career of Islam as a civilizing force. When Christian Europe was experiencing its "Dark Ages," the cities of Islam in Spain, North Africa, and the East were alive with cultural creativity. Within the framework of tolerance provided by Islam, Muslim scholars in Toledo and Cordova, Cairo, Baghdad, and Damascus were feverishly adding new dimensions to our knowledge of philosophy, the sciences, mathematics, and astronomy. In the arts and crafts, in commerce, agriculture, and navigation innovations introduced by Muslims had a lasting effect in the shaping of our Western traditions; traces of such contributions prevail in numerous technical terms derived from the Arabic and surviving in Western languages. While these specific aspects of Islam's growth fall outside the purview of this work, to the extent that they contributed to the image of Islam they become germane to our understanding of this religion.

Scholarship and learning in general went on relatively unhampered by dogmatism or religious injunctions. The fact that Islam boasts of no organized clergy similarly made the task of adaptation to modern life relatively easy. Indeed, the absence of such an institution is one of the unique features of Islam, which only serves to bring out the remarkable capacity of Islamic society to cohere. Coherence was achieved not by the guiding hand of a clerical institution, but by the volition of the adherents, resulting from reasoned individual and communal interests.

The institution of the caliphate was designed originally to rally the believers and centralize their loyalties; but the caliph by the exercise of his will or the force of his personality alone did not always succeed in maintaining the political solidarity of Islam. In the last analysis the solidarity engendered by Islam stems not from a rallying institution or figure, but from *pride of belonging*. This does not necessarily mean that such pride of belonging was successful in preventing schismatic movements. Islam did develop its schisms, but these stemmed mostly from political differences which later became religiously oriented. The overwhelming majority of Muslims until today have remained loyal to the orthodox or Sunni sect of Islam.

According to the historical record, Islam was not able to foster a political coherence commensurate with the religious. Some scholars believe that had Islam succeeded in resolving the problem of successorship to the lay authority of the prophet in the earlier decades, political solidarity might have become more firmly established. But the trend favoring national determination in Muslim lands is not necessarily a modern phenomenon. As early as the eighth century A.D. the conquered Iranian elements resented the refusal of the conquering Arabs to accord them the full social equality ordained by Islam. The challenge to caliphal authority equated with Arab hegemony resulted frequently from such resentment. The nature of the challenge often took on the form of "ethnicism," a movement spearheaded by ethnical elements desirous of asserting their avowed cultural superiority over their Arab overlords even though the basic tenets of Islam opposed the show of preference outside the bond of religion. If from the point of view of Islamic dogma the Muslim must assert his individual identity, he would have to justify this in terms of his superior piousness, not his ethnical heritage.

But repugnant as ethnicism was to the dogmatist, in his religious and philosophical disputations the ethnicist provided an important medium for the cultural enhancement of Islam. To him accrues a good part of the credit in the "internationalization" of the religion and in making it a substantial cultural as well as a religious, social, and political force. By successfully challenging the authority of the self-styled dogmatist to control the realm of the intellect, or even to dictate to it, partisans of the non-religious sciences seized upon philosophy as a weapon of liberation. Soon there developed a rational school of thought spearheaded by Aristotelianism and epitomized by Averroës (Ibn-Rushd). Much of the contribution of Islam in the realm of ideas that inspired the Scholastic movement in late medieval Europe resulted from the disputations of the Muslim Platonists and Aristotelians, culminating in the reconciliation of reason and faith in Islam before Medieval Catholicism and Judaism were able to achieve the same end.

European interest in Islamic scholarship in the Upper Middle Ages was not restricted merely to the influence of Averroism on the Scholastic philosophers, such as Magnus, Abelard, and Aquinas. Advanced concepts in medicine as embodied in the famous *Canons* of Avicenna, in mathematics as articulated by al-Bīrūni, or astronomy as enhanced by al-Majrītī—all of whose works were translated into Latin in the twelfth century—were equally sought by budding European scholars. Frederick II Hohenstaufen surrounded himself by Muslim savants in his semi-Islamized court at Palermo. The abbots at the monastery of Cluny in France, center of the earliest reform movement in the thirteenth century, actively availed themselves of Muslim scholarship. Peter the Venerable busied himself with a translation of the Qur᾿ān into Latin late in the twelfth century. Muslim learning provided an impetus to the revivification of independent thinking in southern Europe in the Upper Middle Ages leading into the Renaissance.

Contacts of this nature in the late Middle Ages provided one of those rare periods of productive exchange between Islam and Christianity when the sword was subordinated to the pen. The courts of Toledo, Cordova, and Palermo attracted Christian scholars in the waning years of the Middle Ages with as much appeal as the riches of Syria attracted Christian warriors in the days of the Crusades. Through such intellectual contacts as were now effected, Christian scholars not only acquired an appreciation of

Muslim scholarship but also came to appreciate also the heritage of the classical age of Greece and of an Aristotle whom Muslim intellectuals regarded as their "first teacher."

But this period of fruitful exchange which contributed to the subsequent general awakening of Europe, and from which Europe became the principal beneficiary, left no immediate imprint on the world of Islam. Europe's rise to prominence—intellectually, politically, commercially, and militarily—coincided with general arrestation in Muslim lands. Indeed, with the exception of the military prowess displayed by the Ottomans in the creation of the last important Muslim empire, the Muslim world for the most part began to experience its own medieval period. During this age, which lasted approximately from the sixteenth to the nineteenth century, the torch of learning was dimmed; creativity slowed down to a trickle; the posture of the Muslim world became defensive and weakened; and wealth hitherto acquired by Muslim control of transient trade diminished when the Portuguese succeeded in diverting such trade from its sources in the farther East. Gradually the enfeebled petty dynasties of Islam either vanished or were overcome by a revitalized Europe. Finally, in the course of our present century, European powers succeeded in imposing their political hegemony—and substantially their cultural—over a much weakened and strife-torn Muslim world.

But out of defeat victory may yet emerge. Modernism in its Western context appears to have kindled in the Muslims not only a fiery resentment of the West, but also a general disposition to investigate the secret of the West's success. There is sufficient evidence to point to a general revivalism in the making, conspicuous recently not only in the political sphere but in the realm of ideas as well.

Contacts with the West in recent decades have set in motion trends that are bound to transform, if not remold, traditional Islamic values. We are on the threshold of witnessing an Islamic version of Europe's "Renaissance" and "Reformation." The Islamic world has the advantage of being able to draw on the wealth of experiences from the Renaissance to the Enlightenment relevant to the task of lifting itself into the twentieth century with the opportunity of avoiding the pitfalls into which Europe stumbled while traversing the same course.

Present religious reformist movements in Islam, while still lacking in momentum, envisage a bootstrap operation that will revitalize Islamic society and tailor the religious ideal to present-day needs. The religiously oriented reformers propose to bring this about by dipping into the reservoir of Islam's accumulated values and beliefs, many of which are valid still for Islam's posture in the modern world. The secularly oriented modernists, on the other hand, believe that they must depend considerably on the accumulated experiences and tools of the West.

The area of conflict between these groups centers on the question whether a general Islamic renaissance can be produced without jeopardizing the fundamental tenets of the religion. The streamlining of religious concepts appears to be the *sine qua non* of modernization in Islam. There are movements today concerned with ways and means to reinterpret Islam. Current efforts seek to plow through the deadweight of medieval accretions back to the puritanical ideals of the Prophet and his companions. Muslim reformers believe they can eliminate these accretions without compromising the essence of the Islamic faith. In this regard such efforts are reminiscent of the Protestants and of the task confronting them in the period of the Reformation.

As Islam girds itself for the twentieth century and prepares to adjust itself to the demands of a modern civilization heavily tinged by the material bounty of a triumphant technology, it must be equally prepared to fight off the competition of rival ideologies. Atheistic communism and secular nationalism are its principal rivals. Both movements are contending for the loyalties of Muslims in a manner which the Islamists interpret as opposed to the basic precepts of their religion. But the gains made by Islam in the face of such competition in Black Africa attest to its dynamism, even at this crucial state of its transition.

The study of Islam in those facets which explain its prominence as a religious force will provide us with an insight into the sources of its strength in its meteoric rise to the status of a major world force today. The remarkable spirit awakened by the preachings of Muḥammad provided the base of this strength and contributed to the dynamism which has not ceased to manifest itself even in times of misfortunes. Such resilience as Islam was able to muster in the face of adverse experiences enabled the religion to gain followers while lacking the external power to withstand the political encroachment of the West. It is probable that the vitality which at one time permeated all levels of Islamic society will still enable Muslims to maintain a religious solidarity notwithstanding the assaults of a powerful secular nationalism that strives to submerge the Muslim's identity in an ocean of national distinctiveness. But be he a Nigerian or a Pakistani, an Egyptian or an Iranian, his historical heritage still favors pride of identity inside the pale of Islam over pride of adherence to nationality. This becomes increasingly evident when the Muslim's loyalty is put to the test.

The secret of Islam's powerful appeal lies in the fact that it is not only a religion regulating the spiritual side of the believer, but also an all-embracing *way of life* governing the totality of the Muslim's being. For this reason no study of Islam can be complete without a commensurate study of the non-religious forces unleashed by it; these, however, can not be treated sufficiently in a study of this nature.

Muslims today actively working to preserve the richness of their faith can count on powerful support in the dynamism characteristic of Islam in the early stages of its evolution. The forces that enabled the religion to surmount earlier crises may serve Islam well as it passes through its own "Reformation" and prepares itself for the role it can play in the general revitalization of the Islamic world. Already in the last few decades enlightened Muslims have wrought changes in attitudes that had stubbornly refused to respond to new stimuli for nearly half a millennium. Very recently the most famous theological center of Islam, the Azhar University—once the fount of conservatism in the realm of ideas upsetting to traditional religious concepts—has begun to bestir itself into new fields of knowledge hitherto regarded as heretical. The Azhar may become the principal agent in the streamlining of the faith, and in accommodating Islam to the exigences of the modern age. Other active groups in Egypt, Turkey, and Pakistan have propounded their own solutions, each predicated on a different set of premises. The puritanical movement of Wahhābi Arabia insists that the only course open for true Muslims is to revert to a literal observance of the injunctions of the Qurʾān.

That some sort of reform will result is beyond a doubt; what is crucial for the future of Islam is the question of whether such reform as will ensue can accommodate traditional concepts and at the same time charter a course for it in an age overrun by technology.

CHAPTER 2

The Setting in Arabia

TO SOMEONE CONVERSANT with the setting in Arabia on the eve of Islam it would have been inconceivable to believe that within the short lifetime of a contemporary of Muḥammad the land should provide the stage for a revolutionary transformation of religious and social values. Considering the geography, topography, ethnical structure, cultural level of development and the religious, social, and political institutions then prevailing, one had little reason to anticipate that out of a land so characterized by sharp and conflicting contrasts there would emerge a powerful force for uniformity and unity generated by a newly ordained system of religious, social, and political concepts. It would have been difficult to envisage that the inhabitants inspired by Islam could shortly be fired by a powerful zeal that would carry them out of the confines of Arabia on a course of conquest leading to their acquiring an empire larger than anything suggested by their wildest imaginations.

The Land

The Arabian peninsula, shaped into a rectangle spanning twelve hundred by nine hundred miles at its extreme measurements and consisting of a little over one million square miles, is set off from the neighboring world by natural barriers: water on three sides—Persian Gulf, Arabian Sea, Indian Ocean, and Red Sea—and the Syrian Desert on the fourth. One can understand why its inhabitants would refer to it as "the island" (*al-Jazīrah*). No foreigner who had set foot in Arabia was able to give us a description of the land until most recent times. A study of its topography reveals why it was so uninviting to outsiders, and also why the inhabitants migrated when the opportunities presented themselves.

The land consists mainly of barren volcanic steppes interspersed by nearly impenetrable sandy wastes—al-Rubᶜ al-Khāli (the empty quarter) in the south and al-Nufūd in the north—with hardly any surface water except for a few rivulets on the western coast which run dry most of the year, a limited number of underground pools which sustain the few oases on the plateau of Najd, and a brief rainy season which benefits mostly the Yaman (Yemen) highlands in the southwest and the Tihāmah plain along the Red Sea littoral. Because of such topographical handicaps, Arabia during most of its history was unable to sustain a population commensurate with its size.

The sharp divisions and contrasts in its topographical features are no less evident in Arabia's inhabitants. A certain dichotomy characterizes not only the racial structure of the people but their modes of existence as well. The predominant racial strain is Caucasian. Arabians subscribe either to the Alpine substratum—prevalent in the south and extreme north—or to the Mediterranean—mostly in the central and northern parts of the peninsula. Geographical barriers and topographical contrasts have contributed to the confinement of the population to less than ten million in a land nearly a third of the size of the United States.

The People

Contrasts of this nature also account for the sharp division of Arabs into settled and nomadic groups. The division is echoed in their inherited traditions which attribute their descent to "Yamani" (southern) or "Qaysi" (northern) origins. According to Biblical and Qur'ānic testimony, the Arabs are descendants of Shem, oldest son of Noah, hence the appellation "Semite." This kind of kinship can apply only to a commonly shared linguistic and cultural heritage, as anthropologically there is no racial unity among them.

Distinguishing characteristics are evident also in the language: the southerners spoke a dialect partly surviving today in the Ethiopic, the result of early South Arabian colonization of Ethiopia, while the northerners spoke Arabic, the language of Muḥammad and the Qur'ān and the prototype of the Arabic spoken today by nearly one hundred million people. The watered depressions of the Yaman and the Tihāmah encouraged the development of agricultural settlements which nurtured the rise of the early civilizations, while the bleak plateaus and steppes in west-central and northern Arabia favored a preponderantly nomadic existence and provided no incentive for the rise of civilizations before Islam.

The impact of climatological and topographical limitations on the type of life led by the Arabian and on the historical evolution of his traditional values is not to be underestimated. Indeed, no real appreciation of the full range of the transformation wrought by Islam can develop without knowledge of the traditions and values of pre-Islamic Arabia. Where a settled mode of life was permitted, in the southwest corner of the peninsula—the *Arabia Felix* ("Happy Arabia") of the ancients—there evolved the earliest civilizations associated with the land: the Minaean, Sabaean, and Ḥimyarite. From the second millennium B.C. until the beginnings of the Islamic era in the seventh century A.D. these civilizations thrived mainly on agriculture and trade. The theocratic-aristocratic concept of government which the Arabians evolved established a tradition with which early Islam did not break.

Another tradition, that of emigration, is also deeply rooted in the history of Arabia. In periods of drought or when the delicate irrigational system broke down—as it did following the fatal breach of the great dam at Maʿrib around 450 A.D.—

large segments of the inhabitants tended to revert to nomadism and to strike out northward into the fertile valleys of Mesopotamia and the Syrian littoral in search of new means of subsistence. From the third millennium B.C. onward, and at nearly five-hundred year intervals, mass emigrations from Arabia accounted for the rise of the earliest civilizations in Syria and Mesopotamia: Amorite, Akkadian, Canaanite, Phoenician, Aramaean, Hebrew, Nabataean, Ghassānid, and last, but not least, the Muslim Arab, which has survived until the present time.

The deep-seated cleavage between the northern and southern Arab was carried over into Islam and tended to distract from the unity of the believers in times of acute crises. The appellation *Arab* is traditionally said to derive from the little town of Araba in the southeast district of the Tihāmah where, according to legend, settled Yaʿrab the son of Biblical Joktan—the eponymous father of the original Arabs—thus imparting his name to the locality and, by extension, to the entire peninsula and its inhabitants. More appropriately, the term *Arab* derives from the Semitic word root referring to "nomad." But as the tribes multiplied and wandered far and wide over the steppes and sandy wastes of the land, they chose to believe that they were descendants either of Qaḥṭān (Joktan) or ʿAdnān from a common ancestor: Ismāʿīl (Ishmael) son of Abraham and Hagar. The Qaḥṭānis, also known as "Yamanis," regard themselves as the pure Arabs and look upon the ʿAdnānis or Qaysis as foreigners domiciled in the land or accepted by the indigenous Arabs. With the Qaḥṭānis we associate the rise of the earliest known civilizations in Arabia. But it is largely with the ʿAdnānis that Islam triumphed. Such cleavages were not eradicated totally with the later claim of Islam on the loyalties of both.

Tradition

Another important factor which contributed to the outlook of the pre-Muslim and later Muslim Arab is the role into which he was cast either as an intermediary or as a pawn in the life and death struggle of clashing imperial interests. From earliest times Arabia occupied a medieval position geographically between the great ancient centers of civilization in the Mesopotamian, Nile, and Indus valleys, the western Indian littoral, and the Ethiopian highlands. This strategic position encouraged its southwest inhabitants to build thriving civilizations as middlemen in the transit of trade, particularly when some of the best utilized trade routes of ancient times were those which traversed the peninsula along the west coast from south to north terminating on the Mediterranean, or in the lower Nile and Mesopotamian valleys. But the land on the whole did not rise to pivotal importance because of its natural limitations and divided peoples. Only with Islam did the peninsula become united in faith and hence able to strike out on an imperial course of its own.

In the period immediately preceding the birth of Islam, tribal states north of the peninsula were drawn into the struggle between the Sasānid and Byzantine empires. The Ghassānids, protégés of Byzantium, had left south Arabia following the collapse of the Maʿrib dam and settled in the Ḥawrān region in southern Syria. Their rivals, the Lakhmids, protégés of Persia, settled in lower Iraq around al-Ḥīrah. Both were active in trade, and they developed prosperous societies in which Hellenic and Persian influences were pronounced. But their primary utility to their Byzantine and Persian overlords was as buffers against their marauding kinsmen from the peninsula. Shortly before the emergence of Islam, the rulers of these buffer states had become discontented with the growing intolerance of their Perso-Byzantine masters, particularly when these overlords cut off the subsidies which their protégés had been receiving from them. Harsh suppressive measures undertaken against them drove the Ghassānids and Lakhmids into the arms of their surging Arabian kinsmen who under the banner of Islam afforded them the opportunity to avenge themselves by participating in the destruction of both empires.

The south Arabians were no less prone to being drawn into the Perso-Byzantine rivalry. Prodded by Byzantium, Christian Abyssinia waged war on the Ḥimyarite state which was suspected of having close ties with rival Sasānid Persia. When the last Ḥimyarite ruler, dhu-Nuwās (d. 525), began to persecute the Christians of neighboring Najrān and to compel his subjects to convert to Judaism, in a "plague-on-both your houses" attitude, Abrahah, the Abyssinian general, crossed the Red Sea with his armies, overran the Ḥimyarite kingdom, then struck out northward to attack the Persians in their own sanctuary. But he was able to reach only the outskirts of Mecca because, according to the testimony of the Qur'ān, his army was overcome by a pestilence which decimated its ranks. Abrahah withdrew, but his son held on to the land until 570 when the Persians reduced it to a satrapy—only a few months before the birth of Muḥammad, whose followers soon regained the south and consolidated the whole Arabian peninsula under Islam.

Trade

Another tradition of important consequence to the birth and shaping of Islam is trade. South Arabians from earliest times engaged in trade. Bedouin tribes served as carriers and middlemen, as did the northerners who built their efflorescent principalities at Petra, the rock-hewn city in southern Jordan, and Palmyra in northern Syria whose Zenobia was hailed as "Queen of the East" until the Romans carried her off in golden chains to Rome in 273. Another key town astride the important artery of trade was Mecca in the Ḥijāz in west central Arabia. Here around 400 an impoverished segment of the Kinānah which had been associated with the Kinda, the only confederation of tribes known to have existed in Arabia before Islam, renounced its nomadism and settled down in one of the bleakest of surroundings where agriculture was impossible. Since trading was about the only means of survival available to them, these once scattered migrating kingroups found common ties as middlemen. Henceforth they are known to history as the "Quraysh." [1]

Muḥammad was a member of an important family of the Quraysh. The extent of their dependence on trade and the fear of being deprived of the special advantages they enjoyed as middlemen and entrepreneurs is reflected in their violent opposition to the preachings of Muḥammad against an order that gained them power and prosperity. Yet in their rise to economic, political, and social prominence, the Quraysh unwittingly paved the way for Islam.

At first the Quraysh merely traded with transient caravans; next they entered the main markets of neighboring settlements and soon gained control over them. Through a series of shrewd maneuvers, the Quraysh extended their trade connections from Syria to Abyssinia and became the dominant force in the commerce of western Arabia. Mecca, their home base, rose with them to pivotal importance in the economy of the entire peninsula. To finance such vast trade investments, Qurayshites of all walks of life—men, women, clients, and associates—reached into their private purses and extended credit in return for a commensurate share of the profits. Khadījah, the first wife of Muḥammad, was a prosperous trader; it was as a dependable leader of her caravans north into Syria that Muḥammad caught her fancy.

Values

Even more than the traditions, the values of nomadic Arabia left an undeniable impact on Islam; indeed, it may be shown that the values shaped the core of Islamic tenets and supplied the believers with a good many of their mainsprings of action, if not their dynamism. Mobility, the struggle for survival, a rugged individualism, a strong sense of loyalty to family and tribe, hospitality, simple concepts of religion, and aggressiveness are among the principal traits which the nomadic Arab carried over into Islam with him.

The need for mobility, dictated by a constant search for the means of livelihood, accounts basically for the Arab's nomadic existence. Roaming the broad lonely steppes seeking pasture and water holes for his flocks, he was afforded at best a life of austerity. The Bedouin subsisted on a limited diet of dates, milk, and occasionally camel flesh; a tent made of camel or goat hair served as his habitat; a few easily transportable implements and weapons provided for his needs; and his closest companions next to his kin were the camel and the horse which he made famous. He tolerated nothing that impaired his mobility because without it his survival would have been in jeopardy.

He battled both nature and man to satisfy this urge; but however much he cherished personal freedom and the ingrained individualism that accompanied it, he perceived the necessity of banding with related families and clans to form tribes, and sometimes tribal alliances, for the purpose of defense. A typical tribe consisted of the *shaykh* (chief) and his family, other free families, certain protected strangers not related by blood, and slaves. Sometimes kinship was acquired through designated rituals, particularly when noble ancestry figured prominently in determining status; this explains why the Arabs even after they were assimilated by Islam maintained a strong fondness for genealogy.

The simple institutions cultivated by the tribe, and which infused the early Islamic polity with a strong democratic spirit, were likewise decreed by mobility. The only elective office was that of the shaykh, who was chosen from the male membership of the tribe on the basis of seniority and unusual personal qualities topped by ability and wisdom—the exact criteria applied in the choice of the first four caliphs of Islam. The shaykh was invested with no executive or legislative functions and enjoyed no special privileges. His voice was heard in council, but in the settlement of disputes the daily assemblies held for that purpose heard equally the recommendations of the wise man or woman, priest, or seer. Not organized law but custom provided guidance; and in the execution of justice the aggrieved party himself served as the instrument. This practice frequently resulted in vendettas, particularly when the *dīyah* (blood money) payment was not enforceable.

The duties of the shaykh, like those of the early caliphs of Islam, outweighed his privileges. He was responsible for the care of the poor, of widows and orphans, for hospitality to strangers and wayfarers, for the payment of dīyah, and for the maintenance of order within the tribe. His supreme task was to lead the tribe into battle, a very common occurrence in pre-Islamic Arabia.

Mobility impaired the development of concrete social organization. In the absence of established political institutions and a defined legal system, blood ties substituted for law in determining the loyalty of the tribesman. With the triumph of Islam, religion served the same end. Hence the Arabian version of "patriotism" was his *ʿaṣabīyah* (clannishness). Kinship became the mark of "citizenship" for the tribe; and once this was established, a member could command the protection and support of the entire tribe. This principle, in Islam, substitutes communal responsibility towards the believer for the former tribal responsibility towards a member of the tribe. The pagan Arabian tribesman was entitled to no rights outside the bonds of the tribe any more than the Arabian Muslim could depend on any rights outside of Islam. The same applied to obligations. Such relationships of the individual to the group account for tribal solidarity, a phenomenon consecrated in Islam. Solidarity to tribal, and later Muslim, Arabia was the *sine qua non* of survival and, in time of growth, of power. The pagan Arab, like his Muslim successor, recognized that his individual fortunes were intertwined with and inseparable from the fortunes of the whole community.

As war was an important means of survival for the tribe, the *razzia,*[2] or raiding, became the instrument of economic need. Moved predominantly by the same consideration, Arabian tribes, united in Islam, struck out on a series of extended raids which netted them an empire greater than Rome's at its zenith. Although booty was a main goal of tribal raids, often the tribes warred upon each other for a variety of reasons such as to defend their honor, to carry on an established vendetta, to exact vengeance for spilled blood when dīyah was denied, or just for the sportiness of war. According to the law of the desert, blood called for blood; and often wars of revenge and counter revenge became long drawn out affairs, attested by the celebrated *Ayyām al-ʿArab.*[3] But more often than not, intertribal warfare resulted from quarrels over water holes, oases, and flocks: the necessities of economic survival. The tribes also raided the caravans of townsmen to supplement their needs, particularly when townsmen refused to purchase protection.

It is important to observe here that in the Ḥijāz on the eve of Islam the line of demarcation between tentdweller and towndweller was not clearly drawn. The nomad could just as readily lead a life of quasi-urbanity as the settled Arabian could indulge in semi-nomadism. The tendency on the whole for both sides was to achieve a *modus vivendi* because of their basic interdependence: the townsman purchased the Bedouin's milk products, meat, and wool, and the Bedouin in turn acquired in the town's market such essentials as weapons, cloth, and other finished commodities. The Islamization of Arabia reduced tribal warfare but did not compromise this basic relationship of nomad and settler.

Being a creature of the desert, the Arab naturally developed such personal qualities and habits as would comport with the exigences of his environment. He led an exacting life which called for tenacity and endurance, self-reliance and egoism; hence only the virtues which stressed manliness (*murū'ah*) could appeal to him. He acquired a rugged individualism which in turn nurtured his democratic leanings. The life of exertion to which he was subjected required no discipline. The Bedouin, consequently, never developed an instinct to obey authority. He jealously guarded his rights, but he did not shun his tribal obligations lest he become an outcast. His egotism reinforced his self-confidence and permitted him to accept a status inferior to none in the tribe. He had strong aristocratic tendencies, evident in his mores and in his pride of lineage; to him the Arab nation was "the noblest of nations" (*afkhar al-umam*).

All in all, the values of the Arab, nomad or settler, were measured in terms of purity of blood as it flowed in the veins of a long line of noble ancestors, in the eloquence of his tongue, in the power of his sword-wielding arm, and in the speed of his mount.

Such was the makeup of the Arab whom the Caliph ʿUmar I (634-644) regarded as the "raw material" of Islam and whose values supplied Islam with the vigor and dynamism in the period of rapid growth and expansion without which its triumph would scarcely have reached the unprecedented limits recorded by history.

Rhetorical oratory and poetry constituted for the Bedouin a dearly cherished source of aesthetic pleasure. He was easily swayed by the power of speech and rhythm and aroused beyond compare by the eloquence of his tongue. Hence poetry and oratory provided the best incitement to valorous deeds on the battlefield. The Qur'ān preserves the rhetorical wealth of the Arab's pre-Islamic heritage; indeed, rhetorical oratory proved itself a strong energizing force in times of war. He who commanded the right word at a crucial moment could bring victory to his tribe. Poetry served as a weapon of "psychological warfare" aimed at demoralizing the enemy through derision. But such powers of eloquence were not for all to share and employ: they were gifts of the spirits (*jinn*).[4]

Cultivated as an art, poetry had the effect of strengthening the Arab's consciousness of a separate identity attributed to a lofty ancestry that transcended tribal affiliations. In this context, a properly uttered poetic expression served as a rallying force in an otherwise divided society. This is particularly manifest in the manner whereby during the months of truce which prevailed over Arabia, thousands of tribesmen converged on the fair of ʿUkāz at Mecca, not only to barter their ware but also to match poetic wit. Each vied with the other for the prize of having his poetic composition adjudged the best, as this meant that it would be suspended from the side of the Kaʿbah.[5] This deep reverence for the powers of speech can be vividly traced in the mass of literary works of all types produced by the cultural efflorescence of Islam. Indeed, the reader would be hard put not to find poetic verse embellishing the pages of a scientific treatise or a historical narrative.

Religion

But of most relevance to any study of Islam in its essential function as a religious force is to establish its relations to the religion, or religions, of pre-Islamic Arabia. Islam, like Judaism and Christianity, is indebted for certain basic conceptual, institutional, and ritualistic ideas and practices to the rudiments of the Semitic religion that evolved in the steppes and settlements of the Arabian peninsula. As an established authority on pre-Islamic Semitic religions has observed, "No positive religion that has moved men has been able to start with a *tabula rasa,* and express itself as if religion were beginning for the first time . . . A new scheme of faith can find a hearing only by appealing to religious instincts and susceptibilities that already exist in its audience . . ."[6]

Certain deities and cultic rituals associated with the simple animistic, then daimonic, worship of the early inhabitants survived in a transformed and highly sophisticated version in the three great monotheistic religions. Tribal deities like Allah and Jehovah, sanctified stones and springs such as the Blackstone of the Kaʿbah (Kaaba), the well of Zamzam, Bethel of the Old Testament, the ritual prayer, the offering of blood sacrifices to the deity, the pilgrimage, and numerous rites—not all of which were absorbed—were popular in the period of Arabian history before Islam, which the Muslims term "*Jāhilīyah,*"[7] and became consecrated in Islam and its kindred religions.

The idea that the deity may reveal itself to the select, as Jehovah revealed himself to Jacob in a dream at Bethel, Jesus to Paul on the road to Damascus, and Allah to Muḥammad through the intermediation of Gabriel in a cave outside Mecca, is familiar to earlier Semites. As a matter of fact, in the anthropomorphic state of worship revelation was indispensable to the formalization of relationships between man and his god, as was the cementing of ties ensuing therefrom by a sacrificial ritual. The concept of blood ties, of man to man and man to his god, whereby tribal affiliation is sanctified and the deity assumes the status of patron and ancestral lord to the tribe, developed from such premises. And as the deity was believed to favor the locality where it revealed itself, the tribe converted the place into a sanctuary and instituted a pattern of periodic revisitation to offer homage. The Kaʿbah in Mecca eventually became the supreme sanctuary in pre-Islamic Arabia, and Muḥammad preserved its status in Islam as well.

The tribes of Arabia selected for their deities those which best reflected their distinguishing characteristics and aspirations; the Semites, whether of the desert or town variety, literally created their gods in their own images. The mood and temperament of the god was a reflection of the worshiper's attitude. There were hundreds of such deities in pagan Arabia; the Kaʿbah alone at one time housed three hundred and sixty-seven of them. Of all those mentioned in the Qurʾān, four appeared to be most popularly revered on the eve of Islam: al-ʿUzzah (power),[8] al-Lāt (the goddess),[9] and Manāh (fate);[10] all three female deities, popularly worshiped by the tribes of the Ḥijāz, were regarded as the daughters of Allah (the god) who headed the Arabian pantheon when Muḥammad began to preach.

Allah, the paramount deity of pagan Arabia, was the target of worship in varying degrees of intensity from the southernmost tip of Arabia to the Mediterranean. To the Babylonians he was *"Il"* (god); to the Canaanites, and later the Israelites, he was *"El"*; the South Arabians worshipped him as *"Ilah,"* and the Bedouins as *"al-Ilah"* (the deity). With Muḥammad he becomes *Allah,* God of the Worlds, of all believers, the one and only who admits of no associates or consorts in the worship of Him. Judaic and Christian concepts of God abetted the transformation of Allah from a pagan deity to the God of all monotheists. There is no reason, therefore, to accept the idea that "Allah" passed to the Muslims from Christians and Jews.

Jewish Settlements

Muḥammad was in contact with Jews in Yathrib (Medina) with whom he disputed theologically but later broke for political reasons. During this brief period of exchanges he acquired a number of ritualistic concepts from them, but the influence of strictly Jewish beliefs is still under debate.

Although the presence of Jewish tribes in Arabia dates back to 1200 B.C.—when the Rachel tribes spent their wandering years in Sinai and al-Nufūd,[11] it was not until the first Christian century following the second unsuccessful uprising against the Romans in 132–135 A.D. that an influx of Jewish tribes and some proselytizing among Bedouins brought them into the Hijaz. On the eve of Islam they had come into possession of some of the best land in the oases of Taymā', Khaybar and Yathrib; in Yathrib alone they constituted nearly one half the population.

Knowledge of superior agricultural techniques, monopoly over important commodities of trade, like iron (used in making arms, coats of mail and agricultural tools), resulted in their control of the rich oases and the important trade fairs of Taymā' and Yathrib. Not only did the Quraysh of Mecca resent their economic ascendance, but the Aws and Khazraj, rivals of the Jewish tribes in Yathrib, engaged in a long feud with them for control of the palm-tree plantations in the neighboring oases. It was to resolve their perennial dispute that they invited Muḥammad to come to Yathrib and serve as mediator; this, as we shall see, was of important consequence to the development of the Islamic polity and crystallization of Islamic institutions.

Although the presence of the Jewish settlements in Arabia did not materially influence the development of Islamic concepts, it did, on the other hand, affect the political destiny of the Ḥimyarites. It was allegedly a certain abu-Kārib Asʿad Kāmil, king of Yaman during Ḥimyarite rule, who first adopted the Jewish faith early in the fifth century A.D. His last successor dhu-Nuwās embarked on the policy of forcible conversion which led to the Abyssinian invasion and ended the possibility of Judaism becoming firmly rooted in this important corner of Arabia at a time when Muḥammad was about to preach the religion of submission to Allah.

Christian Elements

The Christian settlements in Arabia during this crucial period left perhaps less of an impact on the development of Islam, principally because the chief Christian centers were on the periphery of the peninsula: in Najrān north of Yaman, in Syria, and Ḥīrah in lower Iraq. There was a minor settlement in Mecca consisting of caravan leaders, monks, merchants from Syria, curers, healers, doctors, dentists, smiths, carpenters, scribes, Christian women married into the Quraysh, and slaves from Mesopotamia, Egypt, Syria, and Byzantium sold in the market place of the town.[12]

Bedouins of the Ḥijāz on their caravan journeys to Syria and other Christian centers undoubtedly carried back with them a superficial knowledge of Christian beliefs and customs. Dissident Christian sects, mostly of the Monophysite confession, and numerous monks turned ascetics had their retreats in the steppes of north Arabia along caravan routes. As a caravan leader, Muḥammad is supposed to have befriended a Christian monk, Baḥīra; it is said that he even wore tunics which were the gifts of other Christian monks. Two Christianized Arab tribes, Judham and ʿUdhra, roamed the Ḥijāz. According to local tradition, there were even Christian religious artifacts in the Kaʿbah at Mecca.

It is not unlikely that Muḥammad may have exchanged religious views with monks, even with Christians who possessed some formal knowledge of Christian theology. Jacobites and Nestorians are known to have conducted active missionary activities among the pagan tribes of Arabia; indeed, priests and deacons were assigned to each tribe, and in Najrān the Monophysites had established churches which, when persecuted by dhu-Nuwās, invited Abyssinian intervention. Monasteries astride caravan routes were open day and night to traveling caravans and roaming Bedouins. Here, besides receiving food and shelter, they undoubtedly had occasion to observe such practices as praying, fasting, and alms giving—three of the five basic injunctions of Islam. The Nestorians had established schools and some churches in many of the towns frequented by Arab tribesmen of the Ḥijāz.[13]

When Muḥammad began his summons to Islam, Christians were involved in deep theological disputes, not the least of which was over the use of icons, a dispute which culminated in the celebrated iconoclastic controversy in Christianity. Some Christians in South Arabia were accused in the Qurʾān of having departed from the basic tenets of their faith.[14] Such dissensions, coupled with the fact that the Bedouin Arabian, even in the judgment of the Qurʾān, was notoriously inclined to irreligion,[15] could not have disturbed materially the few religious convictions of the Arabs before the preachings of Muḥammad.[16]

Evidence of Transformation

Be that as it may, socio-economic trends long current in Arabian society appeared to converge in the Ḥijāz, and specifically at Mecca, when Muḥammad emerged on the scene. The mustering of economic power through control of transit trade and the housing of pagan deities in the Kaʿbah under their supervision gave the Quraysh an enviable position of influence and contributed to their rising status. Mecca had become the center of pilgrimage and the hub of economic life in West Arabia.

To encourage the flow of pilgrims and trade, the Qurayshites concluded pacts with various tribes securing the inviolability of transients and pilgrims. The Kaʿbah and the area surrounding it were declared *ḥaram* ("forbidden," i.e., to warfare); within a general mile radius from it no blood might be spilled. With their economic power ever on the increase, the Qurayshite oligarchy ruling Mecca deliberately kept extending the ḥaram to assure the stability of social relations in a zone crucial to trade; and in order to enhance the inviolability of their area, Meccan traders ringed the Kaʿbah with the idols of other tribes.[17]

The rise of "Allah" to prominence in the pantheon at Mecca was commensurate with the rising status of the Quraysh. The pagans in and around Mecca at an earlier date had already considered him the supreme deity. The attributes associated with "Allah" before Islam, namely his being regarded as creator of the world and lord guardian of contractual obligations of the wayfarer and fate, were preserved in the Islamic conception of him. That he enjoyed a high status during this period is evident in the deference accorded him by certain Christians[18] and non-

Christians, like the Ṣābians[19] and the Magians,[20] who regarded Allah as a deity and even implored their indigenous gods to intercede with him on their behalf. The Ṣābians not only made ritualistic sacrifices to Allah and sent offerings to the Kaʿbah, but even regarded their astral gods as "companions of Allah." Perhaps it is owing to this recognition of Allah that the Muslims later extended their protection to both Ṣābians and Magians even though they did not strictly qualify as possessors of scriptures in the same context as Christians and Jews.

What is of significance to the mission of Islam is the trend toward socio-religious centralization in Meccan society on the eve of the advent of Muḥammad. While laboring to establish and safeguard their economic ascendancy, the merchant oligarchy of Qurayshites ruling Mecca brought about a transformation of values, most important being the establishment of security under *law* in lieu of *kinship*. Thus when Muḥammad preached social unity and solidarity on the basis of Islam, he was exploiting a trend already in evidence. In the area of the ḥaram a stranger was afforded protection because of the sanctity it enjoyed. The support of a native patron would be called upon only when an injustice was perpetrated against the stranger. To be born or to sojourn in the sanctified environment of the Kaʿbah gave non-Qurayshite Arabs precedence over others.

Such extra privileges as were obtainable in Mecca encouraged Arab tribesmen to forsake their local shrines for the Kaʿbah in Mecca, thus contributing to the growing centralization of worship there. What was happening in effect is that an increasing number of Arabs were discarding tribal ties as a means of protection for the *jiwār* (protection) of the Kaʿbah where Allah reigned supreme. As more and more non-kin Arabs banded in the jiwār of the ḥaram, the prestige of Allah as patron grew concomitantly; so did his functions and responsibility toward his followers "as the guardian of faith and the avenger of treason"; in his name tribesmen were to "fulfill their contracts, honor their relatives by oath, and feed their guests." [21]

Of paramount importance to the development of the central socio-religious function of Allah in Islam as an equalizer and a force of solidarity was this pre-Islamic institution in Mecca. When rights and obligations, hitherto unrecognized outside membership in the tribe, became extra-familial or extra-tribal in the jiwār of the ḥaram, it was the prerogative, if not indeed the responsibility, of Allah to serve as imposer and guarantor. When Muḥammad called upon all Qurayshites to forsake the idols and place all their faith in Allah, it was not the novelty of the preaching as much as the fear of economic loss from having to abandon guardianship over the Kaᶜbah, home of the idols of pagan Arabia and the target of the profitable pilgrimage as well as an all-round stimulant of trade, that impelled them to resist him, even by force.

What is of relevance to our understanding of the new socio-religious bonds constructed by Islam is the fact that the commercial development accruing from the centralization of worship caused the transformation of Meccan society from a social order determined primarily by kinship and ethnic homogeneity of origin into an order in which the fiction of kinship served now to mask a developing division of society into classes characterized by considerable ethnic diversity.[22]

As the Quraysh amassed wealth and gained power, the economic gulf separating its component clans widened. Eventually the clans of Makhzūm and Umayya, who later were very instrumental in the spread of Islam, came to the forefront and occupied the "inner city" around the Kaᶜbah; the other eight and poorer clans dwelt in the outskirts—Muḥammad belonged to one of them, the Banu Hāshims.

When the function of the clan no longer served the economic ambitions of the Quraysh, they placed their destiny in the hands of an oligarchy of rich merchants who with their immediate families and dependents controlled political power in Mecca and dominated its economic and religious life. They decided on general policy, concluded alliances as needed, and entered into formal trade agreements with the courts of Abyssinia and Persia.

As the reorientation of Meccan society on the eve of Islam began to crystallize, it reflected increasingly the growing distinctions which we associate with class gradations rather than those formally attributed to tribal affiliations. In this new Meccan society "class" distinction played a more determinative role, a phenomenon unknown to pastoral tribes. The dependent population of Mecca reflected the gradations of its society into slaves, missionaries, merchants in charge of caravans, middlemen like ʿUmar who became the second caliph, those who became dependents through usury, wage-earners, and finally, clients (*mawāli*).

But the organization of power among the aristocracy of Quraysh was not complete because their council of oligarchs lacked legislative force and the means to execute decisions without having to resort to traditional methods, such as refusing protection to a recalcitrant. In a society now organized around functional classes rather than tribal membership, the threat of a blood feud or a protracted vendetta was no longer an effective weapon of social restraint when friction developed within the society. If restraint existed, it was due largely to fear of repercussions from antagonizing the controlling clans of the "inner city."

But in this crucial period of Mecca, when traditional socio-religious values were giving way to new ones, the evolving system was not free from injustices; otherwise Muḥammad would have lacked the wherewithal for his preaching of a new socio-religious system based on submission to one God. The discriminatory and exploitative policies of the "inner Quraysh" toward the "Quraysh of the outskirts" (clients and slaves), gained for Muḥammad an audience, the earliest target of his preachings, and provided him with a core of early followers. Obnoxious practices instituted by the oligarchy, such as wage payment and debt slavery, contributed to the growing unrest directed against them. Some clients escaped exploitation because of the nominal backing of patrons to whom they were tied by some kin-ritual, but those without such backing and other unaffiliates were exposed to attack or even unobstructed killing in a blood feud.[23]

Mecca at the birth of Muḥammad was indeed a complicated order undergoing considerable fermentation aggravated by social injustices resulting from distinctions based on clan and kin affiliations. And while the trend toward religious unity was pronounced, the social order was far from stable owing to the widening gulf between the "haves" and the "have-nots." The need for a remedial treatment such as that offered by Muḥammad in his message of Islam was timely because demands for reform could not have been avoided much longer. The role of Muḥammad was indeed preordained.

CHAPTER 3

Muḥammad the Prophet

History relates of men who distinguished themselves by deeds and left permanent imprints on their societies; of prophets who delivered the message of the true God to their peoples; of statesmen who distinguished themselves in the service of their nations; of authors who left monumental additions to the literary wealth of mankind; of conquerors who led their followers to victories, wealth, and renown; and of those who by force of personality or unusual calling succeeded in transforming values or completely revamping the societies into which they were born.

The Role

Muḥammad, the prophet of Arabia, has fulfilled for his people a role that combines the functions of a distinguished prophet, statesman, author, and reformer. He has earned for himself as a consequence the respect and reverence of countless people, Muslim and non-Muslim everywhere.

By vocation Muḥammad was a prophet in the true Biblical sense with a message for his people, a message anchored in religious belief but aiming at the realization of fundamental social, economic, and political reform. The religion he founded was hampered by no wrangling creed or barrier to man's relations with God or to his fellow man. He succeeded, both as prophet and as reformer. The fact that Muḥammad's mission was accomplished in his lifetime is a living testimony "to his distinctive superiority over the prophets, sages, and philosophers of other times and countries." [1]

While our knowledge of men who filled similar roles from Moses to Zoroaster to Jesus is shrouded with legend, often incomplete and frequently colored, and while the accounts of Muḥammad's life and deeds contain their share of incompleteness and coloring, the fact remains that he was the first to live and preach in the full light of history. We have more information relating to his career than we have of his predecessors. His life by and large is not wrapped in mystery, and few tales have been woven around his personality.[2]

For the biography of Muḥammad we are dependent on the work of ibn-Isḥāq (d. 767) as preserved in the recension of ibn-Hishām (d. 834). Ibn-Saʿd, a historian of the ninth century, compiled an encyclopaedic work on the Prophet and his followers which contains valuable information on the life and preachings of Muḥammad. But no source or work can yield more dependable information on the genius of Muḥammad or provide a greater insight into his personality and accomplishments than the Qurʾān, the sacred book of Islam.

While the Qurʾān in Islamic theology conveys strictly the word of God, it remains in respect to the message contained therein a true mirror of Muḥammad's character and his accomplishments. Complementary information is obtainable also in the sayings and deeds of the Prophet that have been amassed in voluminous quantities but carefully scrutinized by scholars of the early Islamic centuries. These non-canonical texts, which contain eye-witness accounts of Muḥammad, fall under the category of *hadīth* (utterances) and *sunnah* (observed conduct).

The life and preachings of Muḥammad are in marked contrast with what Arabian society had ordained for his fellow Meccans. The established facts of his life have been subjected to much less variance of interpretation than those of preceding prophets. This is due to the circumspection of available sources.

He was born about 571 A.D., the posthumous son of ʿAbdullāh and Āminah. On his father's side he descended from the impoverished house of Hāshim, adjudged by the Quraysh the noblest of the dominant aristocracy; on his mother's, from the Najjār branch of Khazraj, a major tribe of Yathrib, his adoptive city. His grandfather, ʿAbd-al-Muṭṭalib, formerly the custodian of the Kaʿbah and one time the virtual head of the Meccan commonwealth, took charge of his upbringing upon the death of his mother when Muḥammad was only six years old. When the grandfather died, the care of the child was entrusted to his paternal uncle Abu-Ṭālib.

Most of his youth was evidently uneventful as the lack of biographical information on Muḥammad's early life suggests. The most important landmark in his youth prior to the prophetic call is his marriage to Khadījah, a wealthy Qurayshite widow who was impressed by Muḥammad's personality and virtues when he served as a factor in her caravan trade with Syria. He was twenty-five at the time and she fifteen years his senior. The marriage lasted over fifteen years. During this period Muḥammad would have no additional woman for a wife, an unusual disposition for the times when polygamy was widely practiced by his fellow Arabs. Yet these were the years that afforded him the happiness which escaped him as an orphaned youth.

Khadījah bore him two sons, who died in infancy, and four daughters. Two of the daughters married the future third and fourth caliphs of Islam. His daughter Fāṭimah married his first cousin ʿAli, the son of Abu-Ṭālib, whom he had taken under his wing and raised as an act of gratitude when Abu-Ṭālib, Muḥammad's uncle, died.

The mission of Muḥammad began after a careful period of soul-searching and spiritual reassessment lasting over fifteen years. When the call to prophecy came at last, there was no turning back. He hesitated but he did not fail to respond.

Muḥammad was a mature man of forty when he received the

first revelation. It came to him as he was contemplating in a cave on Mt. Ḥirā', above Mecca, to which he habitually withdrew. The injustices permeating all levels of Meccan society in his days undoubtedly weighed heavily on his mind and caused him much anguish. The wealthy lorded it over the poor; the helpless were at the mercy of the strong; greed and selfishness ruled the day; infanticide was widely practiced by Bedouins who lacked adequate means of sustenance, and there were numerous other evils prevailing on all levels of Arabian society that had the effect of widening the gulf between the privileged aristocracy and the deprived multitudes of Mecca. With such considerations preying on his mind, Muḥammad found himself confronted by a twofold crisis: spiritual and social.

In his early life he had understood only too well what poverty accompanied by orphanage meant. Now he had time to do something about both. It is important to note here that Muḥammad's preaching of monotheism and of social reform went hand in hand. Indeed, no other message is so thoroughly underscored in the revelations received from Allah with so much stress on equal treatment and social justice. To Muḥammad these constituted a vital concomitant of worship. The revelations of the one and only God enjoin consistently the exercise of mercy and benevolence as the necessary adjuncts of belief in Him.

This dual role of Muḥammad as preacher and reformer is largely evident in his life and career. What he sought was the cohesion of Arabian society through uniform beliefs and a unified faith. He knew this could be accomplished only through the worship of the one God alone and through laws authorized by the sanctity of divine command. With such laws Muḥammad would bind the hitherto scattered ends of Arabia.

He preached belief in the one God, God of Abraham, Moses, and Jesus, and the brotherhood of all Arabs in *islām,* or "submission" to God.

To preach such a radical message in Arabia at this time was to be truly daring and, judging by the standards of the day, it was an undertaking fraught with risks and formidable obstacles. Muḥammad himself was overwhelmed when he awakened to the awesome realities of the task he was being charged with. "No incipient prophet," said Edward Gibbon, "ever passed through so severe an ordeal as Muḥammad." Indeed, as the commandments of Allah became increasingly manifest in the revelations that were descending upon him, Muḥammad undertook to show that the whole organization and institutional beliefs of pagan Arabia were not in conformity with the divine will. The voice of Muḥammad amidst the strong chorus of opposition was indeed a lone voice. Yet he persistently challenged the moral and social norms governing Arabia, and particularly the values and institutional practices of Mecca, the hub of Arabia, under the powerful leadership of the Qurayshite oligarchy.

His Ministry

The facts relating to his ministry have been treated in almost every narrative concerning Muḥammad's mission. While the launching date is not exactly fixed, it is commonly accepted that revelation was received by Muḥammad in a dream one night during the month of Ramadān as he secluded himself in the cave on Mt. Hirā'. The deliverer of the revelation and all subsequent ones was held to be Gabriel the archangel. Gabriel brought to Muḥammad the command of God:

> Read in the name of thy Lord who created, who created man of blood coagulated. Read! Thy Lord is the most beneficent, who taught by the pen, taught that which they knew not unto men.[3]

Muḥammad recounted to his wife the facts of his experience and was seriously perturbed over the prospects of being possessed, like the soothsayers of his day, by the jinn. Khadījah reassured him of his sound judgment; so did her cousin Waraqa ibn-Nawfal, a blind man known to his associates as a *ḥanīf*.[4] Waraqa was familiar with the scriptures of the Jews and Christians; he detected in Muḥammad the signs of prophethood and predicted hardships for his mission. "They will call thee a liar," said he to

Muḥammad, "they will persecute thee; they will banish thee, and they will fight against thee."

The gravity of his portended mission gave him much reason to pause and reconsider. It is probable that during this critical period of soul-searching he became particularly receptive to Judaic and Christian concepts of monotheism. For some time before, and probably through the proddings of Waraqa, he had become strongly inclined in that direction. Indeed, the Qurʾān suggests this in the verse:

> And if thou art in doubt concerning that which we reveal unto thee then question those who have read the scripture before thee. Verily thy Lord hath caused His truth to descend upon thee. So be not of those who waver.[5]

Some time lapsed before the next revelation descended. But with the assurance of Allah propelling him forward, Muḥammad no longer doubted that he was being commissioned for a serious mission. All hesitation vanished and the Angel once more spoke to him while he lay with his limbs wrapped in a mantle:

> Oh thou enwrapped dost lie! Arise and warn, and thy Lord magnify, and thy raiment purify, and the abomination fly.[6]

This was the most critical point in Muḥammad's career. It was the climax of a long beginning which stretched back into his youth. As a five-year-old boy, while being cared for by a Bedouin nursemaid, Ḥalīmah, he was supposed to have had his inwards cleansed by "two men in white garments," echoed in the Qurʾān: "Have We not opened thy breast for thee?"[7] When he was twelve he had accompanied his uncle Abu-Ṭālib to Syria, and it was near Busra that the Christian monk bearing the legendary name Baḥīra is alleged to have seen in him the markings of a true prophet. Still while a lad, he was upbraided by Zayd ibn-ʿAmr, an outcast of Mecca because of his monotheistic beliefs, for making offerings to the idols. After that episode, and according to tradition, Muḥammad never knowingly stroked one of their idols nor did he sacrifice to them until God honored him with His apostleship.

Contacts with Waraqa, Jews, and Christians must have given him some familiarization with existing versions of monotheism, although Muḥammad's narration of events attributed to the Scriptures shows that this familiarization could not have been the result of contact with anyone who had an educated knowledge of the sacred texts.

The call to prophecy was not a unique occurrence among Semitic peoples; indeed the details concerning Muḥammad's role as a *nabi* (prophet), *rasūl* (messenger) and *nadhīr* (warner) have parallels in the Old and New Testaments. Pagan Arabs before Muḥammad's time were not as familiar with a nabi as they were with the *shāʿir*[8] who made his ominous predictions through the medium of rhymed prose, a form of expression preserved in the Qurʾān.

When Muḥammad preached the worship of God and God only, the earliest believers consisted of his wife Khadījah, Abu-Bakr, the popular and respected merchant of Mecca who became the first caliph, his cousin ʿAli, and his adopted son Zayd ibn-Ḥārith. His uncle Abu-Ṭālib, who defended him against all his foes and stood by him during the most critical period of his prophethood, never accepted the message of Islam; nor did he, on the other hand, insist that his nephew stop preaching the religion of Allah.

After three years of rather quiet and earnest preaching in his home city in the shadow of the Kaʿbah, Muḥammad succeeded in converting altogether thirty individuals; most of them came from the deprived classes. The Quraysh, who had profited from the existing economic and social order in Mecca based on the worship of the idols, were skeptical of Muḥammad's message and contemptuously unreceptive. Their indifference to his preachings soon turned to anxiety when Muḥammad decided to abandon the quiet and unobtrusive approach for a bolder public appeal, calling upon his fellow Meccans to desist from their worship of the idols. But such attempted inducements as promising them the bounties of Allah or threatening them with the consuming fires of *Jahannam* (hell) appeared to yield no positive results. His audience remained largely unconvinced; indeed, many were beginning to believe that he was beside himself, if not possessed by the evil jinn.

Failing to win over his fellow Meccans, Muḥammad began to work on traders and other individuals who frequented Mecca during the season of the annual pilgrimage. He excited his listeners to heed the call of God and to learn the lesson of those who had fallen; those who had disobeyed God's ordinance: "Set not up with Allah any other God (O man) lest thou sit down reproved, forsaken." [9]

The prophet was becoming increasingly a warner, stressing the inevitable doom awaiting the skeptics and disbelievers on the day of reckoning. "Who so desireth that (life) which hasteneth away, We hasten for him therein that We will for whom We please. And afterward We have appointed for him hell; he will endure the heat thereof, condemned, rejected." [10]

If he gained converts, it was due less to the threats of eternal fire than to the strong justice and egalitarian principles imbedded in his message of submission to God. The promise of sharing with the "haves" had a particular appeal to the "have-nots" of Mecca. The aristocracy of Quraysh did not hesitate to remind him, "Why is it that thou art followed only by the most abject from our midst!"

Opposition

Prudence soon moved the aristocracy of Quraysh to take firmer steps than public derision of Muḥammad, especially when they could not prevent his message from gaining a wider following on account of its appeal to fairness and dignity.

> O ye who believe! Let not a folk deride a folk who may be better than they (are), nor let women (deride) women who may be better than they are; neither defame one another, nor insult one another by nicknames. Bad is the name of lewdness after faith. And whoso turneth not in repentance, such are evil-doers.[11]

The message had another force of attraction in its strong democratic spirit.

> O mankind! Lo! We have created you male and female, and have made you nations and tribes that ye may know one another. Lo! The noblest of you, in the sight of Allah, is the best in conduct. Lo! Allah is Knower, Aware.[12]

The Quraysh could perceive from the spirit and text of such preachings that Muḥammad was in effect undermining the entire structure of their society, founded as it was on a system of privilege. They concluded that the message could have only one enduring effect: the loosening of their political, religious, and commercial grip on Mecca.

The Quraysh, therefore, made the decision to take all necessary steps and adopt all feasible means to wipe out Muḥammad and his followers. Each family of the Quraysh accordingly was charged with the responsibility of stamping out the new belief. This was often accomplished by harsh methods. Muḥammad escaped such treatment largely because of his uncle's prestige among the oligarchs and because Abu-Ṭālib consistently refused to coerce his nephew-protégé into abandoning his mission.

When his uncle, fearing for Muḥammad's life, pleaded with him to give up his mission, the nephew replied with conviction: "I will not forsake this cause until it prevails by the will of God or I perish instead, no not if they (the Quraysh) would place the sun on my right hand and the moon on my left!" [13]

A delegation headed by another uncle, ʿUtbah, also failed to dissuade him from continuing his preaching through such promises as "we are willing to gather for you a fortune, larger than what is possessed by any of us; to make you our chief, and if you desire dominion we shall make you our king, and if the demon which possesses you cannot be subdued we will bring you doctors and give them riches to cure you." To them Muḥammad replied with the words preserved in the Qurʾān:

> Good tidings and a warning, But most of them turn away so that they hear not.[14]

> Say (unto them O Muḥammad): I am only a mortal like you. It is inspired in me that your God is One God, therefore take the straight path unto Him and seek forgiveness of Him. And woe unto the idolaters.[15]

Persecution intensified and became unbearable. Muḥammad advised those of his followers who could not depend on the protection of their kinsmen to seek refuge in the Christian kingdom of Abyssinia. And so in the year A.D. 615 about eleven to fifteen families, followed later by eighty-three individuals, male and female, arrived in Abyssinia where the Negus took them under his wing and refused to surrender them to the Quraysh. Muḥammad and his small party of staunch followers remained in Mecca to continue the struggle against overwhelming odds.

Faced with privation and strong pressure, Muḥammad at one time almost compromised with his hostile kinsmen. It was during a prayer session at the Kaʿbah that, in a moment of weakness, he referred to the three female deities, al-Lāt, al-ʿUzzah and Manāh, ". . . as the most exalted cranes (or swans)" and stated: "Verily their intercession is to be hoped for." The Quraysh were pleasantly surprised; and while they did prostrate themselves before Allah as Muḥammad called upon them to do, they still were unwilling to submit to His worship alone.

Muḥammad, however, was reportedly rebuked by Gabriel for including words in the revelation not transmitted from Allah who ". . . abolishes that which Satan proposes . . . (and) establishes His revelations." [16] After he had repented for having yielded to temptation in a moment of trial, God spoke again to Muḥammad and the idolatrous verses were expunged from the Qurʾān; in their place was substituted the verse, "Shall yours be the male and his the female?[17] This were then an unjust division! They are naught but names which ye and your fathers have named." [18]

His recantation evoked all the more the anger of the oligarchs who stepped up their persecution of Muḥammad's followers and even plotted his death. Besides, the Muslims had for some time boldly and openly carried on their worship of Allah in the environs of the sacred Kaʿbah. The Qurayshites now retaliated by ostracizing their Hāshimite cousins who had pledged themselves to defend their Muslim kinsmen and secluded them in an outlying quarter of the city where for more than two years they suffered extreme hardships. Still they would not deliver Muḥammad to his persecutors.

Prudence decreed that Muḥammad take precautions to safeguard the lives of his followers. Threatening his kinsmen with the wrath of Allah and eternal damnation seemed to make no imprint on them. Pagan Arabians, moreover, had no preconceptions of a life hereafter, or of rewards and punishments in such a life. They had looked upon such notions with ridicule and were not restrained by fear of judgment from pursuing their persecution of the believers.

The Qurayshite oligarchy in another respect had looked upon Muḥammad's claim to prophethood with skepticism because they had been convinced that if Allah really wanted to appoint a messenger, surely He would have chosen one from their midst! Were they not, after all, the leaders of Mecca and the custodians of the sacred shrine wherein He dwelt and was revered?

Their skepticism of Muḥammad's mission manifested itself in another way. If Muḥammad were truly sent, so they argued, why did he refuse to produce a sign in testimony of his declared mission or perform a miracle like other prophets before him?[19] Why did he insist, as he did time and again, that he was not sent by God to work miracles? Was it sufficient to argue that the only miracle he was capable of was to point to God's power as manifested in His divine word and in His creation round about them?

The only miracle attributed to Muḥammad by the believers in him is the Qur'ān. That so illiterate an Arab was capable of such rich utterances was truly miraculous in their eyes. And when the outside observer ponders the powerful impact he wrought on pagan Arabia in a decade of work, he is indeed overwhelmed by the miracle Muḥammad performed.

In the midst of the crisis, death carried off both his faithful wife and the uncle who had been his benefactor and protector. The loss was somewhat mitigated by the conversion to Islam of the future caliph, ʿUmar ibn-al-Khaṭṭāb, a man of strong will and conviction who contributed materially to the strengthening of the Islamic faith and the community.

Muḥammad remained the target of ridicule; his opponents accused him of sorcery and fraudulent lifting of ideas from Christians and Jews. But to be berated and slandered apparently was the normal fate of prophets. The reception accorded his predecessors among Jews and gentiles had not been milder.

> If they deny thee, even so the folk of Noah, and (the tribes of) Aʿād and Thamūd, before thee, denied (Our messengers); and the folk of Abraham and the folk of Lot; (and) the dwellers of Midian. And Moses was denied; but I indulged the disbelievers a long while then I seized them, and how (terrible) was My abhorrence! [20]

The Hijrah

When he first considered seeking outside assistance, Muḥammad went to Ṭāʾif, a town sixty miles east of Mecca; but the inhabitants turned him back after he had spent a month among them fruitlessly endeavoring to win them over to the new faith. Two years later a delegation from Yathrib came to Mecca on a pilgrimage. Impressed by Muḥammad, they swore an oath of fealty to him. This delegation of twelve members represented the Khazraj and the Aws, the two principal and feuding tribes of Yathrib. Ten of the twelve were Jewish, the other two pagan. The Jewish delegates mulled over the possibility that Muḥammad might be the Messiah they had been awaiting. The message he preached and the doctrines he sought to establish had a familiar ring to them. Next year, in 622, an emissary sent by the Prophet returned from Yathrib accompanied by seventy-three men and two women who extended Muḥammad a formal invitation to come to Yathrib.

Shortly thereafter, about one hundred Muslim families slipped out of Mecca and headed for Yathrib where they were warmly received. The Meccans, now fearing an alliance between Muḥammad and the hostile tribes of Yathrib, seriously contemplated killing him. But accompanied by his cousin and followed by ʿAli and Abu-Bakr, he eluded his would-be assassins and reached the city by a round-about route on September 24, 622. This date became subsequently the first year of the Muslim calendar,[21] popularly referred to as the "Hegira" (Hijrah).[22] It is a significant date in Islamic history, because it heralded the dawn of a new era, the Islamic era, and the end of the "Age of Ignorance" (Jāhilīyah).

The migration to Yathrib introduced a new phase in Muḥammad's struggle with his kinsmen among the Quraysh. They were shocked by his abandonment of folk and home city; the desertion of kin in pre-Islamic Arabia was tantamount to committing suicide. The Quraysh implored their deities "to bring the woe upon him who more than any among us has cut off the ties of kinship and acted dishonorably." [23]

In Mecca Muḥammad had preached a predominantly ethical doctrine anchored in justice and social equity, which he maintained the worship of Allah alone could bring about. But in Yathrib he acquired a new role, that of arbiter in the feuds of the Yathribites and of a statesman providing leadership to the Muslims who broke the ties of kinship and organized themselves as a separate community wherein Islam was substituted for blood ties.

This new role changed the character of Muḥammad's preachings. He had become the head of an organized society. The role of a lawgiver accedes to his role as prophet. Muḥammad became increasingly an organizer, and the statesmanship in him emerged. Allah came to his rescue and obligingly caused the appropriate revelations to descend upon him as the occasion called for them.

The citizens of the city, which henceforth becomes known as *"Madīnat al-Rasūl"* (the city of the messenger) or more popularly, *"Madīnah,"* "Medina," consisted of three basic groups: (1) those who helped bring Muḥammad to Yathrib, the *Anṣār* (helpers); (2) those who emigrated from Mecca at his behest, the *Muhājirūn* (emigrants), and (3) a party which embraced mostly the Jewish tribes and those branded as *Munāfiqūn* (Hypocrites) in the Qurʾān. To weld all parties together into a uniform administrative social unit and at the same time to provide them with freedom of internal government, Muḥammad granted each group a charter[24] defining their respective rights and obligations.

The Commonwealth

In this manner the preacher established under the aegis of Islam the first socio-religious commonwealth. Faith and society were merged. Islamic hegemony emerged. Though predominantly non-Islamic in its structure, Islam nevertheless became the commonwealth's guarantor. The believers were committed to safeguard the rights of all citizens irrespective of their religion. The fact that the inhabitants adhered to a variety of religious and non-religious convictions and were willing to accept Islamic leadership is a tribute to the statesmanship of Muḥammad. It is also a measure of Islam's capacity for tolerance. This strengthened their receptiveness to the new ideas propagated by Muḥammad in spite of the presence in their midst of a strong Jewish faith, which presumably had predisposed them beforehand towards monotheism. As a noted scholar points out: "from a religious standpoint paganism in Medina was dead before it was attacked; none defended it, none mourned its disappearance. The pagan opposition to Muḥammad's work as a reformer was entirely political . . ."[25]

Having reconciled the disputing factions, introduced law, and restored order through skillfully transferring the center of power from the tribes to the community represented by the commonwealth, Muḥammad earned the respect of all statesmen familiar with the obstacles he overcame in the process of transferring power. The Prophet was now ready to square off with his antagonists in Mecca. He was not seeking revenge; he was moved rather by the same sense of mission which had impelled him from the start to gain his kinsmen's acceptance of Allah as the only God.

Some scholars are of the opinion that he was moved also by economic necessity. Muslims in Medina had been experiencing considerable hardships because of their poverty. For some two years, moreover, the Quraysh had been provoking him by acts of sabotage directed against fruit trees in the oases around Medina and by theft of flocks belonging to the Muslims.

Mounting opposition came also from many of the Jews who in the two years of theological debate with the new prophet became convinced that he was not exactly the Messiah they had been awaiting. For some time they had been turning against him, and had often sided with his enemies. This not only incurred for them the animosity of Muḥammad, but served also to reinforce his growing conviction that any accommodation of sweeping Jewish beliefs and practices in Islam would dilute its appeal and weaken its role as a dynamic force possessing a strong message of its own. To justify the political break with them he openly declared that the Jews had falsified their scriptures to conceal the foretelling of his mission as the prophet of God. He also accused them of deviating from the true worship of God. He no longer felt inhibited from taking steps to uproot the "deviates" from Medina when the opportunity presented itself. The moment came when formal hostilities broke out between the Meccans and the Medinans.

The Struggle with the Quraysh

In January of 624 a Meccan army led by Abu-Jahl headed for Medina. Though lacking in adequate resources for defense and outnumbered three to one, the Muslims were determined to stand their ground at Badr. This was a new experience for the Muslim community. The believers, furthermore, were not sure whether Allah would give them permission to defend themselves. Surely He would not suffer the believers in Him to perish at the hands of His enemies. He spoke, and Muḥammad relayed the message:

> Allah defendeth those who are true . . . sanction is given unto those who fight because they have been wronged . . . Those who have been driven from their homes unjustly only because they said: Our Lord is Allah . . .[26]
>
> Fight in the way of Allah against those who fight against

> you, but begin not hostilities. Lo! Allah loveth not aggressors. And slay them wherever ye find them, and drive them out of the places whence they drove you out, for persecution is worse than slaughter.[27]

In the encounter that ensued, Allah granted victory to the believers even though their enemies were more numerous and had fought bravely. The so-called "battle of Badr," a skirmish by modern standards of warfare, provided the "day of decision," as Muḥammad termed it and as echoed in the Qur'ān:

> There was a sign for you in the two hosts which met: one army fighting in the way of Allah, and another disbelieving . . .[28]
>
> Lo! Herein verily is a lesson for those who have eyes. Ye slew them not, but Allah slew them . . .[29]

As for the effect of victory on the Muslim community, it represented a turning point in its future development. All eyes now turned to Muḥammad whose temporal power had received a boost by a military victory. The Prophet's career was enhanced: first preacher, then administrator, and now military commander. This *was* a miracle, though not exactly the kind of miracle which the Quraysh had so often sought from their kinsman and now experienced in an unpleasant manner.

Muḥammad had humbled the mighty of Mecca. Skeptical Bedouins flocked to the faith, the zealots were strengthened in their belief, and the disaffected had grounds for fear.

But the Quraysh struck back in the following year, inflicting serious damage to the community and nearly killing the Prophet at the battle of Uḥūd when the archers left their positions of defense and allowed the enemy's cavalry to surround the defenders, who were outnumbered 3000 to 700. Fortunately for the Muslims, the Quraysh did not follow up their victory with the occupation of Medina. Again the community was saved.

The Break with the Jews

During the last two forays, the Jews of Banu Naḍīr had been incited by the fiery poetry of Kaʿb, who ridiculed the Muslims and eulogized the Quraysh, to side with Muḥammad's enemies. the Banu Qaynūqa Jews in the meanwhile openly violated the terms of the charter. Efforts at reconciliation failed, particularly when the "Hypocrites" supported their position against Muḥammad. A military showdown was inevitable. It took place in 626 with Muḥammad launching the assault by laying siege to the stronghold of the Banu Naḍīr. After fifteen days of being hemmed in, they requested and were granted permission to leave Medina with their movable property; their holdings in land and appertinences were turned over to the community. This was a precedent set for the disposal of property gained in warfare in the future. The Banu Qaynūqa had been banished from Mecca earlier, before the showdown with the Banu Naḍīr.

From both religious and political considerations, the commonwealth of believers had to eliminate disruptive forces and consolidate its defenses against the real threat to its independence and existence, regardless of whether the threat was from within or from without.

In the two or three years following the setback of Uḥūd, the Muslims were preoccupied with the task of repelling the forays of nomadic tribes against their possessions. But in the meanwhile, the Qurayzah, another Jewish tribe that had entered into a pact relationship with the commonwealth of Medina, were induced by the dispossessed Banu Naḍīr and the "Hypocrites" to join the Quraysh in a new assault on Medina. This group was being organized and led by Abu-Sufyān, the chief oligarch of Mecca.

The "Confederates" (al-Aḥzāb), as they were called, invested the city in 627 and presented the Medinans with the most serious threat to date. But on the advice of a Persian convert, the defenders dug a trench around the beleaguered city. Revolted by such unwarlike tactics, the assailants, who took pride in the tribal methods of warfare, withdrew after a month of fruitless siege and minimal losses to both sides.

Angered by the betrayal of the Banu Qurayzah in the violation of their oath, Muḥammad submitted them to trial by the chief of the Aws whom they had requested to pass judgment upon them.

Having been mortally wounded in the battle, the chief passed the death sentence; and since they had pledged to honor his decision, six hundred men of the Banu Qurayzah submitted calmly to execution.

Next Muḥammad embarked on an expedition to encircle Mecca and subdue the neighboring tribes who usually allied themselves with the Quraysh. Having accomplished this mission, he next set out with fourteen hundred of his followers on a pilgrimage to the city in 628.

The Quraysh at first were determined to block his entry into the city. But the genius of Muḥammad the diplomat again turned an adverse situation into a victory. At al-Ḥudaybīyah, leaders of the Quraysh concluded an agreement with the Muslims that granted them permission to perform the pilgrimage in the following year provided Muḥammad would accept a ten-year truce. This was an important gain for the Muslims, as the conclusion of a pact with Quraysh was tantamount to their being recognized as equals. The pact went further by permitting them to proselytize. Hundreds of tribesmen consequently accepted Islam.

Only one more major obstacle remained: the stubborn defiance of the Jewish tribe at Khaybar reinforced by numerous refugees from the Naḍīr and Qurayzah. The Prophet and some of his companions had been invited to a banquet given by Zaynab, a female member of this tribe. Zaynab had lost her brothers in the aftermath of Uḥūd, and she seized on the occasion of the banquet to poison Muḥammad and his companions. He survived, however, and resolved to strike back with vengeance. The tribe succumbed to the Muslims and were forced to yield all their lands and wealth to them.

In 629 accompanied by two thousand followers, Muḥammad went on a pilgrimage to Mecca. In accordance with the truce terms the city was vacated of its inhabitants to accommodate the Muslims during their three-day visit to their former homes. It was at this time that the Muslims gained two important converts—ʿAmr ibn al-ʿĀṣ and Khālid ibn al-Walīd. Both men during the next decade were to write a valorous record in the annals of Islamic conquests.

On returning to Medina, Muḥammad dispatched a force of three thousand men under the leadership of his adopted son Zayd to exact retribution from the Ghassānid prince who had murdered a Muslim envoy sent earlier by the Prophet to solicit the conversion of Ghassānid Arabs to Islam. A year before, in 628, the Prophet had dispatched envoys to the Byzantine Emperor Heraclius and the Sasānid "king of kings," Chosroes Parvis, asking them to accept Islam. The Byzantine emperor politely declined the invitation, but the Persian Chosroes tore up Muḥammad's invitation in a rage and insulted the envoy. When the Prophet learned of the results, he was prompted to state "and thus will the empire of Chosroes be torn to pieces"; as indeed came to pass, and at the hands of the Prophet's followers, seven years later.

The encounter with the Ghassānids proved disastrous to the Muslim force which suffered the loss of Zayd, the son, and Jaʿfar, a cousin of Muḥammad. The Muslim force was spared complete annihilation thanks to the ingenious maneuvers of Khālid who succeeded in withdrawing the remnants of the expedition to Medina. But the Muslims avenged this defeat a month later when al-ʿĀṣ forced a number of hostile tribes to submit to the new faith, restoring in the process the prestige which the Muslims had lost during their previous encounter in the borderland separating Syria from Arabia.

The Submission of Mecca

The final episode in the career of Muḥammad and his crowning achievement was the submission of Mecca to Islam, accomplished in the year 8 of the Hijrah. At the instigation of the Quraysh, the Banu Bakr violated the truce of Ḥudaybīyah by attacking the Banu Khuzāʿah, allies of the Muslims, and killing a number of them. "And if they break their pledges after their treaty [e.g., with you, Muḥammad] and assail your religion, then fight the heads of disbelief . . ."[30]

Muḥammad resolved to end, once and for all, the resistance of the Quraysh. He gathered together a force of ten thousand men and set off for Mecca on January 1, 630. When still a day's journey from the city, a delegation of the Quraysh headed by the chief oligarch Abu-Sufyān met the Prophet and offered to submit to the new faith. Muḥammad was spared thereby the unpleasant task of forcibly entering Mecca. Instead, the faithful entered the city in peace. The Prophet's mission was rapidly nearing completion.

Having submitted without bloodshed, Mecca and its inhabitants were treated with a magnanimity that was unearned. Only four criminals, condemned according to prevailing laws, suffered execution. This show of clemency was not unrewarded, however, as thousands of Meccans now formally adopted Islam. The only desecration visited upon Mecca was sustained by the Kaʿbah where Muḥammad personally destroyed three hundred and sixty idols with his staff as he proclaimed "God is great! Truth has come. Falsehood has vanished!" Henceforth Allah was to be the sole dweller of the Kaʿbah which was now made into the principal shrine of Islam. "He only shall tend Allah's sanctuaries who believeth in Allah and the Last Day and observeth worship and payeth the poor-due and feareth none save Allah." [31] With the destruction of the idols Muḥammad destroyed the symbol of wealth and power of pagan Arabia, and the Meccans witnessed for themselves how powerless their idols really were.

The destruction of the idols was followed by a sermon to the swollen ranks of the assembled multitudes in which Muḥammad proclaimed: "Verily the true believers are brethren; wherefore make peace among your brethren; and fear Allah, that ye may obtain mercy." [32] The pagans of Mecca submitted to Islam as had been ordained in Allah's words:

> When victory and triumph are come from God and thou seest hosts of people embrace the religion of God, ye will then praise the glory of your Lord and implore His pardon, as He is ever ready to welcome penitence.[33]

The new converts pledged to adore no other deity save God and to abstain from theft, adultery, lying, and backbiting when they offered their submission to the Lord of the Worlds.

While still in Mecca, Muḥammad dispatched emissaries to all

parts of Arabia for the purpose of preaching Islam to the tribes. Temples dedicated to pagan worship were torn down. The two major tribes of Thaqīf and Ḥawāzin did not submit without resistance. The Thaqīf had turned Muḥammad away in humiliation when he called on their city of Ṭā'if nine years earlier and were now fearing his vengeance. They had to be subdued by force, and Muḥammad's followers were victorious over both. He was much more magnanimous in his treatment of the Thaqīf and Ḥawāzin than perhaps they deserved or expected. They turned consequently to Islam and embraced the faith with an ardent zeal.

This was in the ninth year of the Hijrah, which witnessed an upward trend in the fortunes of Islam. It was a year of decisive triumph, when all of Muḥammad's enemies, the Quraysh, Thaqīf, and Ḥawāzin, submitted to him. Christian and Jewish tribes on the periphery of Arabia reached amicable agreements with the Prophet of Islam, who in return for his promise of protection received from them a consideration in a form of payment later termed *jizyah*. Muḥammad made no attempt to convert them to Islam, as both peoples already had received the Scripture from Allah; Muḥammad, moreover, had been specifically commissioned by Allah to bring the message to non-believers in Him.

This by no means eliminated the possibility of conflict with Christians and Jews. A part of Muḥammad's role was also to set straight those who had formerly received the Scripture but later deviated.

> Fight against such of those who have been given the Scripture as believe not in Allah nor the Last Day, and forbid not that which Allah hath forbidden by His messenger, and follow not the religion of truth, until they offer tribute on the back of their hands bowing low.[34]

In its pronouncements concerning Christians and Jews, the Qur'ān refers to their having succumbed to what Islam regards a deadly sin, namely *shirk* or association in worship; this in itself would justify the visitation of the wrath of Allah at the hands of the Muslims.

> The Jews say Ezra is the son of God while the Christians say Christ is the son of God. . . . They say this with their own mouths imitating the saying of those who disbelieved of old. May God fight them, how perverse they are! They have taken as lords besides Allah their rabbis and their monks and the Messiah, son of Mary, when they were bidden to worship only one god. There is no God but He! Be he glorified by those they associate with Him as partners; He it is who sent His messenger with guidance and the true religion that He may cause it to prevail over all religion, however much disbelievers are averse! [35]

Yet in spite of such strong statements concerning the "deviation" of other Scripturists, Islam still permitted Christians and Jews, wherever they were to be found in lands under Muslim domination, to retain their religious practices unrestrained.

The Submission of Arabia

The year 631 is also known as the "year of delegations" (*Sanat al-Wufūd*) when the tribes of Arabia sent their representatives to Mecca to offer their submission to Allah and their fighting men to Muḥammad. They paid taxes and volunteered tithes, a novel experience for them. Those who once ridiculed and satirized the Prophet now outrivaled one another in their laudatory praise of a man from Quraysh who had triumphed in the name of Allah over every obstacle placed in his path. Muḥammad had thus become a hero of Arabia, the first and the last Arab to accomplish so much from a very inauspicious start.

Following the submission of the tribes, Muḥammad sent out his representatives to the various parts of Arabia to teach the precepts of the new religion, enjoining them to "deal gently and be not harsh." The Prophet's messengers were to bring cheer to the converts and good tidings to those who believed that the key to heaven is "to bear witness to the divine truth and do good."

Muḥammad had now succesfully fulfilled his mission. In ten short years after his flight from Mecca, he had gained over to Islam the whole of Arabia, a land that had never before united under any set of ideals or beliefs. Now they came from all over to proclaim their submission to God and loyalty to Muḥammad.

Thus he witnessed in his lifetime the accomplishment of his mission. Idolatry was destroyed; spirituality now superseded superstition, cruelty, and vice. A land hitherto torn by intertribal warfare in pursuit of plunder and material gain was now united in purpose by ties that made one Arab a brother to every other Arab in submission to the one God and His apostle Muḥammad. *Blood* kinship for the first time was subordinated to a kinship constructed on *faith.* Ideals hitherto measured in terms of worldly gains were lifted to heights the skeptical Arab would never have accepted ten years before: an afterlife with rewards and punishments meted out to the deserving on a day of judgment. Such injunctions from Allah pertaining to charity, goodness, rightdoing, acting justly, observing peace, all would have been deemed unacceptable outside the confines of tribal society before Muḥammad began to preach. These precepts were now made a condition of belief for all those who professed Islam.

The Farewell Message

In February of 632 Muḥammad set out once more with a large contingent of his followers to perform what turned out to be a farewell pilgrimage to Mecca. The city had been purged of all traces of idolatry during the preceding year when Muḥammad had decreed that none but the believers should perform the pilgrimage rite. Before the ceremony was completed, Muḥammad addressed the Muslims from atop Mt. ʿArafāt, a short distance from the city, in a speech which has figured in the pilgrimage ritual ever since. To the assembled multitudes he proclaimed:

> O believers harken unto my words as I know not whether another year will be permitted unto me to be amongst you. Your lives and possessions are as sacred and inviolable (and so you must observe) the one toward the other, until ye appear before the Lord, as this day and month is sacred for all; and

> remember you will have to present yourselves to the Lord who will demand that you give an account of your deeds . . . Listen to my words and harken well. Know ye that all Muslims are brothers. Ye are all one brotherhood; and no man shall take ought from his brother unless it is freely given to him. Shun injustice. And let those here assembled inform those who are not of the same who when told afterwards may remember better than those who now hear it.[36]

Muḥammad concluded his sermon with the remarks: "O Lord! I have fulfilled my message and accomplished my task," to the echo of the assembled: "Verily thou hast." He ended with the words "O Lord! I beseech Thee to bear witness unto it."

The eleventh year of the Hijrah and the last of his life was spent in Medina. There the Prophet busily sought to tidy the affairs of the Muslims, as he sensed the end was near. At this time Muḥammad integrated the tribal and provincial communities that had professed Islam and dispatched deputies to all parts of Arabia to teach the injunctions of the new religion to converts, to administer justice, and to collect tithes.

A new military expedition against the Byzantine prefect who had killed Zayd, Muḥammad's envoy, was in the process of departing when news of the Prophet's illness leaked out. Some anxiety followed and a number of impostors, or pretenders,[37] rose to share the prophetic role with Muḥammad.

The last few days of his life Muḥammad arranged to spend with his wife ʿĀʾishah, the youngest daughter of Abu-Bakr. Though he had grown weak and feeble, he continued to lead the faithful in public prayer up to the third day prior to his death. In his last sermon to the believers he stated: "O Muslims! If I have wronged any of you, I am here to make amends; if I owe ought to any of you, all that I possess belongs to you." He prayed to God for mercy, then enjoined the faithful to observe religious duties and lead peaceful lives, reminding them of Allah's promise: "Abode in paradise We shall grant unto those who seek not to exalt themselves on earth or do wrong; a happy issue will attend the pious."

In a final gesture, an eloquent testimony to the role which he faithfully carried out to the end, Muḥammad told all those near him: "I have made lawful only that which God hath ordained and I have prohibited only that which God so commanded in His Book." Then turning to his daughter Fāṭimah and aunt Ṣafiyah for the last time he said to them: "Work ye both that which will gain thee acceptance with the Lord; for verily I have no power to save thee in any wise." He then rose and returned to ʿĀʾishah's dwelling where he died a few hours later, on June 8, 632 in the arms of his young wife.

"Thou shalt surely die (O Muḥammad)
And they also shall die!"

He was buried on the very spot in ʿĀʾishah's home where later a mosque was erected. Abu-Bakr faced up to the task of announcing the Prophet's death addressing the faithful assembled outside:

> "O Muslims! If any of you has been worshiping Muḥammad, then let me tell you that Muḥammad is dead.
>
> But if you really do worship God, then know ye that God is living and will never die!"

CHAPTER 4

Muḥammad the Man

MUḤAMMAD RATES as one of the truly great personalities of history. Muḥammad's success in accomplishing his mission within ten short years is a tribute to his faith and to his superior moral qualities. His life and his work are a living testimony to his genius. That he towered over contemporaries, many of his predecessors and successors alike, is evident in the radical transformation of fundamental values and mores he wrought for a people who hitherto had excelled in their uncontrollable individualism and insatiable egoism.

The Genius in Him

Muḥammad's insecure early youth wherein misery often prevailed apparently had awakened in him the instincts which in later years relentlessly drove him on and instilled in him the determination to accomplish clearly stated goals: unity in worship and a coherent society for the Arabs. Stimulated by the social injustices he himself experienced, and which reached deeply into his youth, Muḥammad preached religion. By means of religion he sought to accomplish certain important aims, involving a complete social transformation as revolutionary in nature and extent as any of the modern crusading socialistically motivated ideologies.

The idea of religion serving to bring about social revolution was not alien to Semitic societies. From the times of the Pharoah Ikhnaton to the times of Moses and the ethical prophets of Israel; from Zoroaster to Jesus to Muḥammad, when social conditions became intolerable and grew increasingly lacking in equity, in righteousness, and in the fundamental principles of morality, religion not ideology provided the incentive for change.

The success of Muḥammad's mission, based on other-worldly precepts, rests in no small measure on his own worldly gifts. He was thoroughly practical and master of both individual and mass psychology, as is attested by the near fanatical devotion of his companions to him and to the message he preached. Muḥammad's teachings were tailored to the mundane wants of his audience as can be seen in his earthly depiction of rewards and punishments for the skeptics and unbelievers. His message reflected the clairvoyance of his understanding in relation to his milieu and the needs of Arabian society in his time.

He never forgot himself even in the highest moment of triumph, remaining just and temperate in the exercise of authority which, had he chosen, could have been absolutely dictatorial. Had he been lacking in sincerity and genuineness, this side of him would have manifested itself upon his conquest of Mecca. As our sources acknowledge, the city was treated with the magnanimity that doubtlessly he himself would not have received had the Quraysh triumphed instead. There was nothing to prevent him in this moment of victory from gratifying his own ambition and satisfying a sense of lust or revenge if it had been at all present.

His capacity for achievement is evident in the success of his mission. His cardinal aim to assert the worship of one God, and that God alone, was attained, and with it a doctrine that would insure its perpetuation. A new ritual and a new cult were born. The old system of belief based on idolatry was abolished, by force when peaceful persuasion failed. Commensurate with the triumph of Allah was the erection of a new society based on submission to Him, a society which recognized the universal brotherhood of all Muslims. First the Arabs of Arabia and later, with the expansion of Islam outside of Arabia, all those who submitted to Allah in Islam were looked upon as rightful members of this vast fraternity.

At first, and by his own admission, Muḥammad had no intention of founding a new religion. He merely wanted his fellow Arabs to worship one God, the only God, as worshiped by their neighbors, the Christians and the Jews.

> Say, we believe in Allah and in what has been revealed to us, in what was revealed to Abraham, Ishmael, Isaac, Jacob, and the tribes; in what was given to Moses and Jesus, and in what the prophets received from their Lord: we make no distinction between any of them.[1]

Muḥammad did not consider his mission as superseding those of his predecessors, the former prophets of Allah from Abraham to Jesus; he looked upon his mission rather as serving to complete and revitalize these earlier religions and to set straight misconceptions associated with them.

Nor did he look upon himself as superior to any of the former prophets; he was one of them, but the last to be commissioned by Allah to deliver the same message previously delivered by his former colleagues.

Beside reminding his people of Allah's command that they should worship none other but Him, Muḥammad also drew attention, especially where called for, to deviations by other worshipers of the same God from the true worship established by Him. Indeed, it is also to Muḥammad's credit that at the height of his religious and political authority he did not insist that Jews and Christians should renounce their version of monotheism for that which he preached.

It was out of respect for all those who worshiped God alone, Muslim and non-Muslim, that Muḥammad made himself available to them for guidance and comfort. The destitute, the sick and those in need of hospitality had access to him. Muḥammad made no distinction between them on the basis of their worship of the true God. He looked upon himself as the liberator and protector of the other religions.

This strong protective instinct was manifest in his extensive legislation to define and safeguard in the Qur'ān the rights of women. He enforced puritanical injunctions clearly unheard of before his time, such as banning intoxicating beverages, the gratification of illicit sex relations, and the like. He conceived it his sacred duty to promote the moral and material welfare of his people. Some authorities in subsequent decades have advanced the claim that Muḥammad did not purpose the establishment of a formal code of law since, from their point of argument, he only volunteered rules of conduct and ritual when they were extorted from him by questioning. There might be some truth to this argument; at least it would help to explain the absence of a well laid out system of law for political conduct. The absence of a defined system of law had drastic consequences, following the death of Muḥammad, for political solidarity in the Islamic commonwealth.

The study of Islam reveals the eclectic nature of Muḥammad's preachings. This eclecticism, however, did not prevent it from acquiring an identity of its own stamped by Muḥammad's personality and mirroring the basic precepts which guided his life. Islam is the religion of Allah.

> This day have I perfected your religion for you and completed My favor unto you, and have chosen for you as religion AL-ISLAM.[2]

Faith was perhaps the strongest moving force behind Muḥammad's personality. And the central repository of this faith was his conception of the will of God as it finally came to be expressed in the Qur'ān. The strength of his faith did indeed write one of the most dramatic chapters in the history of mankind. The strong and powerful appeal which the Qur'ān has held over the hearts and minds of hundreds of millions during the past thirteen centuries attests to the strength of Muḥammad's convictions.

When we consider that the Qur'ān was the product of the heart and mind of an Arab principally illiterate and unschooled in any formal knowledge, we cannot but admire the faith which moved, and indeed conditioned, the man Muḥammad. While he emphatically denied his ability to perform miracles, arguing all along that God alone was the miracle worker; when considering the effects wrought by the Qur'ān on Muḥammad's people, and when pondering the magnitude of its impact on Arabs and non-Arabs alike, we can not deny that this was indeed one of the greatest miracles ever performed by one who insisted he was a mortal like everyone else. This was the miracle of the non-miracle worker.

By a fortune somewhat unusual Muḥammad, while preaching the worship of God alone, became the founder not only of a religion but also of a nation which later evolved a distinct culture of its own. Circumstances beyond his anticipation transformed Muḥammad from a religious teacher in Mecca to ruler and legislator in Medina, "but for himself he sought nothing beyond the acknowledgment that he was Allah's apostle." [3]

Above all he became the author of a text which is a poem, a code of laws, a book of common prayer, and a bible in one, reverenced to this day by a sixth of the whole of the human race, as a miracle of purity of style, of wisdom and of truth.[4]

While the establishment of Islam as the religion of Arabia and the foundation of its government and society is Muḥammad's supreme achievement, the subsequent development of a coherent commonwealth guided by the precepts of the new faith and the rise of a nation out of the heterogeneous tribes separated by clear geographical and ideological barriers is no less important for our understanding of the full range of Muḥammad's work. The radical transformation of values achieved in the Bedouin Arab, regarded as singularly egotistical in his skepticism and antipathy to change, is perhaps another miraculous achievement.

The Qur'ān provides a contrast between the life and mores of the Arabs in the shade of Islam and their values in pre-Islamic times. Not only did Muḥammad abolish and nearly uproot the institution of blood feuds, the most evil of the institutions governing social relationships in pre-Islamic Arabia, he almost reversed this institution by insisting that rivals engaged in mortal conflict should embrace and accept brotherhood in Islam. He urged upon all true believers a real union of hearts.

The essence of Muḥammad's socio-religious message is embodied in the Qur'ānic text:

> O ye who believe! Observe your duty to Allah with right observance, and die not save as those who have surrendered (unto Him);
>
> And hold fast, all of you together, to the cable of Allah, and do not separate. And remember Allah's favour unto you: how ye were enemies and He made friendship between your hearts so that ye became as brothers by His grace; and (how) ye were upon the brink of an abyss of fire, and He did save you from it. Thus Allah maketh clear His revelations unto you, that haply ye may be guided,
>
> And there may spring from you a nation who invite to goodness, and enjoin right conduct and forbid indecency. Such are they who are successful.
>
> And be ye not as those who separated and disputed after the clear proofs had come unto them. For such there is an awful doom.[5]

His Personal Assets

The question comes to mind: what kind of a person was Muḥammad to cause such a deep and lasting stir in the wastes of Arabia? What kind of a personality did he have?

From what we know, he appears to have been a humble and unpretentious being, if not outrightly austere in his habits and manner of living. He dwelt in a very simple abode in unaffected surroundings. An ambassador to the Quraysh, an outsider who had contact with Muḥammad in the period of exile once stated in this regard: "I have seen the Persian Chosroes and the Greek Heraclius sitting upon their thrones; but never did I see a man ruling his equals as does Muḥammad."

Muḥammad possessed a gentle disposition, and his temperament rarely gave way to anger. He was endowed with high moral standards and qualities of trustworthiness to such a degree that his contemporaries were prompted to call him *al-Amīn* (the trusted one) long before he embarked upon his mission. Indeed, it was his high moral qualities that induced the Yathribites to solicit his mediation in their internecine disputes. Muḥammad was exceedingly loyal to his friends and those near him. His biographer relates the story of the Christian slave Zayd who after a period of association with Muḥammad was given the opportunity to return to his father, but Zayd chose instead to remain with Muḥammad. For this act of devotion Muḥammad subsequently awarded Zayd his freedom and formally adopted him as his son.

The dignity of his personal habits, his stately and commanding stature, tact, equilibrium, and self-control made of Muḥammad a natural leader of men. A patriarchal simplicity permeated his life. He was self-reliant to a rare degree, personally delivering alms into the hands of petitioners, tying up cattle, mending his own clothes, cobbling his sandals, and aiding generally in the household duties of his wives. He never rejected an invitation; he disliked to say no, and he was "more bashful than a veiled virgin," proclaimed his witty wife ʿĀʾishah. He had the unique faculty of making each guest feel that he was the favorite. He exuded joy to those who were happy and tender sympathy to the afflicted and bereaved. Generous and magnanimous, Muḥammad shared his food with the hungry and when he died he left all his modest belongings to the faithful.

Marital Life

Further insight into his personality and character can be derived from a glance into his domestic life. This is one facet of Muḥammad where authorities concede he set an example of virtue emulated by so many millions of believers in subsequent times.

While it is not the aim of this study to make an apologetic presentation of Muḥammad's attitude toward the opposite sex or to narrate his marital indulgences, it suffices for us to state here that the revelations bearing celestial injunctions have often provided his critics with much unwarranted fodder for ridiculing his claim to prophethood. In these, "the latter-day saints" of Christian Europe found cause for dubbing Muḥammad a sensuous man who was reportedly guided to ecstatic visions through the favors bestowed upon him by the opposite sex. Scholars in more recent times have found appropriate answers to such early charges.

Those who have referred to his plural marriages as evidence of his sensuous nature made little mention of the fact that in the prime of his youth and adult years Muḥammad remained thoroughly devoted to Khadījah and would have none other for consort. This was in an age that looked upon plural marriages with favor and in a society that in pre-Biblical and post-Biblical days considered polygamy an essential feature of social existence. David had six wives and numerous concubines,[6] and Solomon was said to have had as many as 700 wives and 300 concubines.[7] Solomon's son Rehoboam had 18 wives and 60 concubines.[8] The New Testament contains no specific injunction against plural marriages. It was commonplace for the nobility among Christians and Jews to contract plural marriages. Luther spoke of it with toleration.

Muḥammad's marriages after Khadījah's, yielding about eleven wives in all, were due partly to political reasons and partly to his concern for the wives of his companions who had fallen in battle defending the nascent Islamic community. In spite of the calumnies heaped upon him by his detractors who, among other things described him as a voluptuary and wife-hungry, a study of Muḥammad's marital inclinations reveals that, besides the political considerations for acquiring more than one wife following the death of Khadījah, pity and elementary concern prompted him in later years to take on wives who were neither beautiful nor rich, but mostly old widows. The wives of companions fallen in battle had to be looked after, and Muḥammad married them in order to offer them shelter and care.[9] His marriage to Zaynab, wife of his adopted son Zayd,did occasion considerable criticism of the Prophet, and his concern over such criticism earned him the rebuke of Allah: "And ye feared men when God had the greater right that ye should fear Him."[10]

Though attentive equally to all his wives after the death of his first, Muḥammad gravitated towards ʿĀ'ishah and was permitted by the others to spend more time with her.

That he realized he was not free from error is attested by his own admission. In the testimony of certain observers:

> His errors were not the result of premeditated imposition but of an ignorant, impressible, superstitious but nevertheless noble and great man. He was excitable like every true Arab, and in the spiritual struggle which preceded his call to prophethood, this quality was stimulated to an extent that alarmed even himself.[11]

His Status as Prophet

An important facet of Muḥammad's character relates to his role as prophet and, specifically, to the question whether he was genuine. Many of his ill-wishers had insisted that he was a "false prophet." The issue here revolves around his sincerity. Certain writers have alluded to his being subject to epileptic seizures, psychic tension, and other abnormal physical manifestations, all of which, it has been argued, inspired Muḥammad to receive revelations from God.[12]

> . . . If epilepsy is to denote only those severe attacks which involve serious consequences for the physical and mental health, then the statement that Mohammed suffered from epilepsy must be emphatically rejected.[13]

What is germane to the discussion is the product, not the means. Many personalities before Muḥammad who were considered "psychologically sound" had less to offer to posterity even when they were accorded the dignity of being official spokesmen for God. We have an example in the Hebrew prophets who preached that the Israelites should return to the worship of *Yhwh* (Jehovah), as Muḥammad called to the worship of Allah.

Like Jesus, Moses, and the prophets in between, Muḥammad

was genuinely convinced of his prophetic role. The triumph of Islam as the religion of Arabia and of hundreds of millions thirteen centuries later would not have been assured, the might of the Islamic imperium notwithstanding, were it not for the powerful appeal of Muḥammad's message. The Qurʾān clearly attests to the magnitude of this message's impact, so strong that only a person endowed with superior qualities of insight could achieve it.

What is relevant for us to observe is the fact that Muḥammad did not announce his mission until after a protracted period of reflection and hesitation. He had advanced well into mature life when he proclaimed his mission to the Arabs. Muḥammad, unlike his predecessors, grew accustomed to believing that the ideas emanating from the depth of a mature soul and a rational mind attributed to the divine will, herein equated with God, must be made known and must gain acceptability.

This was his conviction; this conviction impelled him to act. The role of Gabriel as the intermediary between God and Muḥammad is only symbolic of the process by which Muḥammad became conscious of the mature concepts that we find subsequently enshrined in the Qurʾān, and draped with utmost sanctity. The intent was to insure veracity by means of sanctity, which only the association of Godhood could impart to it. Muḥammad never doubted that these concepts embodied in revelations actually represented the command of that all-pervading will, the will of God.

"Prophecy" is an old and well utilized concept among Semitic peoples. The role of a prophet to the pagan Arab was filled by the shāʿir; to the older Canaanites and their religious protégés, the Hebrews, he was a *nabi* (one who foretells). While the function of the prophet was familiar to most primitive peoples in one form or another, the more sophisticated elucidation of the role, which regards the prophet as the annointed mouthpiece of the deity, was left to the Hebrews to develop.

Muḥammad's treatment of his predecessors, the Biblical prophets, and his image of himself in the general hierarchy of prophets merit consideration. In the manner of his carrying out the requirements of prophecy, Muḥammad followed in the tradition of the other Hebrew prophets, manifesting all the symptoms attending the role—impassioned utterances, use of rhyme in speech, intense preoccupation with God and moral issues, and a sense of compulsion to declare the will of God.[14]

As a result of his intensified disputes with the Jews of Medina and the subsequent theological rift with them, Muḥammad acquired a clearer vision of his own place in the hierarchy of prophets. Of all the preceding prophets starting with Adam, who in the eyes of Muḥammad was the very first, Abraham through his son Ishmael, the eponymous father of the Arabs, becomes the patriarchal prophet. Muḥammad also brought into the picture of prophethood certain individuals who do not occur in the Jewish or Christian scriptures; nevertheless it is the Biblical prophets who play the central role as the annointed agents of God. These are accorded full recognition in the Qur'ān:

> Say (O Muslims): We believe in Allah and that which is revealed unto us and that which was revealed unto Abraham, and Ishmael, and Isaac, and Jacob, and the tribes, and that which Moses and Jesus received, and that which the Prophets received from their Lord. We make no distinction between any of them, and unto Him we have surrendered.[15]

Muḥammad conceived himself a prophet in the true Biblical line, but subsumed no extra prerogatives. He considered himself, however, the seal of prophets. In the testimony of the Qur'ān:

> Muḥammad is but a messenger, messengers (the like of whom) have passed away before him.[16]
>
> Muḥammad is not the father of any man among you, but he is the messenger of Allah and the Seal of the Prophets; and Allah is Aware of all things.[17]

Muḥammad believed he was called to deliver the message of God to his own people and also to set straight distortions in the Scriptures grafted on the message of God by Jews and Christians. Again as preserved in the Qur'ān:

> And the Jews say the Christians follow nothing (true), and the Christians say the Jews follow nothing (true); yet both are

> readers of the Scripture. Even thus speak those who know not. Allah will judge between them on the Day of Resurrection concerning that wherein they differ.[18]

This point receives considerable emphasis in the Qur'ān, as for example:

> And the Jews will not be pleased with thee, nor will the Christians, till thou follow their creed. Say: Lo! the guidance of Allah (Himself) is Guidance. And if thou shouldst follow their desires after the knowledge which hath come unto thee, then wouldst thou have from Allah no protecting friend nor helper.[19]

The sensitive nature of the prophet's task is in juxtaposition to the official view of the Scriptures; this is partially evident in the Qur'ānic verse:

> Those unto whom We have given the Scripture, who read it with the right reading, those believe in it. And whoso disbelieveth in it, those are they who are the losers.[20]

Muḥammad was quite jealous over the message he brought to his people and would not tolerate seeing it mocked or derided. "Take not those for friends who make a jest and sport of your religion from among those who were given the Book before you, and the disbelievers . . ."[21] On a number of occasions he rebuked the Jews when they chided his message with the words of the Qur'ān:

> Say: O, People of the Scripture! Do ye blame us for aught else than that we believe in Allah and that which is revealed unto us and that which was revealed aforetime, and because most of you are evil-livers?[22]

He disputed less with the Christians because he had less contact with them. There were relatively few Christians in his part of Arabia while the Jewish tribes were quite numerous in the environs of Medina where his doctrine of Islam was being molded. He appeared, however, to be equally distrustful of Christians, as stated in the Qur'ānic verse:

> O ye who believe! Take not the Jews and Christians for friends. They are friends one to another. He among you who taketh them for friends is (one) of them. Lo! Allah guideth not wrongdoing folk.[23]

Versatility of the Message

In the socio-religious injunctions and ordinances imposed on the believers and preserved in the Qur'ān, we have a measure of the versatility of Muḥammad's message. He preached to the pagans. When they became converted, he organized them into a separate community. He legislated for this community, then led it through the most trying period of its existence.

In turning statesman he never forgot his principal role as the messenger of God. While the Qur'ān abounds with legislation for the organized community, the strong ethical rejoinders are never lost sight of. Time and again Muḥammad enjoins the faithful to do rightly by the Lord and His creation, to fight for the faith, to perform commendable deeds, and to refrain from what is objectionable in the sight of God.

> . . . thine God is one God so submit ye all to Him. And give thou glad tidings to the humble, whose hearts are filled with fear when God is mentioned, and who patiently endure whatever befalls them, and who observe prayer and give generously of what We have provided them.[24]

The ethical message is strongly intertwined with the social. The full extent of his social legislation encroaches on the civil and ceremonial codes of Islam and is beyond the range of this present study. Much of the revelation enjoining social legislation for the nascent community of Islam belongs to the period of Muḥammad's preaching in Medina. Most of the ordinances and canonical laws of a developed Islamic society in the centuries following Muḥammad's death can be traced to these legislative revelations.

Revelations pertaining to women, their rights and obligations, their status in society and in the family, have been carefully recorded and often portrayed in vivid and realistic terms. Other revelations dealing with slaves, their treatment and liberation; with orphans, minors, the needy and destitutes of all sorts, have provided the cornerstone for the social structure of Islam.

While we endeavor to focus attention on Muḥammad's religious and social achievements, we must also take notice of the moral forces awakened by him in forging a coherent nation out of a most unwieldy conglomeration of tribes and systems of belief. "Half Christian and half Pagan, half civilized and half barbarian, it was given to him in a marvelous degree to unite the peculiar excellences of the one with the peculiar excellences of the other." [25]

By moral persuasion, and by coercion when called for, Muḥammad won Arabia over to the worship of the one and only God. He instilled in its wild tribes the will to fraternize rather than to continue their fratricidal wars and vendettas; to cohere rather than to pull apart when there was no precedent for cohesion in Arabia, and to abandon long established and hallowed practices and beliefs when until his advent they experienced none other.

A partial testimony to the type of change wrought by Muḥammad's message is preserved in the apocryphal statement attributed to his cousin Jaʿfar, the son of Abu-Ṭālib, in his address to the Negus of Abyssinia when the early Muslims had sought refuge there:

> Jāhilīyah people were we, worshiping idols, feeding on dead animals, practicing immorality, deserting our families and violating the covenant terms of mutual protection, with the strong among us devouring the weak. Such was our state until Allah sent unto us a messenger from amongst ourselves whose ancestry we know and whose veracity, fidelity and purity we recognize. He it was who summoned us to Allah in order to profess Him as one and worship Him alone, discarding whatever stones and idols we and our forbears before us worshiped in His stead. He moreover commanded us to be truthful in our talk, to render to others what is due them, to stand by our families and to refrain from doing wrong and shedding blood.

> He forbade committing fornication, bearing false witness, depriving the orphan of his legitimate right and speaking ill of chaste women. He enjoined on us the worship of Allah alone, associating with Him no other. He also ordered us to observe prayer, pay *zakāh* [alms] and practise fasting.[26]

Muḥammad brought to his people what men of faith construe the commandments of God, as Moses and Jesus had brought similar commandments to their peoples before him. These commandments are eloquently enshrined in the Qur'ān in such verses as:[27]

> Set not up with Allah any other god (O man) lest thou sit down reproved, forsaken.
>
> Thy Lord hath decreed, that ye worship none save Him . . . (that ye show) kindness to parents . . . and lower unto them the wing of submission through mercy, and say: My Lord! Have mercy on them both as they did care for me when I was little.
>
> If ye are righteous, then lo! He is ever Forgiving unto those who turn (unto Him).
>
> Give the kinsman his due, and the needy, and the wayfarer, and squander not (thy wealth) in wantonness.
>
> And let not thy hand be chained to thy neck nor open it with a complete opening, lest thou sit down rebuked, denuded.
>
> And come not near unto adultery. Lo! It is an abomination and an evil way.
>
> Slay not your children, fearing a fall to poverty, We shall provide for them and for you. Lo! The slaying of them is great sin.
>
> And slay not the life which Allah hath forbidden save with right.
>
> Come not near the wealth of the orphan save with that which is better till he come to strength; and keep the covenant.
>
> Fill the measure when ye measure, and weigh with a right balance; that is meet, and better in the end.
>
> (O man), follow not that whereof thou hast no knowledge. Lo! The hearing and the sight and the heart—of each of these it will be asked.
>
> And walk not in the earth exultant. Lo! Thou canst not rend the earth, nor canst thou stretch to the height of the hills.

Other verses selected at random equally portray the essence of Islam's commandments as revealed unto Muḥammad and taught by him:[28]

> Fear ye the Lord who from a single soul ye didst create . . . and therefrom its mate . . .
>
> And give to the orphans their due . . . to the women their dowries.
>
> Devour not possessions amongst yourselves by means unlawful . . .
>
> And covet not that whereby Allah hath shown distinction for some over others. . . . Ask Allah of His bounty . . .
>
> And show kindness to parents and to kindred, and orphans, and the needy, and the neighbor . . .
>
> Approach not prayer when you are not in full possession of your senses . . . nor when you are unclean.
>
> Verily Allah commands you to make over trusts to those entitled to them and that . . . ye judge justly between men.
>
> O ye who believe! Obey Allah, and obey His messenger and those who are in authority among you.
>
> Whatever of good befalleth thee it is from Allah, and whatever of ill befalleth thee it is from thyself.
>
> Fight, therefore, in the cause of Allah . . . and urge on the believers . . .

The Qur'ān explicitly enjoins the believer to avoid "the evil of all that is hateful in the sight of thy Lord."[29] Muḥammad is reminded that "this is (part) of that wisdom wherewith thy Lord hath inspired thee . . ." and commanded to "set not up with Allah another God, lest thou be cast into hell, reproved, abandoned."[30]

Muḥammad in his lifetime faithfully carried out what he regarded the will of God. Millions of Muslims never doubted that he was genuinely commissioned by Allah to deliver His commandments to those who believed in Him. Yet for a long time, well through the Middle Ages and up to the Age of the Enlightenment, Muḥammad's prophethood and message remained the object of suspicion and controversy. In his biography of Muḥammad Prideaux treated the Prophet's life as "a mirror to unbelievers, atheists, deists, and libertines." Nearly a century earlier a prominent Orientalist when using the name of Muḥammad felt impelled to qualify it with the statement: "at the mention of whom the mind shudders . . ." [31]

In his *Vie de Mahomet* published posthumously, the Count de Boulainvilliers went to the opposite extreme and attempted to "portray Mohammed as a wise and enlightened lawgiver, who sought to establish a reasonable religion in place of the dubious dogmas of Judaism and Christianity." [32] Two decades later Savary published a translation of the Qur'ān in which he treated Muḥammad "as one of those unusual personalities occasionally appearing in history, who remake their environment and enlist men in their triumphant train." [33] When at about the same time Voltaire attacked the Qur'ān and Muḥammad in his *Mahomet ou le fanatisme,* he was not motivated by Christian disdain for Islam and its prophet but rather by his intense dislike of fanaticism of which Muḥammad in his eyes was a good example.[34] Later in his *Essai sur les moeurs,* Voltaire tones down his judgment and grants recognition to the accomplishments of Muḥammad upon which his claim to fame rests. In 1840 when he delivered his second lecture on "Heroes and Hero-Worship," Thomas Carlyle stated the prevalent view of Muḥammad as "an impostor, an incarnation of falsehood, and that his religion was a combination of charlatanism and stupidity." But he hastened to mention that "such a view is a reflection upon ourselves." "For countless people," he argued, "Mohammed's words have been the guiding star of their lives. Can it be possible that so many creatures, created by God, have lived and died for something which must be regarded as a tragic fraud?" [35]

CHAPTER 5

Foundation of Islam: The Qur'ān

AT THE CORE of Islam lies the Qur'ān, the Word of God. To a religion that has no ecclesiastical organization, mystical ritual, a body of saints whose aid the troubled soul may invoke, the Qur'ān becomes the principal inspiration and refuge for the Muslim. More than representing the supreme embodiment of the sacred beliefs of Islam, its bible and its guiding light, the Qur'ān constitutes the Muslim's main reference not only for matters spiritual but also for the mundane requirements of day to day living.

The Qur'ān is more widely read than any other sacred text; indeed, more portions of it are committed to memory than those of any other similar body of sacred writings. The Muslim's extensive dependence on the Qur'ān makes of it the principal recourse both in the performance of religious duties and in the acquisition of basic knowledge. To him the Qur'ān has profound historical and literary meaning besides serving as his manual of prayer, code of religious and ethical well-being, his guide to social behavior and daily living, and a compendium of useful definitions and maxims of practical value. It is a repository of historical knowledge as unfolded by God and revealed unto the believers as a reminder. It is also the basic textbook for all Muslim youth studying the Arabic language in its present form.

As a magnificent piece of rhymed prose, it yields not only aesthetic contentment but provides also much philosophic truth. It is a valuable tool to the lexicographer seeking to perfect the language, to the scientist probing for clues concerning the existence of man and of the world, to the historian seeking understanding of the purpose of life as ordained by God for mankind, and to the theologian who regards the Qur'ān as the ultimate unchallengeable recourse for all religious knowledge. The Muslim jurist finds in the Qur'ān the basic laws governing Islamic society. Indeed no book, sacred or nonsacred, has served, and continues to serve, so utilitarian a function to so many millions as the Qur'ān, Allah's gift to the Arabs through His prophet Muḥammad.

Conception

The term *"Qur'ān"* in a literal sense means "recitation," "readings," that is, of a proto-type, a "concealed book" or a "well-guarded tablet" which in Muslim theology is supposed to rest in the Seventh Heaven. The Qur'ān more specifically refers to the body of these "readings." Perhaps one may refer to it as a "lectionary," of the type known to the ancient Aramaeans. The Arabs often refer to it as *"al-Kitāb"* (the book), that is, of Allah. Each chapter in the Qur'ān is termed *"sūrah"* (literally, series). Those who studied the Qur'ān called these sūrahs "revelations"; indeed, the term *revelation* is more appropriate in describing the process by means of which Muḥammad received the Qur'ān from God.

The sanctity of the Qur'ān lies in the Muslim consideration of the text as the official word of God and of Muḥammad as the appointed mouthpiece of God. Muḥammad is alleged to have received the sūrahs from the archangel Gabriel, the go-between. The manner of transmission is known as *"tanzīl"* (literally, causing to descend), that is, from heaven, bits by bits, readings from the "prototype of scriptures," the original word which Jews and

Christians previously had received through the aegis of prophets who like Muḥammad had been commissioned to deliver God's sacred message to mankind.

This series of readings for which Muḥammad was called upon by Gabriel to deliver to the Arabs, who hitherto had lacked a body of sacred text, was to be in Arabic, "the language of the angels," as verified by the Qur'ān:

> We have made it an Arabic Qur'ān that ye (Arabs) may see the truth. And it is truly in the mother of books (scriptures) with Us (preserved), most exalted and wise.[1]

The text was revealed to Muḥammad over a span of two decades in parts as the occasion required. The orthodox theologians in the century following Muḥammad's death advanced the premise that the Qur'ān is uncreated, being as it were the word of God. A school of rationalist thinking in the third century of the Hijrah boldly proclaimed the opposite view, namely, that it was created.

Perhaps one reason for the differing conceptions of the Qur'ān's background lies in the seeming contradictions to the untrained eye. The orthodox theologians had insisted that the duty of the faithful was to accept it literally and not to question the tenor or meaning of the revelations. When Muḥammad was alive, the more blatant inconsistencies were usually set straight by further revelations. But when the revelations were gathered and recorded after his death, the only avenue left to cast light on the text was that of exegesis. Apparently Muḥammad himself was not concerned with the exact wording of the revelations; the precision of wording was subordinated to content. Excessive exegesis applied to the text by the interpreters of the Qur'ān in later decades resulted from lexical and philological discrepancies.

Arrangement

To the lay observer the Qur'ān may appear difficult to follow. The arrangement of the sūrahs does not subscribe to a historical pattern; indeed, it adheres to no consistent chronological or topical pattern either. The Western observer may be prone to find "inconsistencies" not only in the text, but in the style as well. A broader understanding of the context wherein the revelation was first received and knowledge of the occasion on which it was applied is indispensable to a meaningful understanding of the Qur'ān.

We have, by way of example, revelations recognizing the two pagan deities, al-ʿUzzah and al-Lāt as the daughters of Allah; we have also revelations rescinding the same; yet both types are preserved in the Qur'ān. To Muḥammad there was no contradiction here because if Allah is absolute and arbitrary, why should there be any restraint on what He commands and forbids? Allah may vary His ordinances at pleasure, prescribing one set of laws for the Jews, another for the Christians, and still another for Muslims.

The sūrahs of the Qur'ān, each treated as a separate chapter, are arranged according to length in descending order: the longest come first and the shortest last, with the exception of the *"Fātiḥah"* (the opener) which is placed at the very beginning of the Qur'ān. Some Western scholars have regarded this arrangement as motivated purely by mechanical considerations. This on the surface may be the case; but actually were we to observe closely the closing lines of some sūrahs and the opening lines of those immediately following each, we would detect some sort of continuity. In the "Fātiḥah," for instance, the believer invokes God to point the right path to Him; immediately following, in the chapter termed *"al-Baqarah"* (the cow) the first six verses provide the principal points of "the path," or what can be described as the embodiment of the cardinal doctrine of Islam. The same type of continuity in trend of thought can be seen in the chapter *"al-ʿImrān"* (the family of ʿImrān) which ends with injunctions carried over into the following chapter, *"al-Nisā'"* (the women).

Sūrahs vary in length from 287 verses ("al-Baqarah") to 3 (*"al-Naṣr"* and *"al-Kawthar"*). The verses themselves are of very unequal length; some consist of two words,[2] while others run for nearly half a page.[3] The manner of dividing or providing breaks in sūrahs varies from version to version. Each sūrah usually received a title based on the occasion that might have invoked the revelation. The process of titling dates back to the second Muslim century. Dividing the Qur'ānic text into four, eight, or thirty parts for a total of sixty sections was done for the practical purpose of committing the Qur'ān to memory.

The longest sūrahs, which come first, relate to the period of Muḥammad's role as head of the community in Medina; the shorter ones, embodying mostly his ethical teachings came earlier, during his prophethood in Mecca; yet in the order followed by the Qur'ān, they are to be found mostly in the latter part. Some of the verses betray clearly traces of amalgamation, fused together for a variety of reasons at the time of the Qur'ān's codification even though they are the result of distinct occasions of revelation.

Each sūrah usually ends with the epitaph "Meccan" or "Medinan" to indicate the place of revelation. In the case of the composite sūrahs, segments thereof belong to entirely different periods, overlapping in terms of place as well as time of revelation.

The novice reading the Qur'ān for the first time is struck by the apparent disjointed fashion in which the sūrahs are arranged and by the rather "odd headings" selected for each. In the choices available for arranging the content of the Qur'ān, a system of classification according to substance was impracticable because of the variety of subjects treated under any one heading. A chronological system, however welcome it may have been, was out of the question because the date of the earlier revelations was imperfectly known, and because a number of passages belonging to different dates had been joined together.

Since an arbitrary mode of arrangement was unavoidable, it is not surprising that Zayd should adopt the one prevailing, arraying the longer ones first and the shorter sūrahs at the end. The exceptions most noticed are the very last two which contextually appear to lack continuity with the main body of the text. Similarly and by reason of its contents, Sūrah I is placed at the beginning, partly because it praises Allah in the same vein that

Psalm I praises the righteous man and largely because it gives classical expression to important articles of faith.

At first the individual revelations were distinguished from each other only by the superscription: "In the name of God the compassionate the Most merciful." [4] Headings and numbering of verses were absent in the original codices and still form no integral part of the holy script.

Style

The style of expression underlying the Qurʾān is a curious blend of poetic rhymed prose and a lyrical flow, familiar modes of expression to the pre-Islamic Arab. Whether owing to accident or design, the sacred text was particularly adaptable for oral recitation, a carry over from the Jāhilīyah when this method of expression was most popular in Arabia. Stylistically the Qurʾān shows the strong predominance of *sajʿ* (rhymed prose), a form of rhyme which adheres to no meter, but was popularly utilized by the soothsayers of pagan Arabia.

The choice of modes of expression available to Muḥammad was limited; for precedent he had either rhymed prose without meter or poetry (*shier*) with meter. The latter he consciously rejected because of his strong antipathy for the pagan poet who was allegedly in league with the jinn, by whom he was supposed to be inspired, while Muḥammad took pains to dissociate himself from being in league with any other spirit by Allah's. His antipathy to the poet is reflected in the Qurʾān: "It is indeed the saying of a noble messenger and not of a poet little of which you will believe."[5]

Some say Muḥammad disdained the poet because he felt himself lacking in poetical talents; others say it was the person of the poet he found repugnant but not his style. Understandably he who considered himself divinely guided could not identify himself with someone moved by the jinn, inferior creatures created by Allah. "And as for the poets, it is the erring ones who follow them; dost thou not see them wandering aimlessly in every vale preaching that which they do not believe." [6]

While the Prophet vehemently denounced the *shāʿir* (poet) and dissociated himself from him, his unconscious affinity with the poet shows up in certain sūrahs like CXIII and CXIV, which for all practical purposes are "charms against magic and diablerie." [7]

> Say, I seek refuge in the Lord of the dawn, from the evil He has created, from the evil of the night when it overspreads . . . from the evil of one who envies . . .[8]
>
> Say, I seek refuge in the Lord of mankind . . . from the evil of the sneaking whisperer, who whispers into the hearts of men, who is of the jinn and of man . . .[9]

This affinity is seen also in the solemn imprecation we find in Sūrah CXI, wherein the Prophet invokes the visitation of destruction upon his own uncle ʿAbd-al-ʿUzzah (servant of ʿUzzah, the female pagan deity) whom the nephew referred to as "Abu-Lahab" (father of flame):

> Perish the hands of Abu Lahab and perish he!
> His wealth shall avail him naught, nor what he hath gotten in fee
> Burned in blazing fire he shall be!
> And his wife, the faggot-bearer, also she.[10]

Neither *sajʿ* nor *shiʿr,* on the other hand, can explain the full style adapted to the text of the Qurʾān. In many of the non-Meccan sūrahs there is a flowing lyrical style which is characteristically the Prophet's; it represents his own contribution, and lacks a precedent in the earlier rhetoric used.

Neither form nor style necessarily follows a haphazard arrangement. The utility seen in both lies in the fact that the Qurʾān was intended to leave an impact on the *listener,* which could be achieved only by means of oral recitation. The motive is somewhat psychologically conceived. His audience being principally illiterate, the word they appreciated most was the oral. Hence by design more than accident, the target of Muḥammad's preachings became sensitized to the power of the rhymed word of Allah which, like the rhetorical utterances of the shāʿir in yesteryears, was to light his aesthetic soul in an era when rhyme reigned supreme in the environs of ʿUkāz.

Biblical Affinities

A Jew or Christian familiar with the contents of the Biblical, Apocryphal, Talmudic, or Midrashic literatures would be struck by the extent of the Qur'ān's dependence on them. With the exception of a few narratives purely Arabian in origin, namely, the stories referring to 'Ād, Thamūd, and Luqmān, and two alluding to dhu-'l-Qarnayn (the two-horned one), Alexander the Great, and the "Seven Sleepers," all other such narratives have their Biblical parallels.

What would be obvious to the Jew or Christian is the discrepany between the Biblical-Midrashic and Qur'ānic version of the same narrative. It is clear to the expert that Muḥammad was concerned less with the details of these accounts and more with the moral underlying them. He cited such narratives not to preserve them in the Qur'ān for their own sake, but rather to support a point he wished to emphasize. His was a didactical approach; and like his predecessors among the prophets of the Semites, he illustrated his themes forcefully and convincingly.

Muḥammad's interest in the sacred literature of Christians and Jews may reflect his own conception of the Islam he preached as the perfection of that religion which God had ordained for Jews, Christians, and now Arabs submitting to Him in Islam. Muḥammad made it amply clear that the religion he preached was the same religion God willed for Abraham, Moses, and Jesus. If Islam were indeed the perfection of God's religion, then the prophets of God, encompassing nearly all those cited in the Testaments, become of singular importance to Muḥammad's mission and his role as a prophet. If Christianity and Judaism, however imperfect they may have appeared to Muḥammad, were expressions of earlier religions willed by Allah, then Muḥammad must show Islam's ties therewith; otherwise from the point of view of basic principles and personalities instrumental in shaping these earlier religions of Allah, Muḥammad's mission would have been deemed redundant and unwarranted.

Hence by force of necessity Muḥammad considered it essential to the credibility of his mission that he set straight the erroneous interpretations given by Jews and Christians to Allah's religion and, more important, to justify his break with his Jewish adversaries when the occasion called for it. This would also account for the frequent occurrence in the Qur'ān not only of Biblical themes, but of Biblical narratives and personalities as well.

The inconclusive manner in which these narratives survive in the Qur'ān, moreover, often in vague and sometimes in erroneous confusion, for example where Muḥammad mistakes Miriam, Moses' sister for Mary, Jesus' mother, suggests that he derived his knowledge of these Biblical accounts and personalities either from uninformed sources or from informants, perhaps Monophysite Christians, whose views of their religion did not comport with the orthodox version of the same. The motive, nevertheless, clearly shows through his narration of these accounts: to illustrate more forcefully the main theme of God's great design for man, namely, to reward the righteous and punish the wicked. His knowledge of the Scriptures, furthermore, though falling short of the expert's, enabled him, at least to his own satisfaction, to meet the criticism of his Jewish adversaries in Medina; criticism which lapsed so strongly into derision that he could eliminate it only by uprooting the Jews from the city and its environs.

Muḥammad's conception of Islam's role in the cosmic order ordained by the great architect may have resulted in the incorporation of Biblical themes into the sacred text. The Qur'ān endorses the story of the creation of Adam and the angels' worship of him. We find in it Biblical narratives relating to the flood and the role of Noah; the patriarchate of Abraham and his deliverance from the fire which Nimrod made to destroy him; the stories of Cain and Abel, Joseph and his brothers, Jacob and the tribes, David and Solomon, and numerous others connected with the Old Testament prophets. New Testament accounts, such as the role of Jesus, his "virgin birth," his childhood, denial of the crucifixion, and how Jesus foretold the coming of Muḥammad are also integrated into the Qur'ān. There are narratives on Mary, John the Baptist, and Zachariah.

Muḥammad musters these personalities and accounts into the

Qur'ān in order to illustrate the purport of his mission; to explain and justify his position in God's design for mankind as it will be revealed on the Day of Judgment. The numerous stories and legends he created "were added for homiletic purposes or to demonstrate the supernatural origin of his knowledge." [11]

The Biblical narratives and tales of wrath suited Muḥammad well in his capacity as *nadhīr* warner battling to win over to Allah his Meccan and his Medinan opponents, whether they were pagan or Jewish. He fought them often with their own weapons, turning the testimony of the Scriptures against the Jews as supporting evidence of Allah's predictable wrath if the unbelievers should persist in their obstinacy, resistance, persecution, or derision of the believers in Him. There were ample supporting tales of vengeance in the Old and New Testaments; also varied samples of the destruction visited upon the disbelievers of earlier times and the persecutors of God's children such as the Egyptians, the "people of Lot," of Noah, ʿĀd, and Thamūd.

The main purport of the Qur'ān in the context of its historical evolution is two-fold: a call to belief in the one God, the supreme repository of all moral law and ethical guidance and, secondly, the establishment of the practical guides and precepts necessary for organizing the believers into a coherent community that would assure the triumph of the religious force that called it into being in the first instance.

This dual aim falls into a sequential order: the pre-Hijrah period, which was devoted to the task of making converts; and the post-Hijrah decade dedicated to organizing the community of believers. A study of the revelations received during both periods, taking into account the overlaps, clearly supports this observation.

The Meccan Period

In the Meccan period of the evolution of the Qur'ān, Muḥammad preoccupies himself with persuading his skeptical listeners to turn away from their idol gods and worship the one God.

Regardless of how he uses his arguments or orients his discourse, the aim is the same; so is his target. He resorted to reason, logical proof, and fair exhortation in his attempts at persuasion just as often as he resorted to threats of impending doom. The central theme plays up the greatness, goodness, and righteousness of God as manifested in nature, history, and His revelations to Muḥammad. God is depicted in most exalted terms. His omnipotence and omniscience are continuously stressed.

There is no god but Allah. Muḥammad is His messenger, the Qur'ān His word. Idolatry and all deification of created beings are imposingly condemned.

> Say, God is one; God who liveth on without father and without son, and like unto whom there is none.[12]
>
> They surely disbelieve who say God is the third of three. There is no God but He. And if they desist not from what they say, a painful punishment lies for the blasphemer in bay.[13]

The joys of heaven and the pains of hell are portrayed in most vivid sensuous terms, as is also the fear and terror which will seize mankind on that awesome day, "When the sky shall be severed, and the stars shivered, and when the seas to mingle shall be suffered, and the graves uncovered."[14] This day of reckoning will bring man before his Creator, "A Day when one soul shall not obtain anything for another soul, but the command on that Day shall be with God alone."

It is then that "A soul shall know that which it hath deferred or delivered" and it will be asked ". . . what beguiled thee against thy gracious Master to rebel, who created thee and fashioned thee right . . . ?" Then comes the confrontation, "Nay, but ye disbelieve in the Ordeal (last judgment)" and the judgment "Surely the pious in delight shall dwell, and the wicked shall be in Hell, burning there on the Day of Ordeal, and evermore Hellfire they shall feel!"

Such are samples of the Meccan sūrahs; they are shorter but more numerous than the Medinan sūrahs, and executed for the most part in a different strain, forming practically a distinct group from the latter.

Not much can be learned about the date of their revelation as we lack reliable traditions on the subject. Indeed, our knowledge of the whole period preceding the Hijrah is insufficient to provide insight into the time and circumstance of the revelation of Meccan sūrahs. These, however, encompass moral legislation, the various stories and legends attributed to Christian and Judaic sources which Muḥammad must have derived from oral narrators, the legends which were adapted to Qurʾānic cosmogony, and the colorful depiction of God's design for man and the world.

The Prophet in the opinion of certain authorities[15] often expressed himself with "utmost vehemence," even allowing himself to be carried away emotionally. The words "seem rather to burst from him," in the fashion of the old soothsayer's utterances. The sūrahs resemble, according to the same view, oracles in their brevity: short crisp sentences in relatively constant but frequently changing rhyme. The oaths with which some begin also follows the pattern of expression used by the soothsayers.

But not all the sūrahs of this period are so vividly expressed. The older ones appear to reflect the calmer moods of the Prophet, yet still it is not possible for us to date them chronologically. One may surmise, however, that the increasing passion of expression was the result of obstinate resistance to the message; otherwise it would be difficult to account for the terrible threats thundered out by Muḥammad against those who ridiculed the preaching of the unity of God, of the Resurrection, and of the Judgment. When his uncle Abu-Lahab rudely repelled him, he immediately consigned him and his wife to hell in a brief special sūrah with which Allah obliged Muḥammad.

In vividly portraying the everlasting bliss of the pious and the torments awaiting the wicked, the lyrical, abrupt, and moving nature of these sūrahs left a strong impact on the imagination of simple men who had not been conditioned in their youth by strong religious preconceptions. While the earlier Meccan sūrahs reflected more the fiery and enthusiastic imagination of Muḥammad and less his ideas and abstract thought on which exact reasoning depends, the later ones were more mundane, animated, and prosaic in tone. The periods are drawn out, the revelations longer; the histories of the earlier prophets, briefly related in the first period, are now more fully detailed.

The first sūrah of the Qur'ān, the Muslim equivalent of the Lord's Prayer, belongs to this intermediate Meccan period; it is simple in wording but full of meaning, though little of it can be termed unique.

> In the name of God, the compassionate, the most merciful.
> Praise is to God, Lord of the worlds.
> The compassionate, the most merciful
> Master of the Day of Judgment.
> Thee alone we worship and thee alone for help we pray.
> Show us the right path,
> The path of those whom Thou hast favored;
> Not of those who have incurred Thine wrath
> Nor of those who have gone astray.

This simple prayer is the most often repeated of all, no less than twenty times a day, by every Muslim who performs his daily ritual prayers with its emphasis on the compassionate nature of God as *al-Raḥmān*. Indeed, so much did Muḥammad refer to God as *al-Raḥmān* that it was a matter of conjecture for a while whether he would not formally adopt *al-Raḥmān* for the proper name of God.

The sūrahs of the later Meccan or third period form a large part of the Qur'ān. They are almost entirely in prose; both the revelations and the verses are somewhat longer. The practical fieriness of the earlier sūrahs is considerably toned down. The Prophet's proclivity for the sermonizing effect is much more accentuated.

Perhaps owing to the fact that the message's effect had been played up, the propagation of Islam through these later Meccan sūrahs was much more successfully assured. Westerners may not find them suitable for carrying conviction to the minds of unbelievers. The fact remains that Muḥammad's mission was not designed for Europeans (even though large numbers did indeed convert in Spain and the Balkans where the political power of

Islam was felt) but for pagan Arabs who "though quick-witted and receptive were not accustomed to logical thinking." [16]

The Medinan Period

It is in the revelations received in Medina that the historical message of Islam as embodied in the Qur'ān becomes easier to perceive. We are able now to trace the event which occasioned the revelation. These sūrahs, by and large, are much easier to assimilate because they allude to accomplished facts and events.

They are more prosaic in style. They also abound in legislative injunctions. Since these sūrahs reflect the triumphant establishment of the religion and of the Muslim community, they are more assured in tone, more aggressive and conquering. It is now the voice of the chief that speaks, the voice of the lawgiver and statesman who is detailing rules of conduct for the believers in God.

These revelations are much more heterogeneous in derivation and practical in nature as they are tailored to meet the sociopolitical needs of an organized community, the community of believers in Medina. The style resembles that of the later Meccan sūrahs: pure prose enriched occasionally by rhetorical embellishments. In them can be detected the injunctions and impressive proclamations of Allah to the faithful.

It is in the Medinan sūrahs that we find the Qur'ān's contextual affinity with Biblical themes. We noted earlier parallels between a number of narratives and interpretations given in the Qur'ān and in Biblical texts. We also observed that a goodly number of these were from Judaic sources. Only a few seem to show connection with Christian topics. The reason for this lies in the relative absence of Christian dwellers in Medina and its environs at the time of Muḥammad's leadership there.

There are certain scholars,[17] however, who believe that concepts and notions of Judao-Christian religious themes were sufficiently established in the principal cities of the Ḥijāz to enable someone interested in them to acquire some sort of a frame of reference. But the historical record, which points to sharp resistance to Muḥammad's preachings, coupled with minimum conversions to Islam of non-pagan tribesmen, does not uphold the theories of such scholars.

Nevertheless, similarities in doctrinal and cultic concepts are too strong and numerous not to suggest some sort of direct affinity, most probably derived from oral sources close to Muḥammad, like his wife Khadījah's cousin Nawfal. Muḥammad in his youth, long before he conceived of himself as a prophet, had occasions to come in contact with Christians knowledgeable in the workings of their faith, perhaps during his caravan journeys north into Syria where the Christian sects were numerous and the monks ready to discuss the principles of their beliefs with listeners. It would be farfetched, however, to accept the views of those who state that Muḥammad may have attended meetings in which a miscellany of missionaries representing Christian sects and other preachers recounted Biblical topics and a mass of Judaic-Christian lore deriving not immediately from the Scriptures but from the post-canonical periphery—Aggada, Targum, Midrash of the Jews, and the apocryphal, patristic, homilitical, and liturgical literature of the Christians.

Affinity with the Scriptures

It is interesting to observe here that during the first period of his mission when Muḥammad took for granted the support of those already believing in the Scriptures, he saw no reason or need to scrutinize the obvious discrepancies between the revelations he received and those already recorded by Christians and Jews through earlier messengers. When the resistance of the Jews mounted during the Medinan period, and when Muḥammad became disappointed for not being acknowledged by the "People of the Book" as a messenger in his own right after he had acknowledged the validity of their scriptures, he was impelled to defend his mission by distinguishing between the *true* content of the Scriptures and what the Jews and Christians claimed them to be.

A consequential development of this rejection of Muḥammad by those with whom he displayed spiritual kinship was the Arabization of Islam. While he did not renounce cultic rituals and rites already adopted, he did give them often a peculiarly Arabian orientation. Instead of Jerusalem, Mecca becomes the primary home of Islam and the Kaʿbah its most sacred shrine; Friday, not Saturday or Sunday becomes the equivalent of the sabbath though officially it is not a day of rest; the faithful are called to prayer by the voice of the muezzin, not by bells, trumpets, or gongs; and Jesus, not Moses, becomes the second most important prophet.

Having despaired of winning over the Jews he referred to the Christians as Jews who believed: *Naṣārah,* or *"Anṣār Allāh"* (partisans of Allah), hoping they would be less hostile to and more receptive of the message even though in the early years he had far less contact with them than he had with the Jews of Medina. Still he did not absolve the Christians of error when thematic or doctrinal conflict arose; they were accused also of having corrupted the Scriptures.

The substance of the Prophet's early utterances shows a broadly derivative and eclectic nature, which suggests that the frame and structure of the early sūrahs may have consciously emulated Christian prototypes. It is not unlikely that later, when the Prophet in Medina faced the problems of legislating for an independent community predicated on entirely new norms and mores, Muḥammad sought relevant prototypes. Facing new issues involving law, cult, ritual, affairs of state and church, and the overriding necessity for immediate and decisive action consonant with the exigencies of the moment, Muḥammad may well have found in related precedents (ordained previously by the same deity to peoples so privileged) the supporting aids he needed to gain credence for his message.

The fundamental similarity in the concepts of the Bible and the Qurʾān show not only the integral relationship and basic kinship of both, but reveal also the conscious identification of the Qurʾān with God's basic design that began on the day of creation of the world and of Adam, and which shall continue until that day, the Day of Judgment, when the Lord's unfoldment of history shall end.

The Allah of the Qur'ān is the Lord, Jehovah and God of the Bible. As He previously entered into personal relationships with those who formerly had believed in Him, so does He again establish ties with those who seek Him out, even though it was necessary for Him to send the "reminder" once more. He is the one and same creator who governs the worlds and the affairs of men, His dependent creatures. As ruler of the universe He rules history; hence rewards and punishments are His way of settling accounts on a day of reckoning, when the dead are resurrected, body and soul together, on that Last Day, the Judgment Day.

While no man can question His will and while His acts are not always according to our desires, He is still the merciful, most merciful and just, the one and only God.

So far the Qur'ān and Bible tally in their view of God; but there is an important difference: the God of Muḥammad does not come to man in incarnate form. Therefore, there are no intermediaries between Him and man; no interceders either. Man's account is directly with his Lord. There is no reference to Him as "father"—He was not begotten nor does He beget. He is detached from the petty annoyances and worries of man.

The concept of divine government reminds us of the Bible. All comes to pass by the decree of God. Notions of preordainment, or predestination or bondage of the will are likewise familiar. God both in the Bible and the Qur'ān plays a determinative role in the unbelief of man, in lending substance to the idea that some beings are led astray with God's knowledge, if not by His will. All is part of His great design for man and the world, which no one has the right to question.

Muḥammad's conception of his prophetic role is also familiar. The doctrine of revelation has both Semitic and Aryan antecedents, the schema may differ but the essence and purport are identical: Revelation is brought by an angel or a spirit, the chosen messenger speaks for God not himself when delivering the message, and as the Bible testifies, "The ego of the prophet disappears before the Higher ego (God)." The idea of the revelation being a transcript of the original preserved in the highest heaven and constituting a rule of faith and a prescription for life are identical in the sacred texts of Christians, Jews, and Muslims.

We see this close identity also in the common usage of terminology referring to the process of worship. Terms like *ṣalāh* (prayer), *sabbiḥ* (praise), *tazakka* (purify), *'abd* (servant), *mathal* (parable), *qara'* (read), *malā'ikah* (angels) are the same in Islam, Christianity, and Judaism.

With language come ideas: what is meant by a prophet, a holy book, revelation, prayer, praise, angels, demons, heaven, and hell. These were known to Muḥammad, mostly indirectly through various media, through poets, monks, ḥanīfs, and traders from the Ḥijāz who alighted at Christian places of worship on caravan stops, and other such contacts.

Muḥammad's Logic

Credit must be given also to the powers of logical thinking within a predetermined framework of reference but emanating from the genius of the Prophet himself. Once you accept the premise "there is no God but God" who is the sole creator and ruler of the destiny of man; who points out the path to life everlasting for those who acquit themselves on the day of reckoning, then the doctrinal and cultic route to salvation, with the exception of detail, assumes a logical pattern. The religion of one God must per se resemble those that preceded it in accepting this premise. One God means one holy scripture, distortions and perversions notwithstanding. If the Christian Bible and the Jewish Torah should contain material that does not conform to the logic of the Prophet's conception of revelation, then the Qur'ān must serve as the final recension of God's testament.

Aids to assist man in his quest for life everlasting are important not because Jews and Christians already had them, but because it is God's desire that they should constitute an essential accompaniment of man on his journey to Him. Fasting was ordained for the believers in Medina after the Hijrah, and presumably following Muḥammad's brief association with Judaic-

Christian cultic practices. Prayer likewise serves an important role, not because monks were observed to pray regularly, but because prayer according to a fixed and prescribed formula would serve a needed disciplinary role once the wild-spirited bedouin was tamed for Allah and Islam. The promise of rewards was an inducement, the threat of Hell a deterrent; these too figured in Muḥammad's strategy for taming the pagan. The pilgrimage was to serve as a reminder of their common brotherhood; the tithe was to remind them of their obligations towards their less fortunate brethren. The stress on the absolute unity of God was to provide no excuse for the new converts to associate any of their rejected idol deities with Allah, and thus to eliminate a source of disunity and its attending strife, the evils of which precipitated the prophethood of Muḥammad.

Codification

The one hundred and fourteen sūrahs of the Qur'ān were revealed over a period of two decades. Many of the revelations were committed to memory upon their "descent." Numerous sūrahs, on the other hand, were recorded on various bits of parchment, palm leaves, smooth stones, and similar objects. Being principally illiterate, the Prophet himself did no writing; he had entrusted most of what had been recorded to his aid Zayd ibn-Thābit.

When Muḥammad died there existed no singular codex of the sacred text. While the memorizers were numerous, no one of them knew the whole. The revelations were scattered and were threatened with being lost. Oral transmission, moreover, was an unreliable method of preserving the Qur'ān because it left the door open sometimes to deliberate, but often to inadvertent alterations. Disputations over the substance of the sacred text obviously could not be permitted, and the need for a uniform codex was soon in evidence.

Shortly after the death of Muḥammad, his father-in-law successor Abu-Bakr (632-634) was compelled to reconquer Arabia for Islam. In the fighting that ensued, a good number of the Prophet's companions, especially the *ḥuffāẓ* (sing. *ḥāfiẓ*: memorizer) among them, were killed. The short, but sanguinary, campaign in 633 against the false prophet or pretender Musaylima also took its toll of the companions. Abu-Bakr was prevailed upon by ʿUmar, who later succeeded him as caliph (634-644), to undertake a formal codification of the Qurʾān.

Abu-Bakr commissioned the twenty-two year-old Zayd, aid of the Prophet, native of Medina where most of the revelations were to be found, to undertake the responsibility of codifying the revelations. Zayd proceeded to assemble the text from scattered sources but chiefly "from the breasts [memory] of men [the companions]" as he put it. His efforts yielded the first assembled copy of the Qurʾān, which he handed over to the caliph. Abu-Bakr at his deathbed bequeathed the codex to his successor ʿUmar who later turned it over to his daughter Ḥafsa, one of Muḥammad's widows.

This first redaction of the sacred text of Islam had no canonical authority, and the format pursued in arranging the revelations is not known. The Muslims had no access to it and not many could recite much of this official version from memory. Furthermore, serious quarrels soon erupted among the Muslim levies from the various districts of conquered lands over the true content of the Qurʾān, owing to a number of interpretations made possible by lexical difficulties.

It was especially during a serious military engagement, the battle of Nehavand in 650-51, that Ḥudhayfa, commander of the Muslim forces, became acutely aware of the serious consequences such disputations over the content of the holy text could have for future campaigns. It was he who prevailed upon the caliph ʿUthmān (644-656) to produce one authoritative universal version of the Qurʾān.

Once again the task was entrusted to Zayd. Assisted by a commission of three leading Qurayshites, Zayd assembled all available copies of the text and proceeded to dictate to the scribes the contents of the final redaction. The work was done in 657, twenty-five years after Muḥammad's death, the year when the caliph pronounced the text the official codex for all Muslims. The main copy was kept in Medina while three others were sent to the principal Muslim encampments at Baṣra and Kūfa in Iraq and Damascus in Syria. All other copies were ordered destroyed.

Scholars have lamented the destruction of these nonauthorized versions of the Qurʾān, a grave loss in their eyes from the point of view of textual criticism. The version established by ʿUthmān for all time is not complete according to certain critics who point to the fragmentary nature of some passages in support of their attestations. It is probable that a few detached pieces were left out of the final redaction when they had been a part of the earlier codex. It is not easy to prove, on the other hand, that Zayd willfully left out passages embarrassing to certain important converts once staunch opponents of Muḥammad. Nor can we tell whether he had been encouraged by the first three caliphs involved in the redaction of the Qurʾān to interpolate.

It is quite possible that Zayd in assembling the revelations, did not have access to all previous versions. There is also the possibility of simple inadvertent clerical errors in the process of recording. Skeptics are of the opinion that Zayd prudently introduced some slight alterations to the wording of the revelations not readily detected. They have accused him also of permitting some "extras" to find their way into the official codex immediately preceding the final revision. These extras are said to ante-date both the Hijrah and, in the view of the extremists, even the Meccan period of Muḥammad's preachings.

Since no devout Muslim would willfully attempt to tamper with the word of God, we must assume that, by and large, the final codex is a faithful reproduction of the earlier version. Critics generally agree that the redaction sponsored by the caliph ʿUthmān contains none but genuine elements even though their arrangement is in disarray.

The content was fixed, but additional problems engendered by the use of the Arabic alphabet remained. These merit some attention if we are to appreciate the full range of the Qurʾān's textual history.[18] There were many words which could be read in different ways and persons who chose could read into the text what they looked for. There were discrepancies not only in the reading of the script, but also in pronouncing it.

Dialectical license in grammatical forms, which had not then been restricted, posed an additional problem. The sense of the words may not have varied, but readings did. Eventually seven possible readings of the Qur'ān became possible as a result of divergences, but with the passing of time they were reduced to two. When vowel signs, diacritical points, and other orthographic signs were invented to distinguish between similarly formed consonants, proper vocalization ensued and arbitrary conjecture on the part of the reader was virtually ended.

Yet the correct recitation of the Qur'ān was not necessarily enhanced thereby. This remains until today an art which even those most fluent in the Arabic language can not readily master. Recitation of the Qur'ān, even today, is aided by a semi-musical modulation which differs from one school to another of those concerned with the study of the Qur'ān.

Exegesis

Owing to the numerous obscurities inherent to the Qur'ān's format, it was very soon after the death of Muḥammad that certain individuals began to apply themselves to the task of interpreting these vague sections. Not all of those who set out on this important undertaking were qualified or honorable in intent. Indeed, even Ibn-ʿAbbās, a first cousin of the Prophet and the earliest of the exegetes, gave currency to a number of falsehoods; some of his students appear to have followed his example. He and his students were less concerned with the exegesis of individual words than with the exposition of the meaning of whole passages.

With the later rise of philology as an aid to the understanding of the Qur'ān, and when with the lapse of time knowledge of the old language declined, more and more effort was expended on the explanation of vocables. Very few results of the hermeneutical efforts invested in the first two centuries of the Hijrah survive. This was the period when not only the opportunists, but also philologists, grammarians, and even philosophers set themselves to the task of explaining the difficulties in the Qur'ān.

One of the fullest and earliest of the important commentaries is Ṭabari's (839-923), executed in thirty parts.[19] This commentary contains elaborate data not only on canonical law but also on the circumstances of each revelation. While not all hopes were realized with this commentary, still in this conservatively faithful work we have the summation of all Qur'ānic knowledge of the first three centuries following the death of Muḥammad.

Another well known commentary is the *Kashshāf* of Zamakhshari[20] (1074-1144) which represents a more progressive tendency than Ṭabari's, but is equally respectful of the Qur'ānic text. Zamakhshari was an adherent of the Muʿtazilite or rationalistic school of philosophy and therefore less concerned with the accumulation of traditions than with the rational interpretation thereof. Zamakhshari delighted in uprooting traces favorable to determinism, anthropomorphism, intervention of the jinns, and in making distinctions between the *essence* and the *attributes* of God. Zamakhshari has been praised for his great insight and still greater subtlety but criticized for his aptness to read his own scholastic ideas into the Qur'ān.

Fakhr-al-Dīn al-Rāzi (d. 1209) was an anti-Muʿtazilite who inserted his own literary dissertations, philosophic and juridic, in what resembles less an exegesis and more a series of monographs. Still he was the last in the great line of exegetes. Later commentators like Bayḍāwi (d. 1286), who bequeathed us a most useful exegesis[21] even though it was but an abridgment of Zamakhshari's work, al-Maḥalli (d. 1495), and al-Suyūṭi (d. 1505) made no new contributions to the task of exegesis.

Numerous other commentaries have been written, some quite prodigious in size; for the most part they contain much that is untrustworthy or irrelevant, yet they provide us with useful hints for a fuller understanding of the Qur'ān.

Translation

Officially the Qur'ān was not to be translated into other languages because Allah declared to Muḥammad: "We have revealed unto thee an Arabic Qur'ān." By this the faithful understood that Arabic was to be the sole language of the Qurʾān, particularly because it is a copy of the archtype preserved in heaven. Moreover, Arabic was the language in which the archangel Gabriel revealed the Qurʾān to Muḥammad and in which it was subsequently to be preserved. So for centuries the faithful, regardless of their native tongue, were taught to recite their Qurʾān in Arabic.

Unauthorized translations have since come into being in forty-three different languages including the interlinear free translations by Muslims into their respective native languages—Persian, Chinese, Urdu, Javanese, Maratti, Bengali,[22] are among the few. The earliest translation was done into Latin by Peter the Venerable, Abbot of Cluny ca. 1141. The *ʿulamāʾ* (ulema) officially accepted a Turkish rendition and in more recent times have managed to tolerate an English translation, that of Muḥammad Marmaduke Pickthall, but under the title *"The Meaning of the Glorious Koran."* [23]

The earliest unauthorized English translation was from the French of Sieur Du Ryer. But perhaps the most highly regarded has been the extremely paraphrastic rendition of George Sale (1734). Rodwell's translation (1861) represented a brave attempt to give the revelations in chronological order. Palmer wisely chose to retain the traditional arrangement in his translation (1880). Since then we have had translations by Bell (1937-39), Arberry (1955), and others.

The more recent translations attempt a critical rearrangement of the sūrahs and are more abreast of modern scholarship. None, however, are entirely faithful to the letter of the original because of certain idiosyncrasies of the Arabic language which the most literate of Arab philologists can not always render with exactitude.

But the need for proper understanding of the holy word of Allah required meticulous and careful study. All relevant tools—philology, grammar, lexicography—were enlisted in the service of hermeneutics. The faithful in the succeeding centuries acquired, as a consequence, a whole body of literature bearing on the sacred text. There are books on the spelling and the right pronunciation, on the beauty of its language, its verses, words, letters, pertaining not only to philological but also to historical disciplines. Indeed, Arabic philology came into being as the handmaiden of the Qur'ānic text, being intimately connected with its recitation and exegesis.

"To exhibit the importance of the sacred book for the whole mental life of the Moslems would be simply to unite the history of that life itself," wrote the imminent German scholar Theodore Nöldeke. "The unbounded reverence of the Moslems for the Qur'ān reaches its climax in the dogma that this book, as the divine word, i.e., thought, is immanent in God, and consequently *eternal* and *uncreated*."

All Muslims with the exception of the Mu'tazilah accepted the dogma of *i'jāz al-Qur'ān* (uncreatedness of the Qur'ān). No combination of man or supernatural forces can reproduce a fragment thereof, as it is a work existing from all eternity and unequaled.

This dogma of the uncreatedness of the Qur'ān may have been influenced by Christian sources. Some Muslim theologians did indeed protest against it, particularly when the rationalist school in Islam was strong during the caliphate of al-Ma'mūn (813-833), who was one of them. But the strong distinctions and sophisms propagated by Mu'tazilite theologians failed to override the view that came to prevail.

CHAPTER 6

The Fundamentals of Islam: Beliefs

MUSLIM THEOLOGIANS have postulated that Islam the faith is anchored in two fundamental conceptions: *īmān* (expression of faith) and *iḥsān* (right-doing). When īmān and iḥsān are buttressed by manifest acts of worship, *ʿibādāt,* the essentials of the religion of submission to Allah are enunciated.

The "Shahādah"

The one prerequisite for becoming a Muslim is to profess the *shahādah* (open testimony): *la ilāha illa 'l-Lāh* [*Allah*] ("there is no god but God") with the essential concomitant that God is the sole and unassisted author of creation.[1] This holds validity not only for Islam, but also for all similarly revealed religions.

The open profession of belief in one God "who begotteth not nor was begotten" is accompanied by the second important pronouncement in the shahādah: *wa Muhammadan rasūl al-Lāh*" [*Allah*] ("and Muḥammad is the messenger of God"). By uttering the first part of the shahādah one becomes a *muslim,* submitter to God; but when he pronounces the second part of the same, he becomes a *Muslim*, an adherent to the religion of Islam.

To be a *practicing* Muslim, the adherent is obligated to acknowledge and apply the two basic fundamentals: Beliefs and Acts. Both are absolutely necessary for the establishment of one's faith as a Muslim. In partaking of Islam the believer acknowledges his dependence on God, his creator, sustainer and guide, and his solidarity with fellow believers.

By a combination of will and design inspired by an uncompromising belief in Allah, Muḥammad succeeded in reducing the essence of the doctrine and cultus which gave form and expression to Islam to the believer's level of comprehension and credibility. He inculcated his followers with the will to abide by the ordinances and injunctions of Allah and molded out of their profession of faith a community unified by belief in Allah and cohering through the common observance of prescribed acts of devotion. He preached complete submission, *islām,* to Allah.

"Al-Islām"

The religion took on the title of "Islam" because Allah decreed it in the Qur'ān:

> Lo the religion with Allah is *al-Islām* (the Surrender) to His will and guidance.[2]

He who professes adherence to the faith is a "Muslim" (Submitter).

> He hath named you *Muslimūn* (Muslims) . . . of old time and in this (Scripture) that the messenger may be a witness against you, and that ye may be witnesses against mankind.[3]

The reference to Muslims as "Moḥammedans" is the result of a false analogy with "Christian," a worshiper of Christ. Muslims do not worship Muḥammad as Christians worship Christ. Indeed, in Islamic doctrine the worship of anyone other than God is *shirk,* or association in worship, and constitutes a major unpardonable sin, *kabīrah.*

Since Allah prescribed the religion of Islam for the Arabs through His messenger Muḥammad, Islam becomes a divinely revealed religion like Judaism and Christianity. It is the same religion which Allah had previously revealed unto Abraham, who is considered the "first Muslim."

> He hath revealed unto thee (Muḥammad) the Scripture with truth confirming that which was (revealed) before it, even as He revealed the Torah and the Gospel.[4]
>
> We gave it unto Abraham against his folk . . . And We bestowed upon him Isaac and Jacob; each of them We guided, and Noah did We guide aforetime; and of his seed (We guided) David and Solomon and Job and Joseph and Moses and Aaron . . . And Zacharia and John and Jesus and Elias. Each one (of them) was of the righteous . . . . and We chose them and guided them unto a straight path . . . Those are they unto whom We gave the Scripture and command and prophethood. But if these disbelieve therein, then indeed We shall entrust it to a people who will not be disbelievers therein.[5]

The official view of Islam, as derived from the Qur'ānic verse "But if these disbelieve therein" is that Jews and Christians erred in their interpretation of Allah's Scripture, making it necessary for Allah to send "the Reminder."

Muḥammad's mission was thus foreordained on two counts: first, to set straight the tenets of the Scriptures; and second, to bring the true Scripture to the Arabs, descendants of Abraham, the first Muslim, but who were not aware of Allah's command to their forefather.

In another respect, Muḥammad's role was to fulfill the mission of his predecessors among the prophets and to eliminate the deviations that had set in. The aim of his own mission was not to replace but rather to complement the mission of his predecessors. With this understanding of his mission, Muḥammad called upon Christians and Jews to recognize his prophetic role and to accord him the consideration and respect accorded his predecessors.

> Say: O people of the Scripture! Come to an agreement between us and you: that we shall worship none but Allah, and

> that we shall ascribe no partner unto Him, and that none of us shall take others for lords beside Allah.[6]

Unlike his predecessors who had forecast the advent of successors, Muḥammad considered himself the "seal of the prophets" (the *khātimah*) even though, like them, he had served to bring "the Reminder."

> Lo! it is naught but a Reminder to (his) creatures. And they measure not the power of Allah its true measure when they say: Allah hath naught revealed unto a human being. Say (unto the Jews who speak thus): Who revealed the Book which Moses brought, a light and guidance for mankind, which ye have put on parchments which ye show, but ye hide much (thereof), and by which ye were taught that which ye knew not yourselves nor (did) your fathers (know it)? Say: Allah. Then leave them to their play of cavilling. And this is a blessed Scripture which We have revealed, confirming that which (was revealed) before it, that thou mayst warn the Mother of Villages[7] and those around . . .[8]

The fact that Muḥammad had not chosen a title for the message he was preaching until after the conquest of Mecca in 631 is significant. It is quite possible to see in this delay of over a decade some consideration of the extent to which he identified the basic tenets of the religion he preached with those he formally acknowledged to be divinely ordained. Indeed, it is commonly accepted by scholars that the verse imparting title to the faith he preached in his prophetic career is the very last in order of descent. It was during his "Farewell Pilgrimage" to Mecca and specifically his last formal address to the faithful at ʿArafāt, when all Arabia had embraced Islam, that Allah spoke to Muḥammad for the last time:

> This day are those who disbelieve in despair of (ever harming) your religion; so fear them not, fear Me! This day have I perfected your religion for you and completed My favor unto you, and have chosen for you as religion AL-ISLAM.[9]

Allah

A most crucial point in Islamic doctrine is the stress on Allah's unity of being. The Qur'ān is replete with the seriousness of the consequences awaiting those who ascribe more than one entity to Allah.

> He unto Whom belongeth the sovereignty of the heavens and the earth, He hath chosen no son nor hath He any partner in the sovereignty.[10]

The orthodox Muslim (Sunni) conception of God may be summed up as follows: God is one; He has no partners; Singular without any like Him; Uniform, having no contrary; Separate, having no equal; Ancient, having no first; External, having no beginning; Everlasting, having no end; Ever-existing, without termination; Perpetual and constant, with neither interruption nor ending; Ever qualified with the attributes of supreme greatness; nor is He bound to be determined by lapse of ages or times. He is both the Alpha and the Omega, the Manifest and the Hidden. He is real.[11]

He is omnipresent, too exalted to be contained in any one place and too holy to be determined by time; for He existed before He created time and place, and He is now as he always existed. There is nothing like Him in His essence nor is there of His essence in any other besides Him. His holiness makes Him impervious to change and He is beyond contingencies. But He abides through all generations with His glorious attributes, free from all imperfection.

While Muslim theology takes pains to describe what God *is,* it conversely specifies what God *is not:*

> God is not a formed body; nor a measurable substance; neither does He resemble bodies, either in their being measurable or divisible. Neither is he a substance, nor do substances exist in Him; neither is he an accidental form, nor do accidentals exist in him.

Allah in His essence is one, as He is in His attributes and acts; He is the all-mighty, judge of the universe and master of the Day of Judgment. He knows, sees, and hears everything. He is the creator of heaven and earth, of life and death. His knowledge is perfect, His will is beyond challenge, and His power is irresistible. All these qualities are manifest in His creation. While everything needs Him, He depends only upon things originated by Him. Allah is not identifiable with man, with whom His only connection is the fact He created him. All that which Allah created will return unto Him.

The principal elements of worship in Islam entail belief in God, His angels, scriptures revealed to believers in Him, the messengers, and the Day of Judgment. Recognition of God is the supreme manifestation of faith; indeed, over ninety per cent of Muslim theology is concerned with Allah as the one real God who is indivisible in nature.

> Say! He is Allah, the one! Allah the eternally besought of all! He begotteth not nor was begotten. And there is none comparable unto him![12]

The role of God as creator is heavily emphasized:

> Lo! your Lord is Allah Who created the heavens and the earth in six days, then mounted He the Throne. He covereth the night with the day, which is in haste to follow it, and hath made the sun and the moon and the stars subservient by His command. His verily is all creation and commandment. Blessed be Allah, the Lord of the Worlds![13]
>
> He hath created the heavens and the earth with truth. High be He exalted above all that they associate (with Him).
>
> He hath created man from a drop of fluid, yet behold! he is an open opponent.
>
> And the cattle hath He created, whence ye have warm clothing and uses, and whereof ye eat;
>
> And wherein is beauty for you, when ye bring them home, and when ye take them out to pasture.
>
> And they bear your loads for you into a land ye could not reach save with great trouble to yourselves. Lo! your Lord is Full of Pity, Merciful.

And horses and mules and asses (hath He created) that ye may ride them, and for ornament. And He createth that which ye know not.

And Allah's is the direction of the way, and some (roads) go not straight. And had He willed He would have led you all aright.

He it is Who sendeth down water from the sky, whence ye have drink, and whence are trees on which ye send your beasts to pasture.

Therewith He causeth crops to grow for you, and the olive and the date-palm and grapes and all kinds of fruit. Lo! herein is indeed a portent for people who reflect.

And he hath constrained the night and the day and the sun and the moon to be of service unto you, and the stars are made subservient by His command. Lo! herein indeed are portents for people who have sense.[14]

The omniscience of Allah is equally emphasized:

He is the Knower of the invisible and the visible, the Great, the High Exalted.[15]

And with Him are the keys of the invisible. None but He knoweth them. And He knoweth what is in the land and the sea. Not a leaf falleth but He knoweth it, not a grain amid the darkness of the earth, naught of wet or dry but (it is noted) in a clear record.[16]

The sovereignty of Allah is related to His omnipotence, and both are conceived of in equal terms:

Say: O Allah! Owner of Sovereignty! Thou givest sovereignty unto whom Thou wilt, and Thou withdrawest sovereignty from whom Thou wilt. Thou exaltest whom Thou wilt and Thou abasest whom Thou wilt. In Thy hand is the good. Lo! Thou art Able to do all things.

Thou causest the night to pass into the day, and Thou causest the day to pass into the night. And Thou bringest forth the living from the dead, and Thou bringest forth the dead from the living. And Thou givest sustenance to whom Thou choosest, without stint.[17]

His attributes distinguish Him from His creatures. These Attributes of Allah are clearly distinguished from His essence; they too are adumbrated in the Qurʾān:

> Allah's are the fairest names. Invoke Him by them. And leave the company of those who blaspheme His names. They will be requited what they do.[18]

According to the renowned theologian al-Ghazāli,[19] Allah has ninety-nine beautiful names (*al-asmāʾ al-ḥusna*); these are frequently repeated by the faithful whose "rosary" consists of a like number of beads. The attributes most pronouncedly stressed are Allah's might and majesty:

> He is Allah, than whom there is no other God, the Sovereign Lord, the Holy One, Peace, the Keeper of Faith, the Guardian, the Majestic, the Compeller, the Superb, Glorified be Allah from all that they ascribe as partner (unto Him).
>
> He is Allah, the Creator, the Shaper out of naught, the Fashioner. His are the most beautiful names. All that is in the heavens and the earth glorifieth Him, and He is the Mighty, the Wise.[20]

Allah's omnipotence is mitigated and tempered with justice because He is equitable. He has complete knowledge of every good deed of man however insignificant, and Allah will take cognizance of it on the day of reckoning. Being transcendent does not preclude Allah's consciousness of all that takes place and He will not suffer the smallest injustice to befall anyone ". . . and they will not be wronged even the hair upon a datestone."[21]

God rewards and punishes, yet He is also the Merciful, Guardian of His servants, Defender of the orphan, Guide of the wrongdoer, Liberator from pain, Friend of the poor, generous and ready-to-forgive Master.

> And, O my people! Ask forgiveness of your Lord, then turn unto Him repentant; He will cause the sky to rain abundance on you and will add unto you strength to your strength. Turn not away, guilty![22]

God is the Merciful (*al-Raḥmān*) and the compassionate (*al-Raḥīm*); these are basic to His attributes, as attests the Qurʾān in every sūrah. He is forgiving and reassuring to the sinner who repents; and although God can overtake with His punishment anyone He wishes, His mercy "encompasses everything" because He Himself has commanded that mercy shall be an unbreakable law. "Mercy is a pillar of Islam and an attribute of God." [23]

Cosmology

Allah created the world in six days. Everything therein is the work of Allah. Beside Himself there are only two other uncreated beings: (1) the prototype of the Qurʾān, "mother of the Book" which was transcribed on a "preserved tablet" (*lawḥ maḥfūẓ*)[24] and (2) the throne (*kursi*) upon which Allah is seated in the Seventh Heaven surrounded by angels, pure, sexless beings, some of whom bear the throne while others are engaged in praising Him continually.

Angels also serve as His messengers who are sent to fight with the believers against the heathen. Some of them, known as jinn, are guardian angels of man accompanying him constantly at close range to watch over his deeds and keep a record thereof to be produced on the day of reckoning. Other angels are watchmen of hell, whose duty it is to usher in the condemned and make sure they do not escape. There are other types, like the "mediate being" between Allah and man, referred to as the "word" (*amr*) from which derives the "spirit" (*rūḥ*) or "holy spirit" (*rūḥ al-qudus*). Another manifestation of Allah to the believers only is the "glory" (*sakīnah*).

Allah creates each new life by breathing into it a soul. Hence man consists of both soul and body. This duality is maintained, even unto death and resurrection. Every man according to Muslim belief is possessed with a good and bad impulse. The fall of Adam was the work of Satan (*Iblīs*). Adam by his fall lost the grace of God, which was restored to him only by the gracious choice of God.

Men are separated from the angels by the *jinn*,[25] male and female, inhabitants of the desert, created from smokeless fire. Before Muḥammad's time they used to roam the heavens spying;

but in the time of the Prophet they could learn no more of its secrets. Indeed, some of the jinn were converted by his teachings.

Lowest of creation in Allah's estate is the devil (*Shayṭān*) or Satan, who at one time was himself an angel but expelled from heaven for refusing to bow to Adam and the Lord's command.

God makes Himself known to men through (1) scriptures and (2) prophets. As He had given to the Jews the Law (*Tawrāt*) (Torah) and to the Christians the Gospel (*Injīl*) so He revealed to Muḥammad the Qur'ān. Each time a revelation is made, God sends it with a messenger, apostle or prophet to each people. He started the process with Abraham and ended it with Muḥammad.

Muḥammad's task was to remind men of Allah's decrees. When he met opposition, he was compelled to turn warner, and ultimately teacher, guide, and ruler, though he had been commissioned at first as messenger. When through the exercise of his natural faculties Muḥammad convinced very few of his fellow Meccans, he announced the doctrine of God's election.

The "Commandments"

Since what we term 'commandments' is not specifically spelled out in any one document, we must learn of the do's and dont's of Islam only through perusing the contents of the Qur'ān. From this we can adduce the following injunctions:

1. *Acknowledging there is no god whatsoever but God—*
   "Thy Lord hath decreed, that ye worship none save Him . . ."

2. *Honoring and respecting parents—*
   "And lower unto them the wing of submission through mercy, and say: My Lord! Have mercy on them both as they did care for me when I was little."

3. *Respecting the rights of others—*
   "Give the kinsman his due, and the needy, and the wayfarer, . . . But if thou turn away from them, seeking mercy from the Lord, for which thou hopest, then speak unto them a reasonable word."

4. *Being generous but not a squanderer*—
"... squander not (thy wealth) in wantonness. Lo! the squanderers were ever brothers of the devil, and the devil was ever an ingrate to his Lord.
"And let not thy hand be chained to thy neck nor open it with a complete opening, lest thou sit down rebuked, denuded. Lo! thy Lord enlargeth the provision for whom He will, and straiteneth (it for whom He will)."

5. *Avoiding killing except for justifiable cause*—
"Slay not the life which Allah hath forbidden save with right. Whoso is slain wrongfully, We have given power unto his heir, but let him not commit excess in slaying."

6. *Committing not adultery*—
"And come not near unto adultery. Lo! it is an abomination and an evil way."

7. *Safeguarding the possessions of orphans*—
"Come not near the wealth of the orphan save with that which is better till he come to strength; and keep the covenant. Lo! of the covenant it will be asked."

8. *Dealing justly and equitably*—
"Fill the measure when ye measure, and weigh with a right balance; that is meet, and better in the end."

9. *Being pure of heart and mind*—
"Your Lord is best aware of what is in your minds. If ye are righteous, then lo! He was ever Forgiving unto those who turn (unto Him)."

10. *Being humble and unpretentious*—
"And walk not in the earth exultant. Lo! thou canst not rend the earth, nor canst thou stretch to the height of the hills . . . and follow not that whereof thou hast no knowledge. Lo! the hearing and the sight and the heart—of each of these it will be asked."

And generally the Qur'ān enjoins Muslims to avoid "The evil of all that is hateful in the sight of thy Lord." It also stresses that "This is (part) of that wisdom wherewith thy Lord hath inspired thee (O Muḥammad)."[26]

Eschatology

The Islamic belief in the hereafter is traceable to the earlier sūrahs of the Qur'ān. The Resurrection, Last Judgment, Paradise, and Hell are all described.

At death the body again turns to earth while the soul sinks to a state of sleep or unconsciousness. At a time unknown to all but Allah and decreed by Him as "the Hour" (*al-Sā'ah*) or the "Day of Resurrection" (*Yawm al-Qiyāmah*), and the "Day of Judgment" (*Yawm al-Dīn*), an angel of the Lord will sound the clarion. At this moment the earth will be rent asunder and the body will issue forth to rejoin its soul. Allah will then appear on His throne surrounded by the angels. The Qur'ān is replete with descriptions of that day:

> A day on which no soul hath power at all for any (other) soul. The (absolute) command on that day is Allah's.[27]
>
> The day when the Trumpet is blown. On that day we assemble the guilty white-eyed (with terror).[28]
>
> And when the trumpet shall sound one blast
>
> And the earth with the mountains shall be lifted up and crushed with one crash,
>
> Then on that day will the Event befall.
>
> And the heaven will split asunder, for that day it will be frail.
>
> And the angels will be on the sides thereof, and eight will uphold the Throne of their Lord that day above them.
>
> On that day ye will be exposed; not a secret of you will be hidden.[29]

The object of the Resurrection is to judge the deeds of men for the purpose of rewarding the faithful and punishing the guilty. Not only mankind but also the jinn and irrational animals will be judged.

Judgment does not immediately follow the Resurrection. Mankind resurrected must wait a long time during which period anxiety and suspicion will torment those in doubt. Men will resort to their respective prophets for intercession that they may be redeemed from the painful situation and be called upon for trial.

> On that Day no intercession availeth save (that of) him unto whom the Beneficent hath given leave and whoso He accepteth.[30]
>
> (On that day) neither the riches nor the progeny of those who disbelieve will aught avail them with Allah. They will be fuel for fire.[31]

At the given time the great book in which the deeds of mankind have been recorded will be opened and a list of each one's deeds will be given, to the good in his right hand and to the evil, in his left.

> And the Book is placed, and thou seest the guilty fearful of that which is therein, and they say: What kind of a book is this that leaveth not a small thing nor a great thing but hath counted it! And they find all that they did confronting them, and thy Lord wrongeth no one.[32]

A balance will be present to weigh the deeds of all, and sentence will be passed depending on how the scales are tipped. He whose balance is laden with good works will be saved; he whose balance is light will be condemned.

> Thou seest the wrong-doers fearful of that which they have earned, and it will surely befall them . . .[33]

There will follow a period of mutual retaliation when those who were made to suffer unjustly will have satisfaction. The injurer will be made to yield a measure of his good works to the injured proportionate to the injury. This could spell the difference between Hell and Paradise.

Brutes will be made to pay the penalty for cruelty. Then God will command that they be turned into dust. The wicked, however, are destined to protracted suffering in Hell where they will cry out "would that we were also turned to dust."

When the trial is over those destined to Hell or Paradise will be made to pass over a narrow bridge to their respective destinations. The bridge is so fashioned that the favored will cross with ease and facility while the condemned will tumble off into Hell.

As for the idolators, the jinn will testify against them and they will be condemned to eternal damnation. But those who had embraced the revelations of Allah, even if they had sinned, will spend a term in Hell proportionate to their sins. They will be delivered therefrom upon expiating their sins by the right amount of punishment. The Sunni Muslim, however, insists that no infidel who denied the existence of God or any person who did not believe in the unity of God shall ever be redeemed. While, on the other hand, no one who acknowledged the existence and unity of God will be made to suffer eternal fire.

The Qur'ān goes into considerable detail to portray the nature of punishments and rewards. The righteous will gain eternal peace and joy in the garden of Allah, studded with trees, flowing water, and all the niceties of earthly dwelling which the desert Arabian considered the chief attractions of his ideal of paradise.

> And hath awarded them for all that they endured, a Garden and silk attire;
>
> Reclining therein upon couches, they will find there neither (heat of) a sun nor bitter cold.
>
> The shade thereof is close upon them and the clustered fruits thereof bow down.
>
> Goblets of silver are brought round for them, and beakers (as) of glass
>
> There serve them youths of everlasting youth, whom, when thou seest, thou wouldst take for scattered pearls.
>
> Their raiment will be fine green silk and gold embroidery. Bracelets of silver will they wear. Their Lord will slake their thirst with a pure drink.
>
> (And it will be said unto them): Lo! this is a reward for you. Your endeavour (upon earth) hath found acceptance.[34]

The wicked condemned to eternal damnation will be cast into the fiery ditch *Jahannam* (Hell) where pains of body and soul are united.

> They will abide therein for ages.
>
> Therein taste they neither coolness nor (any) drink

Save boiling water and a paralysing cold:
Rewards proportioned (to their evil deeds).
So taste (of that which ye have earned). No increase do We give you save of torment.[35]

The rewards of Paradise and punishments of Hell vary in degree, depending on earned merits or demerits. Yet as seen in the verses of the Qur'ān, if taken literally, both types of rewards are depicted in sensuous and material terms with body and soul together being subjected to them.

Still there is a greater joy than those expressed in mundane terms; indeed, the greatest joy of all to the happiest soul is to ". . . see the face of his Lord, night and morning, a felicity which will surpass all the pleasures of the body, as the ocean surpasses a drop of sweat."

Rewards will exceed the measure of man's good deeds, but punishment will be in proportion to his evil work.

> For those who do good is the best (reward) and more (thereto). Neither dust nor ignominy cometh near their faces. Such are rightful owners of the Garden; they will abide therein.
>
> And those who earn ill deeds, (for them) requital of each ill deed by the like thereof; and ignominy overtaketh them—They have no protector from Allah—as if their faces had been covered with a cloak of darkest night. Such are rightful owners of the Fire; they will abide therein.[36]

The type of sin a Muslim may commit is defined in the Qur'ān in terms of the judgment to be passed thereon. The greatest sin, known as the *kabīrah*, which earns the perpetuator eternal fire, is committed by those who associate others with God in the worship of Him.

> Lo! Allah forgiveth not that a partner should be ascribed unto Him. He forgiveth (all) save that to whom He will. Whoso ascribeth partners to Allah, he hath indeed invented a tremendous sin.[37]
>
> . . . We shall expose them to the Fire. As often as their skins are consumed We shall exchange them for fresh skins that they may taste the torment. . . .[38]

Another major sin is causing the death of an innocent being. "The guerdon of an ill-deed is an ill the like thereof. . . ."[39]

The category of lesser offenses (*ṣaghā'ir*) cover all other types of sinning. While the sūrahs of the Qur'ān do not definitely specify, a number of them assert that Allah in His omnipotence can deliver the damned if He so wills; other revelations seem to imply that, for Muslims, hell is only temporary.

> If Allah afflicteth thee with some hurt, there is none who can remove it save Him; and if He desireth good for thee, there is none who can repel His bounty. He striketh with it whom He will of his bondmen. He is the Forgiving, the Merciful.[40]

Predetermination and Free Will

The question of the "bondage of the will" or "free will" preoccupied Muslim theologians as it had their Christian counterparts. By and large all Muslim sects do not agree on this crucial element of Islamic dogma. The one important principle of agreement held by all, however, is that Allah in His divine justice allows man the freedom of those actions upon which he will be judged. From this point of view man *does* possess free will. The notion that man is totally dependent in all aspects of belief and deeds on God as the author of virtues and vices, crimes and punishments is beginning to be discarded by recent Muslim theologians. The modernists among them have reverted to the idea of placing responsibility for man's actions upon man's own conscience.

The path to Allah is open to everyone, even the wrongdoers should they seek to tread it. Allah grants all of His creatures the powers to do good deeds and shun evil. He welcomes the one who seeks Him on his journey to Him even though the underling may commit some mistakes along the way. Man will earn his rewards on the basis of his faith and good deeds because of God's mercy and benevolence. The one who does not occupy himself with good deeds will be left alone. God may not stretch

His arm towards him, but at the same time He will not be the one who puts him on the evil path.

Certain authorities consider belief in predestination a pillar of the faith. The Qur'ān appears to lend credence to this concept in the verses:

> All things have been created after a fixed decree . . .[41]
>
> No soul can ever die except by Allah's leave and at a term appointed. . . .[42]
>
> Thy God hath created and balanced all things, and hath fixed their destinies and guided them . . .[43]
>
> Say: Naught befalleth us save that which Allah hath decreed for us. . . .[44]
>
> . . . nor is there anything not provided beforehand by us or which We send down, otherwise than according to a foreknown decree.[45]
>
> . . . He hath created everything and hath meted out for it a measure.[46]

The sayings of the Prophet are replete with his insistence on God's role as preordainer and determiner of all that takes place. On one occasion Muḥammad told his listeners that God had said to him: "I have created this family for Hell; and their actions will be like unto those of the people of Hell." To Adam God had said the opposite: "I have created this family for Paradise, and their actions will be like unto those of the people of Paradise." But the servant of God from the Muslim theological point of view will have control over his actions from the time of birth until his death. "When God createth His servant for Paradise, his actions will be deserving of it, until he dies [*sic*] when he will enter therein; and when God createth one for the fire, his actions will be like those of the people of Hell, 'til [*sic*] he dies, when he will enter therein." [47]

The tendency of the Bedouin Arab to allow his "predetermined role" to come in the way of the fulfillment of his moral and religious obligations as a convert to Islam was curbed by the Prophet. Muḥammad insisted that the righteous will do good works and obey the word of God, while the wicked will perform evil deeds.

> To him who giveth alms and feareth God, and yields assent to the excellent creed, to him We will make easy the path to happiness. But to him who is worldly, and is indifferent, and who does not believe in the excellent creed, to him We will make easy the path to misery.

According to the sayings of Muḥammad: "The first thing which God created was a (divine) pen, and He said to it, 'Write'; it said, 'What shall I write?' And God said: 'Write down the fate of every individual thing to be created,' and accordingly the pen wrote all that was, and that will be, to eternity."

When pressed, Muḥammad stated: "God hath predestined five things to his servants; their duration of life, their actions, their dwelling places, their travels, and their portions."

To the debates and inquiries aroused by belief in predestination, Muḥammad would answer with the injunction to his followers: "Your forefathers were undone through debating about fate and destiny. I conjure you not to argue on those points."

The official orthodox view concerning the essence of the doctrine of predestination is summed up in the statement:

> A Muslim should believe in his heart, and confess with his tongue, that the most exalted God hath decreed all things; so that nothing can happen in the world, whether it respects the conditions and operations of things, or good or evil, or obedience or disobedience, or sickness or health, or riches or poverty, or life or death, which is not contained in the written tablet of the decrees of God. But God hath so decreed, good works, obedience and faith, that He ordains and wills them, that they may be under His decree, His salutary direction, His good pleasure and command. On the other hand, God hath decreed and does ordain and determine evil, disobedience and infidelity; yet without His salutary direction, good pleasure and command; but only by way of temptation and trial. Whosoever shall say, that God hath not indignation against evil and unbelief, he is certainly an infidel.[48]

The apparent contradictions ensuing from belief in predestination have posed as much a psychological problem for the believing Muslim as they have for the devout Christian. Muslim theologians have attempted to resolve such a contradiction by the explanation that man is not acquainted in this life with anything of what God has predestined for him. The lack of this knowledge, it is argued, allows him personal freedom of choice and action, which are in no way affected by his ignorance, and which ought not interfere in his fulfilling the normal obligations attending his belief. Bondage of the will in such a situation is not recognized. From this point of view the Muslim is free to act to make an intelligent choice, the choice of the agent, a choice plainly in contrast with the mechanical determination governing the physical world.

If what God has willed for man is concealed from him, the will of God is made manifest to him periodically through messengers, God's prophets, who familiarize man with duties to perform and injunctions to respect, so no act of disobedience can be justified on the plea of ignorance of what man is supposed to do or not to do, or the pretext that he was actuated to disobey or to sin by divine decree. Man is not cognizant of what he was predestined to do until the act is committed, by his own choice and free will, of which he is quite conscious. It is then and only then that he realizes that the act committed was preordained. By such an argument faith in divine predestination can neither require denial of human consciousness of freedom of will nor eliminate the factor of individual responsibility from human conduct.

Man's ignorance of his fate is deliberately presaged by God. If he knew from the beginning of his consciousness that he was doomed to perdition, he might naturally make no effort to resist his destiny or to attempt progress; or seeing that he was predestined to salvation, he might not attempt to earn it. By having no foreknowledge of his destiny, man's duty would be to adhere to the law ordained by God and revealed unto man by His prophets. Man's intelligent free action, it is agreed, must simply respect God's eternal decrees and have faith in them.

Hence belief in God, His oneness, His role as the sole Creator and absolute Disposer is dictated by reason and logic, not blind faith. As the cultivator can not rightly claim to be the creator of his own harvest, so man cannot rightly claim to be the author of his own actions.

> Lo! Allah enjoins justice and good deeds, and that ye be kind to kinfolk as He condemns indecency, illicit deeds and all wrong.[49]
>
> Say, my prayers, my offerings, my life and my death are for God, Lord of the Worlds Who has no partner with Him. This I have been ordered (to believe), and I am the first to submit (unto Him).[50]

It is also argued that belief in predestination prevents fortune or misfortune to sway the believer from the "right path." Inasmuch as good and bad have been predetermined and decreed by God, no amount of human effort can hold back the inevitable. Hence the Muslim submits himself with resignation to all trials with the knowledge that this is a part of God's design.

> And We shall try you with fear and hunger, and loss of property and life and blessings; (therefore, O Prophet) give good tidings to those who are patient,
>
> who when misfortunes befall them say: Verily we belong to God, and to Him we shall verily return. Those (the patient) are they, on whom blessings and mercy from their Lord (will descend), and those are the followers of the right path.[51]

Being alive to the purpose of divine will enables a believing Muslim to accept cheerfully his fate and to endure conditions of hardship and misfortune without loss of faith. Reliance on fate under such circumstances may have its salutary side: it allows him to perceive that which enabled the world of Islam collectively to weather the misfortunes of periods of sharp decline and to preserve a sense of solidarity in the face of surging political and ideological pressures from a Western world that was simultaneously on the ascendancy.

The omnipotence of God does not prevent man from enjoying freedom of will. Muḥammad did not dispute the right of man to make a choice between good and evil. The Qurʾān is strong on this matter of free choice:

> Say the truth is from your Lord, whosoever wisheth he may believe; and whosoever wisheth he may disbelieve.[52]

By pointing what path man should follow in Islam, the Qurʾān clearly enunciates that (1) God has determined the destiny of man from the foreknown character of those whose fate He determined and because it is in conformity with His own will—a fundamental concept shared by both Judaism and orthodox Christianity; (2) man is directly responsible for his own actions so long as he is master of his free choice. God has endowed man with intellect and revelation, and left him with a vast sphere of human activity where he enjoys freedom of control and direction. For that reason man will be held accountable for the right or wrong exercise of his faculties. Hence it is a matter of serious concern that man should ascertain the right way to guide him in his conduct. "And show us the right path, the path of those thou hast favored and not of those who have strayed," appeals the Muslim daily to God.

By the aid of his intellect and God's guidance, the Muslim is expected to work out his moral and spiritual endeavors in his dealings with the Creator and the created. It is the Muslim's theological view that human intellect is susceptible to error resulting in the violation of human or divine laws and necessitating direct guidance and injunctions from God to compensate for such frailties of reason.

In obeying the laws enjoined by the Creator, the believer is better equipped to carry out his duties and attain the right path to Him. God, however, does not compel him to do so.

"Verily, We have shown to man the right path; he may be grateful or ungrateful." The lack of compulsion is further evident in the Qurʾānic verse "Verily this is a reminder to all people, for those of you who wish to take the right course." Man's freedom of choice stems from God's will. "It is for Allah only to furnish strong proof, for if He so willeth He would have guided ye all."

One of the strong points of Islam's beliefs is that God has entrusted man with the moral freedom that enables him to master himself. This moral freedom exalts him over the rest of God's creations. It is for man either to reap the benefits of a righteous act or earn condemnation for evil deeds.

CHAPTER 7

The Fundamentals of Islam: Obligations

THE QUR'ĀN specifically reminds the believer: "Lo! those who believe and do good works and establish worship and pay the poor-due, their reward is with their Lord and there shall no fear come upon them neither shall they grieve." [1]

Obligations in Islam are of two types: moral and ceremonial. Under the category of moral falls the concept of Iḥsān or right-doing. Fundamental Islamic law has elaborately defined the precepts of right-doing as embracing categories relating to man's relations with man and man's relations with God.

Moral Obligations

Right-doing entails morally acceptable works, the responsibility of which reposes with both the individual and society. In the area of personal morality much emphasis is placed on *selflessness* as a form of *gratitude* towards God. "And feed with food the needy wretch, the orphan and the prisoner, for love of Him, (Saying): We feed you, for the sake of Allah only. We wish for no reward nor thanks from you."[2]

Man's gratitude constitutes an element of *love for Allah,* an article of the Muslim's faith. "Say, (O Muḥammad, to mankind): If ye love Allah, follow me; Allah will love you and forgive you your sins. Allah is Forgiving, Merciful."[3]

Obedience to Allah and His messenger, Muḥammad, is equally stressed. "Say: Obey Allah and the messenger. But if they turn away, lo! Allah loveth not the disbelievers (in His guidance)."[4]

Kindness is decreed and boastfulness condemned. "Lo! Allah loveth not such as are proud and boastful, who hoard their wealth and enjoin avarice on others, and hide that which Allah hath bestowed upon them of His bounty . . ."[5] Having been orphaned early in his childhood, Muḥammad was particularly sensitive to Allah's decree, "And We have commended unto man kindness towards parents" and the Muslim's prayer, "Arouse me that I may give thanks for the favour wherewith Thou hast favoured me and my parents, and that I may do right acceptable unto Thee."[6] Allah insists, "If one of them or both of them do attain old age with thee, say not 'Fie' unto them nor repulse them, but speak unto them a gracious word."[7]

Consideration for others, namely the destitute, the orphan and the needy, is eloquently taught as an integral part of the Muslim's beliefs and his religious duties. In the words of the Qur'ān:

> Hast thou observed him who belieth religion?
> That is he who repelleth the orphan,
> And urgeth not the feeding of the needy.[8]
>
> . . . but righteous is he who . . . giveth his wealth, for love of Him, to kinsfolk and to orphans and the needy and the wayfarer . . .[9]
>
> . . . (Show) kindness unto parents, and unto near kindred, and orphans, and the needy, and unto the neighbour who is of kin (unto you) and the neighbour who is not of kin, and the fellow-traveller and the wayfarer and (the slaves) whom your right hands possess. . . .[10]

> Give unto orphans their wealth. Exchange not the good for the bad . . .[11]
>
> And when kinsfolk and orphans and the needy are present at the division (of the heritage), bestow on them therefrom and speak kindly unto them.[12]

Dreadful punishment awaits those who choose the opposite path.

> Lo! Those who devour the wealth of orphans wrongfully, they do but swallow fire unto their bellies, and they will be exposed to burning flame.[13]

Chastity and restraint are decreed for women, who are enjoined to be decent and modest and to display their charms only to their husbands or very near relatives. Men, on the other hand, must treat their wives kindly and be gentle with them, just and considerate.

Other decrees command the faithful to be *honest* in their dealings with others, *true* to their commitments, *loyal, humble* and *peace-loving.*

> The (faithful) slaves of the Beneficent are they who walk upon the earth modestly, and when the foolish ones address them answer: Peace.[14]

Social morality in Islam requires one to place *duty* before *right.* Duties in Islam are incumbent on all the faithful, regardless of status in society. Indeed, Islam recognizes no social gradation, though in reality it may exist. In this regard the Qur'ān specifically states: Verily there is no preference for any of you except by what ye enjoy in good health and your deeds of righteousness.

In no other religion besides Judaism is the leveling process so strong. The wealthy are obligated by a precept of the faith's fundamental concepts to aid the poor as a *duty,* not a privilege. To be helpful and kind are recurrent themes in the Qur'ān. The establishment of a fair and just society was one of the strongest motivations in Muḥammad's mission. The faithful are urged to be *just* and fair-minded in their transactions.

> O ye who believe! Be ye staunch in justice, witnesses for Allah, even though it be against yourselves or (your) parents or (your) kindred, whether (the case be of) a rich man or a poor man, for Allah is nearer unto both (than ye are). . . .[15]

In several instances the Qur'ān stresses the need to deal justly, and the Sharī'ah[16] has made of justice one of the inviolable precepts of social morality. Justice in this content provides guarantees for rights, reinforced by ordinances enjoying the full sanctity of the faith. To be equitable is a duty that stems from brotherly relations.

> O ye who believe! Be stedfast witnesses for Allah in equity, and let not hatred of any people seduce you that ye deal not justly. Deal justly, that is nearer to your duty. . . .[17]

Justice underlies also the stress on fraternity and equality in Islam. The Sharī'ah treats believers as brethren, regardless of their nationality or place of abode. As a member of a fraternity reposing in faith and buttressed by it, the Muslim has the right, and commensurately an obligation, to respect freedom, protection, security and the loyalty of his fellow Muslim. With justice as his guiding precept, the Muslim's duty is to weigh in an equitable balance between Muslim and non-Muslim.

> . . . and let not hatred of any people seduce you that ye deal not justly . . .[18]
>
> . . . Allah commandeth you . . . if ye judge between mankind, that ye judge justly . . .[19]
>
> . . . And if ye give your word, do justice thereunto, even though it be (against) a kinsman; and fulfill the covenant of Allah. . . .[20]

To be *beneficent* is another duty of each Muslim who respects the commandments of his religion. In its broader application beneficence (*birr*) obligates the faithful to act rightly in all circumstances: comfort the poor with material gifts, be truthful in his transactions, good in his communal relations, and constantly mindful of God's will in every aspect of his dealings, all of which must conform to the principle of right-doing. It is the duty and the privilege of the one who has to give to him who has not. "And in their wealth the needy and the deprived have due share,"[21] states the Qurʾān.

Ostentation and vulgar display are frowned upon, if not forbidden. The leveling forces of Islam were to work through two powerful media: the decrees of the Sharīʿah and the conscience of the individual. Islam, like Christianity, denies the blissful life in the hereafter to those who deny the needy a fair share of the provisions of this life. Indeed, the conscience of the true believer would not rest were he to "eat, dress and make merry while his neighbors and relatives were unable to earn a living."[22]

The Muslim is not to be subjected to derision on account of poverty. While Islam depends partly on the believer's faith and respect of decency to take positive measures for mitigating the circumstances of the poor, the Sharīʿah nevertheless empowers the state to appropriate from the excess wealth of the individual when necessary what is required to satisfy the needs of his less fortunate brother. As a matter of fact, the Qurʾān threatens:

> . . . They who hoard up gold and silver and spend it not in the way of Allah, unto them give tidings (O Muḥammad) of a painful doom,
>
> On the day when it will (all) be heated in the fire of hell, and their foreheads and their flanks and their backs will be branded therewith (and it will be said unto them): Here is that which ye hoarded for yourselves. Now taste of what ye used to hoard.[23]

Islam also condemns usury.

> Those who swallow usury cannot rise up save as he ariseth whom the devil hath prostrated by (his) touch . . . Allah will blot out usury, and causeth charity to prosper.[24]

To be *respectful* of a fellow believer's welfare in the society of Islam is another article of faith.

> . . . They are the loyal. Those who entered the city and the faith before them love those who flee unto them for refuge, and find in their breasts no need for that which hath been given thee, but prefer (the fugitives) above themselves through poverty become their lot. . . .[25]

Qur'ānic verses strengthen the notions making for solidarity between the individual and society.

> The believers are naught else than brothers. Therefore make peace between your brethren . . .[26]
>
> And the believers, men and women, are protecting friends one of another; they enjoin the right and forbid the wrong. . . .[27]

The strongest concomitant of solidarity is abiding by individual and communal responsibilities as ordained by the religion and the canonical law of Islam. "Help your brother whether he is the doer of wrong or wrong is done to him," decrees the Prophet of Allah. The individual is the cornerstone of Islamic society; "he perfects it and is perfected by it, he gives to it and receives from it, and he protects it and is protected by it." [28] Both the conscience of the individual and of society collectively are held to account.

"Everyone of you is a shepherd and everyone of you will be questioned about those under him," said the Prophet. "Unto me it has been revealed that you should be humble that ye may not be proud over others."

Personal morality is as important as social morality; indeed, the one may not be realizable without the other. The Prophet and the Qur'ān stressed the need for purifying the individual's moral character as the *sine qua non* of achieving individual and collective responsibility. Allah in the Qur'ān addresses Muḥammad: "Lo! thou art of sublime morals." The qualities enshrined in the character of Muḥammad are those which God commands the Muslims to respect. Foremost among these are: truthfulness, ". . . in truth they give not thee (Muḥammad) the lie, but evil-doers give the lie to the revelations of Allah."[29]

Courage is another important quality stressed, and acts of bravery performed by the believers in nascent Islam contributed to its rise and spread. The Muslim is taught to fear not death, as his life is in the hands of the Creator who directs it to life eternal if dedicated to the fulfillment of Allah's will. Hence numerous deeds of martyrdom attest to the courage inculcated in the true believer.

Qualities making for sociability are equally emphasized. A properly trained Muslim youth is "well-mannered, sociable, faithful and sincere because such traits are essential for the perfection of his faith . . ."[30] Concomitantly, the true Muslim "does not deceive, cheat, or swindle."[31]

Unrestrained individualism has been the major blight of pre-Islamic Arabia. Muḥammad the messenger of Allah was armed with revelations to curb it and to destroy bigotry and false pride, evils accompanying such individualism.

> O Mankind! Lo! We have created you male and female, and have made you nations and tribes that ye may know one another (and be friends). Lo! the noblest of you, in the sight of Allah, is the best in conduct.[32]

Instead of manifesting their individualism, Allah through Muhammad decreed that the faithful show *brotherly love* towards one another. This was indeed a strange decree, for the Arabs hitherto had gloried only in chauvinistic clanishness (*ʿaṣabīyah*) and considered it beneath their dignity to fraternize with those whom they looked upon as inferiors. Early in his mission he was derided, as was Noah before him, with the words of his distractors: "We see thee but a mortal like us, and we see not that any follow thee save the most abject among us, without reflection."

This type of solidarity between the individual and society is the basis of its health; it is the means whereby social ills are resisted and reforms are achieved. Islam through the decrees of God that prod the believer's consciousness stresses this responsibility of the individual to the community in almost a filial and beneficent vein and the community's towards the individual in a motherly and protective attitude.

> And the believers, men and women, are protecting friends one of another; they enjoin the right and forbid the wrong . . .[33]
>
> And there may spring from you a nation who invite to goodness, and enjoin right conduct and forbid indecency. Such are they who are successful.[34]

The practice of mercy is perhaps one of the most stressed injunctions of the message of Islam and the rock upon which right-doing rests. Indeed, in the view of a knowledgeable devout Muslim "the entire Islamic law (Sharīʿah) does no more than elucidate, sanction, order, or prohibit that which does or does not constitute righteous action." [35]

Mercy is not only strongly enjoined, but it is regarded also as an essential characteristic of God. In the early days of Muḥammad's preachings he stressed *raḥmah* (mercy) and *Raḥmān* (the merciful) so much that his listeners believed he was calling upon them to worship a god called *al-Raḥmān*.

The Ḥadīth stresses the all-encompassing mercy of God.

> When God had perfected creation, He wrote in the book which He kept near Him: 'My mercy triumphs over my anger.' God divided mercy into one hundred parts; He kept ninety-nine of them for Himself and released one for the world, from that alone comes all the grace which mankind enjoys.[36]

The Qurʾān contains numerous revelations on mercy ending invariably with the words "Allah is Forgiving, Merciful." [37]

> . . . My mercy embraceth all things, therefore I shall ordain it for those who ward off (evil) and pay the poor-due, and those who believe Our revelations.[38]
>
> And We reveal of the Qurʾān that which is a healing and a mercy for believers . . .[39]
>
> It was by the mercy of Allah that thou wast lenient with them (O Muḥammad) . . .[40]
>
> There hath come unto you a messenger (Muḥammad) of

> yourselves, unto whom aught that ye are overburdened is grievous, full of concern for you, for the believers full of pity, merciful.[41]

The stress on mercy has had a strong effect on Muslims everywhere whose every move and each little act is "in the name of the most Merciful" (*al-Raḥmān al-Raḥīm*), and who greet one another with "may peace and the mercy of God be upon you." To them it is the foundation of society and progress. Hence the practice of mercy is a duty of every believer.

Muḥammad's preaching of mercy was undoubtedly founded also on practical considerations. Mecca was a city given to extremes of wealth and poverty, particularly in the area of social relations where the old Arab custom of meeting the social needs of the member of a family or a tribal affiliate did not apply to those who had no familial or tribal ties. Numerous Meccans, accordingly, had no status but sought protection in the jiwār of the Kaʿbah, or the ḥaram area.

> And when it is said unto them: Spend of that wherewith Allah hath provided you, those who disbelieve say unto those who believe: Shall we feed those whom Allah, if He willed, would feed?[42]

The fact that the general standard of living in West Arabia was pitifully low by any method of comparison and that the Bedouins, like the poor of the city, were subsisting at near famine level, did not rule out the major inducement for preaching mercy. Pious gifts preached in Islam are partly for accumulating stores with Allah and partly for "cleansing" the soul of the believer.

The effect of solidarity was not lessened by low subsistence levels, nor was the motive for displaying benevolence entirely religious. The old tribal acceptance of the social practice of helping one's own is reinforced in Islam but not by religious conviction. The Arab's reputation for charity was not to be diminished when Islam upended the mores of pagan Arabia. Charity in Jāhilīyah Arabia was a mark of nobility; in Islamic Arabia it becomes a precept of the faith, albeit restrained and circumscribed.

> Give the kinsman his due, and the needy, and the wayfarer, and squander not (thy wealth) in wantonness. Lo! the squanderers were even brothers of the devils, and the devil was even an ingrate to his Lord.[43]

Ceremonial Obligations

Ceremonial obligations play a special role in drawing the faithful nearer to God and in helping them fulfill their duty to Him. They also have certain disciplinary effects in curbing the excess desires of the believers in teaching them to do things together for the welfare of the group and for the purification of their souls.

Manifest acts of common worship strengthen the awareness of one Muslim for the other in times of gain or of adversity. In many respects they serve to cement communal bonds by stimulating the individual's sense of belonging. Meeting the devotional requirements of the faith is the basic prerequisite of being a Muslim.

Shahādah

The most important and oft repeated act of faith among the Muslim's ceremonial duties is his testimony to the unity of God *la ilāha illa 'l-Lāh,* "there is no god but God," commonly termed *al-Shahādah* (bearing witness). The Shahādah is more of a necessary reminder than it is a prescribed religious duty. When fully uttered the two-fold formula of Islam reads: (1) *ashhadu anna la ilāha illa 'l-Lāh,* (2) *wa anna Muḥammadan rasūlu 'l-Lāh,* (1) "I bear witness that there is no god (whatsoever) but God, (2) and that Muḥammad is the messenger of God." The mere uttering of this phrase makes a Muslim of the reciter. The "doctors" of Islamic jurisprudence have confirmed the fact that the title "Muslim" is due him who pronounces the *Shahādah.*

It is the first few words spoken in the ears of a newborn babe and the last on the lips of the dying. The *mujāhid,* fighter for Islam in the holy war, becomes a *shahīd* ("witness"), or martyr for the faith, if he falls in battle. No words are more often uttered than these; they are repeated by the average believer no less than twenty times daily. They constitute the basic part of the muezzin's call to prayer from the top of a minaret.

Ṣalāh

Of the five ceremonial duties incumbent on the Muslim, *Ṣalāh*, or the ritual prayer, is an essential obligation of Muslim worship and the supreme act of righteousness. Without rendering it, the Muslim in fact ceases to be one in practice.

Muḥammad placed greater importance on prayer than on any other religious duty. Prayer in Islam is not the same as in Christianity as it "does not mean the conversation of the heart with God," [44] but resembles rather public worship with readings from the Qur'ān, already committed to heart, commencing with the "Fātiḥah," followed by other short verses and the confession of faith (*shahādah*) and of the benediction or petition for the Prophet, and of brief praises. At prescribed moments in the ṣalāh there is room for personal invocation of God's aid and His guidance in what the Muslims call *duʿāʾ*.

The act of prayer is not left to the whim of the believer to perform; it constitutes rather a well-defined ritual, faithfully executed according to a prescribed pattern. Five times a day, at dawn, midday, midafternoon, sunset, and nightfall the muezzin mounts the balcony of slender minarets throughout the world of Islam and intones in the melancholy modulation of a resounding voice the call to prayer: "God is great (four times). I bear witness that there is no god but God (twice). I bear witness that Muḥammad is the messenger of God (twice). Come to prayer (twice). Come to contentment (twice). There is no god but God." During the call at dawn the muezzin reminds the faithful that "prayer is better than sleep."

The believer may perform the prayer ritual wherever he finds himself at the prescribed time, although city dwellers usually gather in mosques[45] for praying. The only time he is obligated to pray with his fellow Muslim is at the noon service of Friday,[46] the Muslim's sabbath but not really a day of rest. According to the Qur'ān:

> O ye who believe! When the call is heard for the prayer of the day of congregation, haste unto remembrance of Allah and leave your trading. . . .
>
> And when the prayer is ended, then disperse in the land and seek of Allah's bounty, . . .[47]

In every mosque there is a semi-circular recess called the *miḥrāb* that sets the direction of prayer, which is always towards Mecca. All worshipers face the direction of Mecca as they pray. At this given moment in the Muslim world, the rendering of the devotional requirement would project the image of Mecca and the sacred Kaʿbah at the middle with concentric circlese of believers around the world focusing their sights towards the middle.

In the mosque the faithful stand in straight lines facing the miḥrāb that points to Mecca; and up front with his back to the first row stands the *imām,* the leader in prayer. The procedure is supposedly modeled on that used by the Prophet who provided the broad outlines for it; details were worked out later, after considerable haggling by jurists, as were the five distinct and independent orisons per day. In Mecca during the early years of nascent Islam, only two seemed to have been prescribed.

> Establish worship at the going down of the sun until the dark of night, and (the recital of) the Qur'ān at dawn.[48]

Later, in the Medinan period, a third was added, presumably in keeping with the Jewish tradition of praying three times a day. This addition took place during the early period of rapport between Muḥammad and the Jewish community. The number of five daily prayer performances evidently was affixed by the jurists as a compromise reportedly between this number and forty which Allah allegedly asked of Muḥammad when he visited the Seventh Heaven on that night of the journey.

> Glorified be He Who carried His servant by night from the Inviolable Place of Worship[49] to the Far Distant Place of Wor-

ship[50] the neighborhood whereof We have blessed, that we might show him of our tokens!

The time of performance is fixed as follows:

ṣubh—when the sky is filled with light but before actual sunrise
ẓuhr—immediately after midday
ʿaṣr—sometime between three and five o'clock in the afternoon
maghrib—after sunset but before the onslaught of darkness
ʿishāʾ—any hour of darkness

The worshiper is enjoined to approach this sacred duty in a state of legal purity or ceremonial cleanliness, *ṭahārah.*

> O ye who believe! Draw not near unto prayer when ye are drunken, till ye know that which ye utter, nor when ye are polluted, save when journeying upon the road, till ye have bathed. And if ye be ill, or on a journey, or one of you cometh from the closet, or ye have touched women, and ye find not water, then go to high clean soil and rub your faces and your hands (therewith). . . .[51]

As seen from this revelation the Muslim must be also free of every defilement (*ḥadath*), great or small. For the prayer to be valid, the believer must approach it with purity of body, which implies purity of soul, and of dress and place. Ablutions prepare the believer for prayer; no other restrictions exist as "neither priests nor sacrifices nor ceremonies are needed to lift the heart of man towards his creator." [52]

Ablution is of two types: *ghusl,* a general form, and *wuḍūʾ* or the limited type. Ghusl is necessary after acts of great defilement (*janābah*) such as sexual intercourse; *wuḍūʾ* after small defilements arising from satisfying the calls of nature, from sleep, simple contact with the opposite sex, etc. The wuḍūʾ is the most commonly performed, either in the private dependencies of the Muslims or in the court itself of the mosque.

The process entails the use of legally pure water with which the worshiper washes first his face, then his hands and forearms to the elbows; the right hand next passes over the head, followed by the washing of the feet, all in this order. Cleanliness in this sense also prohibits the worshiper from performing the ritual prayer while wearing a garment stained with blood, excrement, and other such defilements; the efficacy of the prayer is immediately destroyed if such defilement takes place in the midst of it.

After having readied himself for prayer, the worshiper selects a *templum* or an immediate sanctuary where he takes up position facing Mecca, center of the shrine, the *qibla*[53] of Islam, after making sure that the ground he has taken up is not defiled, and preferably delineated by some visible object; hence the use of a "prayer rug."

The ritual is begun with the Muslim standing erect, his repeating the call to prayer (*iqāma*), and next putting into words his intention (*nīyah*) to undertake so many bowings (*rakʿāt,* sing. *rakʿāh*). This intention is important to the validity of the prayer as it represents the conscious will of the worshiper. Then raising his open hands to the level of the shoulder, the worshiper utters the *takbīr* (lit. "magnification") or the formula: *Allāhu akbar* which signifies the beginning of his dissociation for the duration of the prayer with all earthly affairs. The insertion at this point of any word or gesture foreign to the ritual immediately cancels the prayer, as such distractions interrupt the union of the worshiper with God. Muslim jurists laid so much stress on this formula that they called it *takbīr al-iḥrām* (the *takbīr* of sanctification).

The principal postures assumed in executing the prayer ritual are:[54]

1. From standing position, left hand placed in the right, worshiper recites the first chapter of the Qurʾān or the "Fātiḥah" followed by a few other verses usually from Sūrah CXII: "Say, God is One, the eternal God, begetting not and unbegotten; none is equal to Him."

2. Upper part of body is next inclined forward from the hips, and another takbīr is recited while the palms of the hands rest on the knees in an obeisance or *rukūʿ* and the performer recites the words "(I extol) the perfection of my Lord the Great."

3. Erect posture (*iʿtidāl*) is resumed while the worshiper utters the words "Allāhu akbar."

4. Next follows the posture of greatest surrender to God, *sujūd* (prostration), the high point of the prayer, with the worshiper uttering the same words over again.

5. Kneeling on the ground follows; then with hand outstretched in front of him the worshiper touches the ground with his brow at the base of nose.

6. He raises his body and sits on the base of his heels while still in a kneeling position and his hands stretched along his thighs in a *julūs* or *quʿūd* (sitting) position.

7. He prostrates himself for the second time preceded and followed by the takbīr.

8. Back to a julūs position, the shahādah is repeated, the intercession for Muḥammad, *"ṣalla-'l-Lāhu ʿala sayyidina Muḥammad,"* follows, then the ending with the worshiper turning his head first over his right shoulder then over the left pronouncing the *taslīm: "al-salāmu ʿalaykum wa raḥmatu 'l-Lāh."*

Having followed through uninterruptedly from the recitation of the "Fātiḥah" to the second prostration, the worshiper is said to have completed a *rakʿah.* A full complement of daily prayers contains a ritual number of *rakʿāt.* The *ẓuhr, ʿaṣr* and *ʿishāʾ* have four each; the other two, two each.

The Friday Prayer or *ṣalāt al-jumʿah* is performed in the mosque wherever feasible and when forty or more have assembled, hence the application of the term *jāmiʿ* (place of assembly) to the place of worship. The leader in prayer (*imām*) has no special religious function, and no ecclesiastical status or religious authority to issue injunctions as "there is no priesthood in Islam."

The imām may come rather from any walk of life; he is chosen by his coreligionists to lead them because of his reputation for knowledge of the faith and piety.

The prayer is followed immediately by the central function of the ritual, namely a *khuṭbah* (sermon) delivered by an *imām khaṭīb* and consisting of a general eulogy, according to a nearly fixed formula (*khuṭbat al-naʿt*), and pious exhortations (*khuṭbat al-waʿẓ*) in which the *khaṭīb* (deliverer of the sermon) can display his eloquence. He ends the khuṭbah by invoking the blessings of Allah upon the community and its heads.

In the early days of Islam the caliph either in person or through his representative presided over the solemn Friday Prayer; later for protection purposes he prayed within an enclosure of wood (*maqṣūrah*). In the days of Muḥammad, women attended mosque prayers standing behind men. Later they too prayed behind the maqṣūrah; and with the passing of time, fewer of them came to the mosque (*jamiʿ*) because, according to a prophetic tradition, it was preferable that they pray at home.

What is most striking in observing the faithful carrying out their prayer obligations is the marvelous simplicity and sobriety of the Qurʾānic ritual "which leaves the maximum of freedom in respect of the most elevated of spiritual functions." [55]

> The utmost solemnity and decorum are observed in the public worship of the Muslims. Their looks and behaviour in the mosque are not those of enthusiastic devotion but of calm and modest piety . . . they appear wholly absorbed in the adoration of their creator; humble and downcast, yet without affected humility, or a forced expression of humility.[56]

The peaceful and serene manner in which the worshiper carries out his prayer in congregation with others has a certain advantage. In the first instance the prescribed formula for the ritual has a disciplinary effect on the Muslim. It develops in him a greater awareness of his equality with the Muslim next to him and a stronger consciousness of solidarity. Praying in congregation promotes in the worshiper a sense of fraternal kinship with the one beside him, so lacking in pre-Islamic days when the only tie recognized was that of *blood* not *belief*.

The ceremony attending worship concentrates the thoughts of the worshiper "beyond the realm of the body, and enables him to express his devotion and to render thanks for divine bounties in the most profound manner." [57] "By bringing all Muslims together in the same ritual of humility and submission to the Lord, it makes them feel that they are all His creatures and thus brothers." [58] Following the imām in prayer gives the worshiper a real experience in discipline and obedience. Facing in the direction of Mecca provides him a constant reminder of the birthplace and mainspring of his faith, and of the center around which his religious sentiments hover.

Establishing worship may serve the moral elevation and purification of body and mind—"Surely, prayer preserveth one from lewdness and iniquity . . ." [59] But in the final analysis neither the permanence of prayer nor the offering of sacrifices to God can alone endear the Muslim to God; ". . . it is your righteousness that reacheth Him."

Zakāh

Invariably referred to as the "poor tax" or "poor-due" and "almsgiving," the *zakāh* literally means giving back to Allah a portion of His bounty as a means of avoiding the sufferings of the next life, and as an "expiation" or "purification" of what the Muslim retains for himself of material possessions.

While the *zakāh* may be regarded as an act of beneficence, a precept of right-doing and a charitable act in a moral sense, zakāh is less of a voluntary and more of a required religious observance; indeed, it is a fundamental of the faith.

> Establish worship and pay the poor-due and obey the messenger, that haply ye may find mercy.[60]

At the beginning of Islam, the *zakāh* was rendered as an act of piety and love; with the passing of time it took on more and more a legal connotation until it became obligatory, a ritual act, a legal duty. It was levied either in currency or in kind—cattle, grain, produce, or commodities.

> Lo! those who give alms, both men and women, and lend unto Allah a goodly loan, it will be doubled for them, and theirs will be a rich reward.[61]

It was in the days of the Prophet that the habit of bringing alms to the leader of the community began. From this habit was engendered the process that transformed it into a permanent type of taxation. In due time the Muslim community appointed officials to gather the poor-due from the communicants of the faith.

The Qurʾān specifies for whom the zakāh is due:

> The alms are only for the poor and the needy, and those who collect them, and those whose hearts are to be reconciled, and to free the captives and the debtors and for the cause of Allah, and (for) the wayfarers, a duty imposed by Allah.[62]

The distribution of alms is prescribed in the Qurʾān according to fixed categories of utilization:

1. First and foremost to the poor and needy (*fuqarāʾ*); then for
2. Officials (*ʿamalah,* sing. *ʿāmil*) who gathered the zakāh;
3. "Those whose hearts are to be reconciled"—in early Islam these were the recalcitrant Meccans whose hostility often had to be bought off;
4. Slaves to purchase their freedom;
5. Paying back debts incurred as a consequence of acts of benevolence;
6. Arming the *mujāhidūn* (sing. *mujāhid,* fighter) engaged in a holy war (*jihād*) against infidels;
7. Supporting institutions dedicated to the service of God (*fī sabīl-'l-Lāh,* in the way of Allah), and for
8. Aiding poor travelers.

The exact amount was never spelled out; but the average was usually between 2 and 3% of earnings or possessions. Later on, both the percentage levied and the mode of payment were worked out according to carefully laid down and specifically defined rules. Products of the soil, chattel and precious metals and merchandise become liable to zakāh when such items attain a certain minimum value called *niṣāb*. It is paid in kind; but when values exceed the *niṣāb*, then it is subject to fluctuation; when levied on harvests or fruits, the amount is between one-tenth (hence the *ʿushr*) and one-twentieth. There are set rules as to when cattle, precious metals, and manufactured products become liable to *zakāh*. The basic rule is that they must remain in the hands of the same owner for one year.

Both obligatory (*zakāh*) and non-obligatory (*ṣadaqah*) taxes were assessed and collected by a functionary called *ʿāmil* in the early period of Islam. In addition to determining and levying the precise amount, the *ʿāmil* arranged also for its transport to the depots where he personally was responsible for its safekeeping.

The zakāh or statutory alms was supplemented by the ṣadaqah, voluntary or non-obligatory alms. These were not defined or delimited; the faithful volunteered them as his proclivity for doing good or acquiring merits when Allah moved him.

Ṣawm

Ṣawm, or fasting, is another prerequisite of faith, also decreed by the Qurʾān:

> O ye who believe! There is prescribed for you the fast, as it was prescribed for those before you, that ye may ward off (evil) . . .[63]

"Those before you" alludes to other devotees of Allah, such as the Jews who fasted on the Day of Atonement, but more probably to the Eastern Christians, who fasted for thirty-six days. Ritual fasting was not known to Arabia of the *Jāhilīyah*. The fast is to be observed "in the month of Ramaḍān in which was revealed the Qurʾān . . . and whosoever of you is present, let him fast the month, and whosoever of you is sick or on a journey, (let him fast) the same number of other days." [64]

The month of fast varies constantly because the lunar calendar followed by the Muslims may move Ramaḍān through the whole course of the solar year.[65] The day of fast accordingly can be unusually long and, in a thirty-year cycle, it may coincide with the longest day of the year. Under such circumstances fasting can be an occasion of severe mental and physical strain for the faster.

During the fast the Muslims may not partake of any food or drink; nor may he smoke, or have sexual intercourse with the opposite sex, from the time when a white thread may be distinguished from a black one before sunrise until sunset.

> . . . Then strictly observe the fast till nightfall and touch them not, (i.e., opposite sex), but be at your devotions in the mosques . . .[66]

If a Muslim is able to fast and does not, he may make up for it by feeding a poor man; but "if ye fast it is better for you." If the believer in full control of his health and faculties (*ʿāqil, bāligh*) does not accomplish his fast obligations as prescribed, then he must give expiatory alms (*fidya*). If the sexual prohibition is violated, then he must free a slave or fast two months or feed sixty persons.

The validity of the fast is determined by the nīyah (intention) of the Muslim. "But whoso doeth good of his own accord, it is better for him . . ." [67] Mosques are well attended during Ramaḍān, and the rakʿāt accompanied by recitations from the Qurʾān and interspersed after each four by meals may well last the whole night.

The fast is broken immediately after sunset with a *fuṭūr* (light meal). The faster may "eat and drink until the white thread becometh distinct to you from the black thread of the dawn." [68] This culminates with a *suḥur* (dawn meal), the time when it may be taken at the latest is announced by a crier in towns called the *muwaqqit* (time determiner) or *musaḥḥir* (dawn determiner).

The beginning of the month of fast is determined by the appearance of the new moon. The end is likewise determined by a similar astronomical observation. If atmospheric conditions do not permit proper determination, the *qāḍi* or another religious authority of the locality may make the decision. The period of the fast may last from 28 to 30 days.

The fast ends on the first day of the month of Shawwāl with a great feast termed *ʿĪd al-Fiṭr* in the Eastern lands and *al-ʿĪd al-Ṣaghīr* in the Western lands of Islam. The feast of breaking the fast calls for a solemn prayer, *Ṣalāt al-ʿĪd*. On this day the statutory alms marking the end of the fast (*zakāt al-fiṭr*) are given and the head of each household gives to the poor a prescribed quantity of the customary food of the country as an act of piety.

The feast is an occasion for festivities lasting three full days during which time Muslims rejoice and exhibit their new clothes and exchange embraces. This feast of Ramaḍān is one of the most warmly and strictly observed holidays of Islam. Those who seek to avoid it incur severe approbation from their brethren.

Ḥajj

The fifth religious duty of the Muslim is the pilgrimage or *ḥajj* to the sacred monuments of Mecca, at least once in a lifetime for those who are physically able or can afford to perform it. The pilgrimage takes place during a certain period of the Muslim year, namely from the 7th to the 10th of dhu-'l-Ḥijjah. As an institution the pilgrimage is a carry-over from the pre-Islamic period. It was practiced by ancient Semites as a farewell to the harsh effects of the burning sun so characteristic of this part of the world.

The trek to Mecca *"al-Mukarramah"* (the Highly Honored) is more or less constant. Pilgrims from the remotest corners of Asia, Africa, the western hemisphere, and Europe work their way by every conceivable mode of transportation known to man, from airplanes to camel backs, to the birthplace of Islam and to "the Greatly Illuminated City", by which Medina is known.

The Muslim may perform either the ḥajj, the major pilgrimage, or the *ʿumra,* the lesser. Muḥammad referred to them by these terms in 630 when he negotiated with the Qurayshites to enter Mecca. While the revelations received in Mecca make no mention of the *ḥajj*, we have no reason to doubt that Muḥammad prayed to Allah before the Kaʿbah in the early years of his mission as later.

A number of sites are the target of the pilgrimage, and to understand the ritual performed round about them a note of explanation is necessary. Nature condemned most of central and west central Arabia to aridity. Violent thunderstorms, rare but furious, lash the surface with raging waters, very little of which furrow through to yield the few permanent springs upon which the inhabitant of this land depends.

The well of Zamzam is one such a spring. Indeed, it was around it, a stopping place of the caravan trade from Yemen to Syria along the Red Sea, that Mecca was built. According to Muslim legend, it was here that Abraham's wife Hagar and their son Ishmael were abandoned and where the angel Gabriel answered their plea for water by causing the spring of Zamzam to leap forth where Ishmael kicked his heels after his mother had run desperately in search of water between two hills. Abraham, according to the same tradition, came later to Zamzam and with the help of his son Ishmael rebuilt the Kaʿbah, the House of God (*Bayt al-Lāh*) on the very spot where Adam had built it before it was swept away by the Great Deluge of Biblical lore.

The other important monument is the Kaʿbah (literally the cube), located in the middle of a square enclosure surrounded by a wall measuring 36 x 30 x 18 feet high. There is nothing special about it. The façade is of undressed stone covered by the *kiswa* (vesture), made usually by the sovereign of the leading Islamic state. Egypt in the past led in presenting the kiswa, which is of a woven green cotton material inset with gold silk girdled by a black band two thirds up, on which are inscribed verses of the Qur'ān. The kiswa is carried annually to Mecca and the Kaʿbah during the pilgrimage season in the *maḥmal* (planquin).

At the southeast corner of the Kaʿbah is the Black Stone; not far from it at the northern side is the door which is opened on fixed days of the year to the faithful. Surrounding the Kaʿbah is the ellipsoidal roadway (*maṭāf*) on which the pilgrims make the ritual circuits (*ṭawāf*). Opposite the Black Stone, on the other side of the maṭāf, is the little mosque of Zamzam surrounded by the great courtyard (*ṣaḥn*) measuring 300 x 180 feet and bounded with galleries punctured by twenty-two gates.

The shrine of Mecca and the city's environs to the extent that the light of the sanctuary can be seen from beyond the city, which limit is marked off by pillars on all sides, constitute the ḥaram or the hallowed grounds. This concept was known to pre-Islamic Arabia. Within this ground, consecrated to the gods of the pagan Arabs beasts grazed in peace, the yield of the soil was respected, and none but those in a state of ritual sanctity could enter. Islam placed an interdiction on all non-Muslims, barring their entry to the sacred city.

Every able-bodied Muslim must perform this important religious duty once in a lifetime provided he has the means to undertake the long journey entailed should he live far from Mecca.

"And pilgrimage to the House (*Kaʿbah*) is a duty required by Allah from those (of you) who can find a way thither." [69]

A woman may also undertake the ḥajj if the husband permits it, and if she is accompanied either by him or by another person serving as protector. In some cases the performance of the pilgrimage may be delegated to a substitute who will undertake it for him. In this eventuality he would still get credit for it.

Should a believer die without having performed the pilgrimage when he could have and should have, arrangements may be then made for it to be done post mortem on his behalf by his heirs, who would thereby be performing a pious act subject to rewards on the Day of Judgment. In some cases bodies are sent to Mecca for burial.

The act of pilgrimage is attended by certain ritual ceremonies commencing from the moment the faithful declares his intention to undertake it; but it is on the borders of the ḥaram that it truly begins, although it is at certain prescribed stations called *mīqāt* (plural *mawāqīt*) along the route approaching the ḥaram that he performs the rites which prepare him to enter the sanctuary. It is here that he sheds his daily clothing and dons two seamless wrappers, one around the loins reaching to just above the knees (*izār*) and the other about the shoulders (*ridāʾ*) after ablution and prayer. With the exception of two pieces of leather soles (*naʿl*) strapped to his feet, he goes without head cover or shoes. After these necessary preliminary preparations, he enters the ḥaram and does not thereafter shave, trim his nails, or anoint his head during the entire ceremonial period.

Highlighting the ceremony of the ḥajj are the following encumberances: a visit to the *Masjid al-Ḥarām* (the sacred mosque), kissing the Black Stone, circumambulating the Kaʿbah seven times (*ṭawāf*) three times at a run and four at a quick pace, a visit to *Maqām Ibrāhīm,* where there is a sacred stone upon which Abraham allegedly climbed while laying the upper courses of the Kaʿbah. There is also the ascent to Mount Ṣafa whence the pilgrim runs to Mount Marwa seven times, then to Mount ʿArafāt, on the ninth day of the pilgrimage. The *wuqūf* at ʿArafāt, "station before Allah" as it is called, constitutes the culminating point of the pilgrimage without which the ceremony would be nil and void.

The wuqūf takes place in the afternoon of the ninth day. The pilgrim stands erect before Allah and recites pious formulae under the leadership of an imām who also gives a solemn khuṭbah, one of the four ritual khuṭbahs of the entire pilgrimage. Then immediately at sunset the pilgrims proceed to another valley, Muzdalifah, situated between ʿArafāt and Mina. Here they spend the night of the tenth day, the last of the pilgrimage, which culminates at sunrise. At Mina the final ceremonies of the *ḥajj* take place.

The wuqūf at Muzdalifah is followed, like that of ʿArafāt, by a "flight" (*ifāḍah*) that brings the pilgrims back to Mina at sunrise. Here at the edge of a steep slope (*ʿaqaba*), where the road to Mina starts, and before a stone stele with a sort of large basin in front of it the pilgrim casts seven little pebbles picked up at Muzdalifah while reciting *Bism 'l-Lāhi, Allāhu akbar* (in the name of God, God is great). The casting of the seven pebbles is in commemoration of Abraham's escape from Satan, when tempted by him at this spot, by his throwing seven stones at him. The stele is referred to popularly as *al-Shayṭān al-Kabīr* (the great Satan).

The ceremony ends with the sacrifice of an animal at Mina, usually a sheep or goat, which the pilgrim had consecrated during the ḥajj. Part of it is eaten by the owner, or owners; the remainder is distributed to the poor of Mecca. A few pieces dried in the sun are carried back by the pilgrims, while the rest of the carcass is imperfectly buried. The pilgrims continue to live at Mina for a few days more.

This sacrifice on the 10th of dhu-'l-Ḥijjah is one of the most important feasts of Islam, although it is not considered as significant as the wuqūf at ʿArafāt in the ceremony of the ḥajj. On this day throughout the Muslim World the head of each family sacrifices an animal in the same ceremonial manner followed at Mina. The feast is invariably known to the Arabs as the *ʿĪd al-Aḍha* (feast of the offerings) or *ʿĪd al- Qurbān;* to the Turks as *Büyük Bayram;* and to the Muslims of North Africa as *al-ʿĪd al-Kabīr* (the great feast).

At the end of the sacrifice ritual the pilgrim has his head shaven and nails cut. The waste is carefully buried at Mina. Henceforth he is in a state of partial desanctification (*taḥallul al-ṣaghīr*). Full desanctification occurs only after the pilgrim scurries back to Mecca and performs at the Kaʿbah the *ṭawāf al-ifāḍah.* At this point he has fulfilled the ceremonies of the pilgrimage (*manāsik al-ḥajj*) and is entitled to be called "Ḥājj", or "Ḥājji" to the Turks.

After a few days more at Mecca, the Hājj departs for home with a strong sense of accomplishment as he has just fulfilled the crowning act of his religion and acquired an enviable reputation among fellow believers who have no claim to the title. More important, he is instilled with a keener awareness of the power of Islam which can bring together each year men of so many different nationalities and races. This is one of the strongest forces working for solidarity among Muslims devoted to their faith. The pilgrimage is the "plenary assembly as well as the fair of Islam." [70]

A visit to Medina is the next step; it is here as he stands before the tomb of the Prophet that the believer is moved most deeply. Some might visit also Jerusalem, site of the *Miʿrāj*[71] and home of so many prophets, especially ʿĪsa (Jesus). Upon reaching home, the pilgrim performs the same ceremonies which he underwent on departure. He also distributes souvenirs, water of Zamzam, and pieces of the *kiswa*, to relatives and friends.

CHAPTER 8

Solidarity Through Institutional Unity

A MEANINGFUL UNDERSTANDING of the unifying powers of Islam the religion can be derived from a perusal of the institutions it sired. The full impact of the religion can not be fully appreciated without some knowledge of its political, social, and cultural ramifications.

The doctrinal requirements of Islam, together with the obligations imposed by the Qur'ān and the traditions that developed therefrom, gave rise to institutions and usages which transformed a primitive religious community into a highly organized socio-political society cohering through the forces engendered by its religion and in turn strengthening the sentiment of belonging among Muslims. Islam in this respect served as the catalytic force that induced the formation of a distinct identity among the believers in the first few centuries which centrifugal forces in later centuries could not break down, not even in more recent times when the concept of nationality differences gained sway in Muslim lands.

The teachings of Muḥammad as enshrined in the Qur'ān and Ḥadīth provided the framework and the legislative basis of Islamic society, reaching into almost every aspect of individual and group life in this society with emphasis on duties and obligations. Such legislation gave rise to a variety of institutions and practices which, with the passing of time, shaped the pattern and norms governing Islamic society in its multifarious aspects.

The Accident of Circumstance

Circumstance played an equally important role in the first century of Islam's existence. Sustained military probes on the periphery of Islamic Arabia, resulting from a carry-over of the razzia institution from pre-Islamic times and encouraged by ineffective resistance to these probes, culminated within a short century in the establishment of an extensive empire. Islam had banned internecine warfare but it could not subdue the militant zeal of the desert Arabian; indeed, his newly acquired beliefs served to strengthen rather than lessen his zeal for gain and, if he should fall in battle, for martyrdom. Raids in search of gain led to campaigns, campaigns led to wars of conquest, and these ultimately to the establishment of an Islamic empire.

Islam undoubtedly provided the moving force, although one can not state that the zeal to convert non-Muslims to Islam was the major inducement. Far from being destructive, the desert Arabian as conqueror under the banner of Islam exhibited strong qualities of restraint and discipline in his relationships with the conquered people, who represented a variety of ethnic and sectarian groups with strongly differing cultural backgrounds. The credit for such restraint belongs to the tenets and precepts of Islam as clearly enunciated in the Qur'ān. Indeed, under the influence of Islamic injunctions, the conqueror was duty-bound to respect and protect the conquered, especially those who already acknowledged their belief in Allah in Christianity and Judaism. Not by the sword, but by the exemplary conduct of these zealous Muslims and gains anticipated therefrom, did so many of the conquered—pagan, Christian, Shaman, Zoroastrian, Hindu, and Jew—convert to Islam, faith of the conqueror, and adopt for their own the values sustaining this faith.

Contrary to hitherto accepted judgment, it was not by force but by the appeal of his readily comprehensible faith and the example of personal and communal living that the Arab in Spain or Turkistan turned into a magnet for Islam, not a repellent.

Islam in many instances gained from the conversion of those peoples who had evolved a more distinct culture than that of the conqueror. The conquered first as clients and later as a dominant force in Islamic society continued to acquire and utilize the products attending Islam, namely, the language as well as cultural and social norms. The resultant interaction of Islam, the religion, and its medium of expression, the Arabic language, with the cultural background of the converts—Persian, Hellenized Syrian and Egyptian—abetted both the "internationalization" of Islam and its acquiring a distinct culture of its own.

The Arab supplied the broadened Islamic fraternity with Islam and the Arabic language, the two principal media of coherence, together with a broad spirit of tolerance through a deliberate policy, carefully defined, of non-interference in the communal affairs of the conquered. In the resultant diversity Islam found its greatest enrichment, and to the religious nurture of unity and solidarity a new dimension, the cultural, was added.

The survival of indigenous cultural values introduced by converts to Islam, while imparting to the faith a local coloring tolerated by it, did not transgress or compromise the prerequisites of belief as defined by the *Sharīʿah*, the fundamental law of Islam; nor did the acceptance of them override the exigencies of communal solidarity which the Islamic theocracy imposed on all believers.

Not by force of arms nor by administrative fiat did the Arab Muslim, by far the minority element in the lands conquered, impart cohesion and solidarity to the society of converts. By a combination of magnanimity tempered with justice and exemplary conduct, the soldier in earlier centuries like the merchant in more recent times opened up wedges for the expansion of Islam into southeast Asia and sub-Saharan Africa, areas where the force of Islamic arms was never felt. While valor and example played significant roles in the spread of Islam, we can not discount the impact of Qurʾānic legislation and the qualities of leadership exhibited by the caliphs and those close to Muḥammad in his lifetime. Legislative fiat and circumstance combined to create, assimilate, and consolidate a monolithic Islamic society.

To understand the range of the religious impact on the growth and consolidation of the organized Islamic community and on the institutional structure of this cohering body before transformation set in during the period of decline, and more recently when modernism began to cause radical changes in institutional beliefs and practices, a perusal of the fundamental structural basis must be made.

The Caliphate

We noted that the Qurʾān played a vital role in defining the path of growth followed by the religion. The Qurʾān and Sunnah together shaped the institutions attending the rise of Islam to socio-political as well as religious heights of attainment. Among the earliest and most germane to the rise of Islam is the institution of the caliphate.

When Muḥammad ruled the destinies of the faithful, Allah assisted him generously with properly timed revelations which enabled him to attend to the basic administrative needs of a nascent community that looked to itself for the means of coherence and development. Muḥammad served in all capacities as minister, judge, and ruler. He made all important decisions and was the ultimate recourse for all. Upon his death the faithful in democratic council elected the much respected Abu-Bakr successor (*khalīfah*) to Muḥammad's temporal but *not* spiritual authority. Thus began an important institution that lasted until 1924 when it was abolished by Kemal Ataturk of modern Turkey.

The caliph was not only ruler but also *amīr al-muʾminīn* (commander of the faithful) and the *imām* (guide) of the community. To the Sunni orthodox Muslim the office was elective;

but with the first Umayyad caliph Muʿāwiyah (661-680) it became hereditary in his line and continued that way until the end.

The Shīʿites, however, have insisted on legitimacy, namely, that the *imām* must come from Muḥammad's line through his daughter Fāṭimah and her husband ʿAli, the Prophet's closest associate, with full unchallengeable authority due him as God's successor on earth. This "divine right kingship" notion reflected the old Persian theory and was not unfamiliar to the Byzantines. The Persians today are the largest Shīʿite group in Islam.

The caliphate in its heyday was a powerful instrument working for solidarity and coherence in Islam. The caliph enforced legal decisions, safeguarded the divinely revealed restrictive ordinances, maintained the armies and guarded the community of Islam from external attack, enforced order and security, meted out justice, received and distributed the *zakāh* and other alms, maintained the Friday services and public institutions, decided between disputants, served as supreme judge in matters bearing legal claims, married minors who had no guardians, distributed booty gained in war, and generally catered to a variety of needs brought before him by the faithful. Later in the ʿAbbāsid period of the caliphate, particularly from the ninth century onward, under mounting Persian influence the caliph became more withdrawn from public accessibility. With the creation of a bureaucratic machine, his functions were whittled away gradually, until finally the caliph became a mere ceremonial figure.

The first caliphs were elected from amongst the companions of Muḥammad. They faithfully carried on the tradition established by him and ministered to the needs of the community along lines set by the Prophet himself. For this they were titled by historians as *al-khulafāʾ al-rāshidūn* (the rightly-guided caliphs). Even though the community expanded militarily under ʿUmar I with the conquest of Syria and Egypt from Byzantium (636-641) and the Persian Empire from its Sāsānid rulers (637), the first three caliphs took no active part in war. They regarded themselves primarily as custodians and enforcers of the *Sharīʿah,*[1] canon law with which they had been charged. By and large, they were pious men who followed the Prophet's example of austere living and personal accessibility to the faithful.

The Umayyad caliphs[2] who succeeded them were more interested in acquiring and enjoying the benefits of this life and its material enrichments. With them the caliphate became more nearly a form of kingship and lost much of its spiritual orientation. This materialistic orientation notwithstanding, the Umayyad caliphs were careful to safeguard the temporal interests of the Muslim community and to organize it formally into a state administered by an expanding bureaucratic machinery that reflected the strong influences of the assimilated conquered peoples and their traditions of government.

The ʿAbbāsid successors[3] to the Umayyads had forcibly usurped their caliphal authority under the pretext of restoring the pure and pious traditions of the Prophet to caliphal rule. But they were also heirs of the Sāsānid "King of Kings" and of the traditions associated with him. Now under the influence of Persian advisers and courtiers they began to emulate Persian ways and their love of pomp and splendor, familiar to the reader of the tales popularized by the *Arabian Nights*. The caliph no longer regarded himself as the *primus inter pares* of the community, the imām who led by personal example the faithful along the righteous path. He was now an absolute sovereign served by all the prerogatives due the despot; unlimited powers were at his disposal; he was beyond reach, and fully capable of exercising such powers at will.

But a bureaucracy, ever on the increase since Umayyad days, eventually surrogated for itself most of the powers which the caliph once held in his hands. An imām took over leadership of the Friday prayer and delivered the important khuṭbah; a qāḍi dispensed justice as decreed by the Qurʾān and embodied in the Sharīʿah; a ʿāmil was in charge of gathering taxes, and an amīr commanded the army and often the administration in the various far-flung provinces of the caliphate. The numerous decrees issued in the name of the caliph were drawn up by *kuttāb* (sing. *kātib*) *al-sirr* (scribes, secretaries) constantly multiplying in numbers.

With the ʿAbbāsids the institution of vizierate entered the scene, and the vizier, who enjoyed no special function at first other than that of a general aide-de-camp and confidant to the caliph, now took charge of a whole hierarchy of viziers constituted as a sort of "cabinet" and began to exercise powers not much unlike those of the most developed modern cabinet systems.

There came into being also the office of the *ḥājib*[4] (chamberlain) who served as a screen between the caliph and his subjects. When the Seljuk Turks appeared on the scene in the tenth century, the much abused and incapacitated caliph found himself under the tutelage of his rescuers upon whom he gratefuly bestowed the title of *amīr al-umarāʾ* (the prince of princes) and then *sulṭān* (sultan—possessor of supreme authority), an office which distracted from the caliphal image of authority and prevented the caliph from exercising full power.

The gradual whittling away of caliphal authority rendered the caliph almost totally powerless towards the end of the ʿAbbāsid era. He was now no more than a ceremonial figure, isolated from his subjects, and little aware of their problems. They fell prey as a consequence to the exploitation of powerful local amirs who acknowledged only nominally the caliphal office.[5] The effect was to decentralize the empire and give vent to *shuʿūbīyah*[6] movements with their strong centrifugal tendencies. Indeed, one observes that such a tendency was the unavoidable consequence of the caliph's withdrawal from the public exercise of the prerogatives of his office and his retreat, often voluntary, from the active display of his powers.

The result is that regions which possessed a geographical and independent historical personality before Islam began to assert themselves again under some sectarian adhesion in Islam like Fātimid Egypt, Umayyad Spain, Shīʿite Persia, Khārijite Oman, Sharīfian Morocco. The dynastic structure and control of such and similar countries by the nineteenth century maintained very loose ties, when at all, with the Ottoman caliph in Istanbul.

The story of how decentralization took place and how influential it was in creating schismatic movements in the Islamic polity constitutes a separate study. Our concern here is with those institutions that have had a centralizing and binding effect; some of which have not ceased to do the same until today. The Qurʾān and the traditions associated with Muḥammad, his companions, and the Orthodox caliphate are among them. The ideals persisting from pre-Islamic tribal society with emphasis on loyalty, kinship ties, and the pilgrimage also served to bind together the polity.

Jihād

The idea of *jihād* in a military context with its emphasis on the notion of continuous struggle against non-believers in God as the sole deity tended to keep alive the spirit of solidarity in the community over and against outsiders. While the Qurʾān does not make of *jihād* in the "holy war" context an article of faith, it is the Ḥadīth which renders it into a formula for "active struggle" that invariably tended toward a militant expression. What makes of *jihād* a binding institution in Islam is the fact that it is a *communal* not an *individual* obligation. The incentive for *jihād* lies in its two-fold benefits: booty for this life and martyrdom with its immediate promise for a blissful eternal hereafter for those killed in battle, the *shuhadāʾ* (sing. *shahīd*: martyr).

The exercise of *jihād* was the responsibility of the imām, or the caliph when the powers of the office were still in his hands; the territory of sanctioned war, *dār al-ḥarb,* invariably was on the frontier of *dār al-Islām* (abode of Islam). The yearly raids against the Byzantines by the ʿAbbāsids, and later the Turkish thrusts into Byzantine holdings in Asia Minor, which ended ultimately in the destruction of the empire altogether, were sanctioned by *jihād*, as were the raids into Hindustān by the Ghaznāwids in the tenth and eleventh centuries.

Jihād has also an important non-military connotation, namely, that each Muslim must strive to live up to the tenets and requirements of his religion by constant manifestations of charitable deeds. This is the side of *jihād* which Western scholars tend to ignore.

Jihād in a militant context did not affect non-Muslim subjects and residents. The governing institutions of Islam affected directly the communicants and only superficially non-communicants whose residence among Muslims was accepted, tolerated, and indirectly regulated.

The conquerors permitted full juridical and administrative control to Christian and Jewish communities whose protection the Qurʾān enjoins and who are known as *ahl al-dhimmah* or *dhimmis* (dimmis), in exchange for the *jizyah*, a sort of personal tribute-tax levied on all those capable of paying it. Their social and religious status with few exceptions[7] was respected. The bishop, rabbi, or the head of the protected community was directly responsible for its affairs and welfare to the Muslim caliph, and later, sultan.

In the principal cities of Islam where strong pockets of tributaries survived, dimmis filled important offices and professional positions. The ruler's physician invariably was a Christian or a Jew; they engaged freely in a number of professions, practiced banking, carried on trade, indulged in scholarly pursuits, enjoyed authority, and led relatively prosperous lives, which sometimes made them the target of mobs incited by the dimmis' more fanatical Muslim neighbors. Non-Muslim foreigners in Muslim lands, increasingly more numerous from the eighth century onward as members of foreign missions, traders, and the like, enjoyed *amān* (formal safety) in keeping with the ancient Arab custom of granting *jiwār* (quarter) to outsiders. While they were still looked upon as *kuffār* (sing. *kāfir:* infidel), they nevertheless acquired the status of protégés and came to enjoy the same privileges extended to dimmis.

The Sharīʿah sanctioned the residence of Muslims in non-Muslim lands provided they were permitted to carry on their religious duties unencumbered. In the twelfth century, Syrian Muslims lived under the jurisdiction of Frankish Crusader and non-Crusader princes in the Norman kingdom of Sicily. They dwelt in relative safety of person and possessions and were not treated as "colonials," as were their coreligionists during the Spanish regime of the Reconquista. Today no less than a hundred million Muslims live under predominantly non-Muslim jurisdiction.

The Sharīʿah and Fiqh

The *Sharīʿah* encompasses legislation derived from the Qurʾān and the Ḥadīth. Tradition and the juridical consolidation of life molded under the stimuli of the Qurʾān and the Ḥadīth, with no distinction between spiritual and temporal law, served to rally the believers throughout the Muslim world. Only in recent times did decisions sustained by the *Sharīʿah* begin to affect the institutions and livelihood of Muslims, supplemented and sometimes supplanted by modern legal practices.

The *Sharīʿah,* unlike laws developing from the precedents established by Roman law, stresses individual cases. Through the use of analogical reasoning, a doctrinal point resting on the *Sharīʿah* can apply by extension to like points without following any carefully defined formula for such extended use. The jurist could almost always find one case from the multitudinous accumulation over the centuries that would provide him with the proper precedent for a given legal matter. This is what kept the *Sharīʿah* alive and functional in pulling Islamic society together.

The *Sharīʿah* is Islam's constitution. The function of evolving useful effectual legal principles from the *Sharīʿah* gave rise to the *Fiqh,* without distinguishment between the spiritual and the secular. The process of evolving a fiqh started when Muḥammad first began to adjudicate for the nascent Muslim community in Medina. While Allah provided him with revelations suitable for certain cases, often the Prophet drew on the customary law or usages of Arab tribes, and sometimes of Jewish tribes, in and around Medina as long as elements of the faith were not compromised thereby.

Thus the eclectic nature of legal development in Islam can be said to have been predetermined in the lifetime of the Prophet. With the exception of frequently recurring subjects pertaining to inheritance, marriage, enactments concerning children, the treatment and emancipation of slaves, laws dealing with murder and theft, property and commercial matters, where more careful attention to detail is given, Muḥammad was content to treat "legal problems" on their individual merits with no conscious effort to build up a uniform system or code.

Hence, upon his death the faithful inherited a few specific prescriptions in the Qur'ān and a mass of recorded decisions of the cases he handled. Specifically, Muḥammad had left behind his particular use of what would be analogous to common law, equity and legislation, and to enactments and recordings based thereon. The death of Muḥammad may be considered to have ended constitutional legislation in orthodox Islam. What we note instead in subsequent years is the exposition and systemization of Islamic law deriving from the Sharīʿah through fiqh.

At first the *fuqahā'* (sing. *faqīh:* jurist) followed entirely practical precedents. When confronted with a problem, the Qur'ān was their first recourse; if no satisfying answer was found therein, they resorted next to the specific decisions made by Muḥammad himself. If this procedure proved unsatisfying, the jurist had the choice of following Muḥammad's precedent by consulting the common law of Medina. Should this also fail to yield a proper precedent, then the *faqīh* was empowered to follow his personal judgment or, as another resort, to use equity as a standard of decision.

The Sunnah

The *Sunnah* (literally, path) relates to the body of tradition associated with the conduct of Muḥammad in his discharge of prophetic responsibility and to the manner in which he handled himself as guide, judge, and ruler of the organized Muslim community *when not specifically directed by Allah.*

To emulate the way of *the man* as well as *the prophet* becomes exceedingly important in later decades for successors and jurists unable to find specific revelations coping with the demands of an expanded and more complex society. The study and adaptation of Muḥammad's sunnah to rising needs became a considerable enterprise. But in the meanwhile there had come into being literally hundreds of thousands of *ḥadīth* or sayings attributed to Muḥammad, but not all verifiable. Before this vast corpus could enjoy official sanctity, it had to be carefully screened and the genuine traditions ascertained.

In the course of time the *Sunnah* acquired special merits for a variety of purposes. It was useful to Muslims who sought to justify dissenting views over important doctrinal interpretations. The traditions, and particularly the sayings of Muḥammad, served to bolster a variety of causes ranging from personal ambitions to complex doctrinal and institutional decisions. These were more often in situations that would have incurred for Muslims embarked on a course of deviation the approbation rather than the approval of Allah and the Prophet.

The evolution of the *Sunnah* as an important legal corpus had its start with the companions of Muḥammad. These associates of the Prophet were dedicated men who found in his conduct and sayings much to emulate. Hence they made careful mental notations of Muḥammad's life and deeds. To follow in his footsteps was the desired end, the end which every properly brought up young Muslim does not cease to strive after.

Muḥammad to the believers was a mortal like themselves who lived a life pleasing to God and served his fellow Muslims well. Thus his sayings and doings, manners and customs, his answers to questions on religious life and faith and, above all, his decisions in legal disputes became a source of important reference for the layman and the jurist, the philosopher and the theologian, the rebel and the law abider, the respectful of tradition and the innovator, according to a process of challenge and response that gained much validity for the Islamic society in the stage of its development and institutionalization.

The *Sunnah* in later centuries, when confronted by Western ideals and institutions that challenged Islamic traditional beliefs and usages, lent much support to the traditionalists seeking to combat foreign influences on all levels of Islamic society. This resistance has been particularly evident in very recent times. Such concern for tradition gave rise to the extensive literature termed *Ḥadīth* in Islam, the study of which preoccupied Muslim scholars for generations.

Specific schools came into being in the ninth century for assembling and categorizing the sayings of Muḥammad in support of all sorts of arguments and disputes. Theologians and jurists made of these a legal system of reference for passing decisions on important theological and juridical questions. Liberal thinkers in the ninth century were less concerned with Ḥadīth arguments than they were with rational or speculative theories to support their contentions. The conflict that ensued between these "rationalists" and their antagonists the "traditionalists" accounts for much of the philosophical and theological studies of Islam in the heyday of its cultural development.

When the conquests brought Muslim jurists in contact with Roman law in the provinces they, like the Muslim administrator, found much of value and practical utility in it. As long as local customs and usages did not conflict with the basic tenets of the Sharīʿah, they tried to avail themselves of them. The presence of Roman legal terminology in Arabic legal nomenclature attests to the influence of Roman codes on Islamic legalism. When Muslim law permits the qāḍi to exercise his *raʾy* (personal judgment) we are reminded of the use of "equity" in Anglo-Saxon law. The use of *istiḥsān*[8] (preference) as a legal principle, even when the analogy of the code decreed another course, represents another concession to a non-doctrinaire approach. Resorting to *istiṣlāḥ,*[9] deciding on that which would bring the greatest benefit to the community at large, is another nontraditionalistic recourse.

But in the heated controversy that ensued over such principles of legal decision, liberty of opinion was in the end narrowed to *qiyās,* use of analogy, the nearest the Muslim *Sharīʿah* came to the principle of "legal fiction" as applied by Western jurists.

The Umayyad caliphate ended the somewhat pious theocratic empire of the Orthodox caliphs. In the following eras, public life tended to exhibit with few exceptions far less religious sentiment; indeed, the pious said that it was "godless." Law was still needed, but in its development it became more speculative and opportunistic. The study of *Sunnah* and *Ḥadīth* passed into the hands of private individuals noted for their personal piety. The result was that interpretation of the *Sharīʿah* became more idealistic and less in keeping with the realities of Islamic society, and that Ḥadīth with, until now, its handmaiden Fiqh came to a parting of the ways. Students of *Ḥadīth* gathered traditions for their own sake with the idea of providing prophetic guidance and dicta for the details of life as they faced them, on the assumption that any caliph, amīr or responsible individual who went beyond the patriarchal form developed at Medina was of this world "imperiling his soul at every turn."

The subscribers of *Ḥadīth* were seeking to apply it to the details of human experience, and in so doing they were diluting from its universalistic appeal. Yet both the *Sharīʿah* and the *Fiqh* still possessed a much broader applicability than Western secular law. Herein lies the significant role of the *Sharīʿah* as the builder and sustainer of Islamic society in the totality of its earthly existence and in the projection of its promises for eternity. The *Sharīʿah* regulated the essentials of man's relationships to God, neighbor, and self. It was a system of duties that the *Sharīʿah* created, a system which was not only religious and ethical but legal in a non-canonical sense as well. It specifically defined for the faithful what actions are *forbidden* unto them (*ḥarām*), what are *required* of them (*farḍ, wājib*), and what is recommended (*mandūb, mustaḥabb*), or what is tolerated (*mubāḥ, jāʾiz*), and what is disliked or frowned upon (*makrūh*).

The role of the *Sharīʿah* and *Fiqh* may be likened unto a combination of canonical law and the "law of the land." It not only defines for the faithful the prescriptions for the exercise of religious, ceremonial, and ethical obligations, but governs the private lives of all pious Muslims. In one or the other of its four juridic schools, the *Sharīʿah* regulates certain aspects of the Muslims' semi-public relationships, e.g., marriage, divorce, inheritance. It also compels respect for itself, if not acceptance from the state.

The *Fiqh* administered a scheme of duties but had only partial ties with the real legal systems of Muslim peoples in more recent centuries, with the exception of the Wahhābis of Arabia and the Ibādis of ʿUmān where it still constitutes the whole law. The changes in the *Sharīʿah's* role in governing the broader aspect of the Muslim's life were due partly to the converts clinging to their inherited usages and partly to the fact that what sufficed for the nascent community in Medina was not sufficient for an empire embracing a heterogeneous populace and permitting whole communities of Jews and Christians to govern themselves without being integrated into the Islamic fold.

ʿĀdāt

Peoples conquered by the Islamic polity were willing to apply a veneer of Islamic phraseology to conceptions of their own religions. The Muslims themselves, particularly the new converts, conversely allowed themselves to be influenced by local customs or *ʿādāt* of the conquered peoples. *ʿĀdāt* consisted of a variety of local usages having the sanctity of law; such usages not only differed from place to place, sometimes radically, but often obscured, if they did not contradict, the Sharīʿah.

ʿĀdāt as a form of "local law" crystallized into a legally applicable corpus in lands ruled by the Ottoman Turks. It developed two systems of legal procedure, one administering ordinances of the *Sharīʿah* with emphasis on private and family affairs and pronouncing decrees on purely personal religious questions, e.g., details of ritual law, law of oaths and vows, and the other sustaining the working courts of the land by administering codes based on local custom and the decrees of local rulers.

The canon laws of Islam, like the institution of the caliphate, served as a binding force in the organization and management of the affairs of Islamic society. There were in addition other forces at work cementing the ties of the community. These relate to concepts and practices engulfing a much broader and more intimate side of the Islamic community, namely, family bonds and common observances that permeated the whole social and economic life of the community.

The Family

The family to Islam is the cornerstone and the mainstay of the community, as it had been to the Arabs before Islam. What Muḥammad did was to take the Arabian conception of the family and to fit it into the framework of Islam. Essential ingredients carried over into Islam are those relating to plural marriages, the place of women and children in the persisting patriarchal family, and the rules governing the conclusion of marriage. These would encompass also the preliminary steps like the *mahr,*[10] *khiṭbah,*[11] and *ʿaqd al-nikāḥ,*[12] without which marriage cannot be finalized; there is also the matter of verifying intent, i.e., when the parties declare their consent to marriage and the husband pays the dowry. All such Muslim steps toward marriage are survivals of pre-Islamic practices.

Islam on the other hand did introduce some changes. The mahr, for instance, is assigned by the Qurʾān to the wife as a form of surety, which adds the material element to the spiritual bond of marriage and makes of this innovation a more honest and forthright approach. The marriage contract, moreover, possesses no specifically religious character. It may be formalized either in the mosque or in the home of one of the parties according to a defined ritual and a legal procedure. The contract spells out the terms by which marital relations are to be conducted and under what conditions dissolved. It also defines the respective rights and obligations of both sides, delineating the role of tutors, specifying when minors or those adjudged legally incompetent can marry, stipulating the terms of inter-faith marriages, the marriage of slaves, and related matters.

The occasion of marriage is one of great celebration and festivity throughout the Muslim world. It provides one of the great outlets for social intercourse and enjoyment. In a way it serves to emphasize the great significance attached to family life as a force for unity in Islamic society.

Social Institutional Observances

Numerous social practices and ceremonies continuously observed have strengthened the notions of belonging and common identity in Islam. The birth of a son to the Muslim family, no less than the marriage fetish itself, is a special joyful event. Animal sacrifices are made and the flesh is distributed to the poor; alms are offered and Muslim prayers are whispered into the child's ear. When named, seven days after birth, he usually carries a name by which the Prophet was known—Muḥammad, Maḥmūd, Ḥāmid, Muṣṭafa—or one of the ninety-nine variants by which God is addressed—al-Qādir, al-Ḥāmid, al-Razzāq. The daughters usually receive the names of the women in the Prophet's family—Khadījah, Fāṭimah, ʿĀʾishah, Zaynab.

The circumcision rite is strictly observed by all Muslims like the marriage ceremonies; it provides an important landmark in the life of the youthful Muslim. If it is performed at age seven, it signifies his passing from the strict care of his mother, to whom the Muslim infant belongs, to a helping relationship with his father; at this date he begins his life as a man or launches his formal study of the Qurʾān at school.[13] The daughter by contrast stays close to the house and there receives what education the social status of the family permits. The great concern of the parents is a properly arranged marriage; and most of their training is dedicated to the cause of turning them into good housewives and mothers. Modernization has undermined much of this custom.

Memorization of the Qurʾān used to be at the core of the Islamic educational program. When completed, the youth became a *ḥāfiẓ*[14] and with it he acquired considerable prestige in society. After memorizing the Qurʾān, he began the formal study of such related subjects as the exegesis of the Qurʾān (*tafsīr*), the traditions (*Ḥadīth*), law (*Fiqh*), grammar (*naḥw*), lexicography (*lughah*), rhetoric (*bayān*), and literature (*adab*). With the diminishing role of Qurʾānic schools in the educational systems of Muslim countries during the last century, increasing numbers of Muslim students have been studying in Western schools.

Here they enroll in broader secular courses pertaining to the sciences and the humanities; indeed, the role of the traditional Islamic curriculum outside of specialized religious schools has been increasingly circumscribed in recent years.

Teaching usually took place either in the courtyard of the mosque or in the master's house. Students formed a *ḥalaqah* (circle) around the master who devised a curriculum as he thought best and stressed memorization of passages from the Qur'ān and commentaries as well as the master's own writings. Assiduous and attentive listeners received his authorization (*ijāzah*) to repeat his lessons in another city. In this manner the works of distinguished masters were disseminated throughout the Muslim world. Thus do we have a scholarly tradition serving to provide Islamic society with a unifying intellectual response.

Regular institutions were founded and maintained by the caliphs for the purpose of promoting the "religious sciences," such as the *Dār al-Ḥadīth* (House of Tradition) and *Dār al-ʿIlm* (House of Knowledge) of the early ʿAbbāsids. The al-Azhar of Cairo evolved from the *Dār al-ʿIlm* prototype; it was founded by the Fāṭimid caliphs of Egypt at the beginning of their reign in the tenth century. The al-Azhar, oldest living university in the World, is emulated by two other institutions, the Zaytūnah of Tunis and the Qarawīyīn of Fez in Morocco.

These schools were later supplemented in the eleventh and twelfth centuries by *madrasahs,* which really amounted to seminaries for the study of the practice of religion and the propagation of the orthodox Sunni doctrine. Examples of these *madrasahs*, teaching according to the Shāfiʿi rite,[15] are the Niẓāmīyah of Baghdad and the Nūrīyah of Damascus, founded and named after Niẓām al-Mulk and Nūr-al-Dīn Zangi respectively. Ṣalāḥ al-Dīn (Saladin) also founded madrasahs. Later the Mamlūk Sultan Rukn-al-Dīn Baybars created a madrasah pattern which included all four rites within its walls, but with separate quarters.

These madrasahs represented a sort of state education and served to popularize a uniform conception of Islamic law, the sinew of the cohering Islamic society. From the eleventh century onward, certain esoteric groups such as Ikhwān al-Ṣafā' (Brethren of Purity), Qarmaṭians (Carmathians), and Ismā'īlīyah began to develop their own schools; so did the Ṣūfis. These specialized centers of learning, though interested primarily in preserving their own peculiar practices, nevertheless maintained a body of teaching which served to enhance the general and lasting aspects of Muslim culture.[16]

The impact of modernism has induced a marked contrast in many aspects of Islamic life. While the madrasahs are still functioning and attracting students, primarily as schools of canon law, the exigencies of the modern age and the new areas of knowledge opened up by great technological discoveries have led to the establishment of ultra modern "houses of knowledge" in almost all the chief urban centers of the Islamic world supported often by well organized elementary and secondary school systems along the French or British models.

Feasts

The pattern of day-to-day living scarcely varied from one end of Islamdom to the other and served no less than other institutional practices to reflect the common imprint of the Islamic way on adherents of the faith. Preoccupation with feast celebrations brought the faithful together on frequent occasions.

While various feasts peculiar to a locality in the Islamic world are celebrated with all the attending fanfare that makes for greater regional and communal identity, there are certain feasts celebrated simultaneously throughout the Muslim world. The *'Id al-Aḍḥa* (Feast of the Sacrifice)[17] commemorates the 10th of dhu-'l-Ḥijjah which marks the end of the pilgrimage. Not only the pilgrims but also Muslim families everywhere sacrifice according to ritual a sheep or camel and in the banquet that ensues the poor are invited to share.

Another popularly observed feast, the *'Id al-Fiṭr* (The Feast of bread-breaking),[18] is celebrated on the first of Shawwāl according to the Muslim calendar and is the occasion for the display of new attire for those who can afford it. Another feast celebrated throughout the Muslim world is the *Mawlid,* the Prophet's birthday, on the 10th of Rabīᶜ I, one of the younger feasts, observed officially from the twelfth century and undoubtedly instituted as a result of the fanfare associated with the Christian observance of Jesus' birthday.

Other Muslim feasts that enjoy regional or sectarian observance include the *ᶜAshūrā* mostly in Berber lands, with its carnival-like atmosphere while the Shīᶜites on that day commemorate the death (680) of Husayn (Hussein), the Prophet's grandson, at Karbalāʾ, in Iraq with a Passion performance and a *taᶜziyah* (consolation) procession in which it is not unusual for the devotees to cut up their flesh and beat their bodies in a form of self-mortification long abandoned in the Christian world. There are in addition numerous other celebrations localized in nature and mostly carry-overs from ethnical pre-Islamic backgrounds.

Funerary rites are distinctly governed by Islamic religious concepts and are the occasion not only for the pious to gain credit on Judgment Day but to be reminded of one of the most significant transitory movements on their path to the hereafter. The special Islamic ritualistic observances in preparing the dead for burial, the resting position of the body with the head pointing to Mecca, the funeral banquets on various days, the special prayers recited at each stage, alms giving, annual sacrifices and numerous other performances all tend to remind Muslims of their common institutional observances both in pleasure and in sorrow.

The "Public Good"

The purely Arabian pre-Islamic concept of *murū ʾah* (manliness) left a strong imprint on Islamic society. Its effect was felt in a different context than originally conceived. Originally murū ʾah impelled the Arab to defend *ᶜirḍ* (honor). In Islam murū ʾah compels the defense of *dīn* (faith), with a strong emphasis on morality and the near identification thereof with piety and beneficence. The spread of mysticism and its legitimization in the twelfth century added a new dimension, that of love. While love to the mystics was the love of God, a personal expression of feeling, the stress of love by extension to the group provided Islamic society with one of its strongest media for strengthening the notion of "public good" or "general welfare" (*maslahah*).

The Calendar

The Muslims have many lesser yet important unifying institutional observances. Their calendar, for instance, is peculiarly their own. It consists of twelve lunar months each alternating between 29 and 30 days in length for a total of 354 days. To compensate for the eleven-day discrepancy, the Muslims follow the old Arabian practice of adding a day to the last month of the year eleven times in a thirty-year period. The months are known by purely Arabo-Islamic terms.[19] The days begin and end at sunset, Friday being the day of rest or congregation; but the night of a day, which ends at dawn, is that which precedes not what follows it. The divisions of the day conform to the astronomical movements of sunrise, apogee, and sunset; they are regulated, however, not by these but by the times of prayer. Because of its sharp discrepancies with the solar calendar, and as modernization continues to permeate Muslim lands on a larger scale, the tendency of the secularists has been to follow the Western Gregorian calendar. The Muslim calendar, however, remains operative because of religious requirements. The Muslim era commenced in 622, that being year one of the Hegira.

Economic Factors

Economic practices in the heyday of Islamic communal strength and the institutions built thereon reflected a certain commonness among Muslims, namely, preference for agriculture and cattle-raising at home and trade abroad. This is shown also in the type and range of taxation sanctioned by the *Sharīʿah* which appears to stress the products of the soil.

The *sūq,* bazaar or marketplace in the towns and cities of

Islam, constituted the hub of social as well as economic activity. The overland trade from the chief Muslim cities in the East—Baghdad, Damascus, Aleppo, Alexandria—which was funneled eastward and westward made for considerable diffusion not only of wares but of usages, ideas, and common institutional practices clearly stamped with an Islamic spirit which foreign travelers could not help but observe in the Muslim trader. Traders in East Asia and sub-Saharan Africa were instrumental in the spread of Islam in the ninth and tenth centuries of the Christian era.

Muslim merchants formed a very important social class, controlling prices and trade with far-off lands. The tales of Sindbād the sailor, the recordings of Ibn-Baṭṭūṭah in his far-flung journeys, even the stories consecrated in the *Arabian Nights* all mirror the spirit and genre of adventure associated with the Muslim trader.

The articles of manufacture, increasingly diffused throughout the Muslim World and abroad from the late eighth century onward, reflect very clearly the peculiarly Islamic imprint. Materials used, as well as design and execution in vases, tapestry, leather and metal works, textiles, silks, embroideries, fine linens, brocades, all still bear the name of the cities that excelled in their manufacture—Damask, (Damascus), Muslin (Mosul), Cordovan (Cordova).

Commercial transactions over vast areas and on a broad scale gave rise to a number of commercial institutions which were clearly adopted by the merchant states of Renaissance Italy and thence disseminated throughout Europe. Among these are practices relating to sale, hiring, warehousing, wages, interest, exchange, banking, and the like. The stress on contractual obligations, the good faith associated therewith, surety guarantees for the debt of a traveling merchant by a creditor, the promissory note and bill of exchange, the contract of deposit or warehousing, the injunctions against usury as forbidden in the Qurʾān,[20] are some specific examples. The lender by not seeking to profit from his loan is registering an act of pious generosity for which Allah will reward him on the Day of Judgment.

Yet in the areas of commerce where the Qurʾān did not prevail, Europe became the beneficiary and the inheritor; we refer chiefly to the banking institutions and commercial practices of Muslim traders as they developed principally in the ninth and tenth centuries.

In conclusion, the institutional observances and practices that caused Islamic society to cohere are not exhaustive. Attitudes of mind conditioned by religious stimuli are most difficult to delineate. There is what may be termed an "Islamic spirit" which gave vent to a pattern of individual and communal behavior that placed a characteristic stamp on the devout member of this society, a society theocratic in structure yet not altogether restrictive.

What we have related are some of the more tangible institutions and related observances at work. But the strong not always distinguishable ethical undertones motivating behavior are not to be dismissed lightly. Morality as ordained by the Qur'ān was a strong binding element in Islamic society. This we have already seen in a number of instances: in the stress on family ties, which is at the foundation of the Islamic community. There is so much emphasis placed on respect for elders that this emphasis has acquired nearly the sanctity of law. The injunctions in the Qur'ān and Traditions prescribing behavior for women are universally honored where the faith is practiced. The stress on justice and fidelity in dealings, the sanctity of oath and trust, the honoring of obligations prescribed by the Qur'ān for the faithful, and the general prevalence of an egalitarian sentiment, all have left a distinguishable mark on Muslims in their relationship with each other and with outsiders.

CHAPTER 9

Heterodoxy and Orthodoxy

THE OVERWHELMING MAJORITY of Muslims today subscribe to Islam of the *Sunnah* or Sunni Islam with its faithful adherence to the doctrine evolved in the nascent Medinan period of Islam under the four Orthodox Caliphs. Subscribers to this doctrine are known as orthodox or "Sunnis," and they constitute over eighty-five per cent of all those who call themselves Muslims today. The Sunnis form one major sect but juridically they may belong to one of four recognized rites or *madhāhib* (sing. *madhhab*): Māliki, Shāfiʿi, Ḥanafi, or Ḥanbali. An adherent may pass from one into the other without ceasing to be known as an orthodox or Sunni Muslim.

Heterodoxy in Islam owes its origin basically to two historical factors. One resulted from political challenges to existing authority, with the disputing parties invariably taking on the sanctity of religious protection and thus giving rise to a multitude of sects. The other resulted from attempts to provide rational bases for the basic tenets of the faith, leading to the proliferation of philosophical schools of approach to theological beliefs. This trend was abetted by efforts to reduce the rather legalistic and somewhat impersonal implements of the faith to a more personal experience, thus encouraging the mystical approach to religion. The one impact they all had in common was to distract from the theological, political, and consequently social unity of Islam.

The first blow to Islamic unity took place twenty-five years after Muḥammad's death; and it was the result of political, not religious, considerations which arose from Muʿāwiyah's desire to wrest the caliphate from ʿAli, Muḥammad's son-in-law, the fourth and last of the Orthodox Caliphs. Muʿāwiyah was then Muslim governor of Damascus, and the son of Abu Sufyān, Muḥammad's chief Meccan opponent, the Umayyad head of the Qurayshite-ruled Meccan commonwealth, who was intensely disliked by many Muslims who had suffered strong privations at his hands before the conquest.

In the ensuing first civil war in Islam, ʿAli won the battle (Ṣiffīn, 657) but lost the aftermath when he was compelled to submit to arbitration the matter of his caliphate, which he legally possessed, at the behest of the claimant Muʿāwiyah.

Khārijites

A group of ʿAli's followers, mostly desert Arabs inspired by the democratic free spirit of their environment, objected to ʿAli compromising his stand by responding to the appeal for arbitration and broke away from him, insisting that there should have been no appeal save to the Book of Allah. These, known later as *Khawārij* (Khārijites), went a step further and insisted that the caliph should be elected from all Muslims, not just the Quraysh. They turned on fellow Muslims and hunted them down as renegades, refusing to have social intercourse with those who did not share their religio-political views and went so far as to put to death the children of unbelievers. A moderate faction of the Khawārij known as *Ibāḍis,* named after the leader ʿAbdullāh ibn- Ibāḍ, still exists today in parts of Algeria, East Africa, and Oman.

Shīʿites

Another party, mostly city Arabs influenced by Persian ideas, clung to ʿAli with worshipful affection insisting that only he and his descendants had the *legitimate* right to be caliphs. They were undoubtedly influenced by the divine-right-monarchy concepts of pre-Islamic Persia and were joined by Persians on a permanent basis after 1500. They called themselves *Shīʿat ʿAli* (The partisans of ʿAli) to be known later as plain "Shīʿah" or "Shīʿites." They are today the largest single sect next to the Sunnis, constituting about fourteen per cent of the total, and numbering no more than sixty million, including all splinter and radical groups.

Shīʿism for all practical purposes is the religion of Iran, modern Persia, and over fifty per cent of the Muslims of Iraq are also Shīʿite. During the Umayyad caliphate they, like other religious minorities, particularly the Christian, were tolerated and left primarily to themselves. The early Umayyads put up with them because they were anxious to enlarge their secular powers and expand their dominions. Indeed, the Umayyad caliphs with the exception of ʿUmar II were considered by their adversaries as "irreligious" and "unpious."

This toleration, however, soon disappeared under the ʿAbbāsids when the Shīʿah had helped wrest the caliphate from the Umayyads in 750. One hundred years later in 850 the caliph al-Mutawakkil became particularly harsh with the Shīʿah, destroying their venerated shrines: the tombs of ʿAli at Najaf and his more venerated son Ḥusayn at Karbalāʾ. In the ensuing atmosphere of increasing hostility, the Shīʿah in their bid for survival began to practice dissimulation (*taqīyah*), that is, they outwardly purported to be espousing other than what actually constituted their real beliefs.

Unlike the Sunnis who were loyal to the duly empowered caliph, the Shīʿahs professed loyalty to an *Imām*, leader or guide, who was a direct descendant of ʿAli, on the grounds that ʿAli allegedly had inherited from the Prophet both his spiritual and secular sovereignty, i.e., the power both to interpret and to enforce the canon law. Thus in the place of the secular guide of the Sunnis whose religious authority was confined solely to setting an example of piety—long absent with few exceptions after the third caliph of Islam—the Shīʿahs recognized an Imām who, until his disappearance, was regarded as an infallible teacher and the only source of religious instruction and guidance. When the twelfth Imām mysteriously disappeared, the collective body of Shīʿah *ʿulamāʾ* (ulema) began to exercise the prerogatives of his office pending his expected return.

The infallibility of the Imām's teachings, according to Shīʿah conceptions of divine successorship, comes first from Allah, then from His chosen mouthpiece Muḥammad, then ʿAli, and finally his legitimate descendants. By reason of kinship with Muḥammad through blood and marriage of his daughter Fāṭimah, ʿAli not only sired the Prophet's only grandsons, al-Ḥasan and al-Ḥusayn, but initiated at the same time a "legitimate" line of successorship divinely ordained and guided.

The line from Ḥusayn produced nine of the twelve Imāms acknowledged by the main body of the Shīʿahs, commonly known as "Twelvers" (*Ithna ʿAsharīyah*). Their fate, however, was not very pleasant—four died of poison, and most of the others either fell in battle against the caliphs or were executed for sedition. The twelfth, youthful Muḥammad, simply disappeared in 878 in the cave of the great mosque at Sāmarra without leaving any heir. Hence he has become known as the *Muntaẓar* (awaited) Imām whose return will usher in the golden era of true Islam shortly before the end of this world. Thus the messianic concept so dear to Christianity finds an equivalent of a sort among the Persians of today, as it had with their spiritual predecessors of yesteryears like the Zoroastrians and related sectarians.

This hidden Imām, who is not dead but merely in a stage of occultation, is destined to reappear as the "Mahdi." Some false alarms had been sounded by the famous Mahdi of the Sudan at the end of the last century, and a little earlier by the so-called "Bāb" (lit. "the gateway," that is, to the Mahdi's reappearance) whose movement inside Persia was ruthlessly suppressed but succeeded in flourishing outside the country in such areas as Chicago and Los Angeles under the guise of Bahāʾism.

The Twelvers' variety of Shīʿism was formally and forcibly imposed on a then predominantly Sunni Persia by the early Safawid Shahs in the year 1502. These Shahs subsequently claimed themselves to be descendants of the seventh Imām, Mūsa al-Kāẓim, each regarding himself as a place-holder (*locum tenens*) of the hidden Imām until such time as he chooses to return. His spokesmen and intermediaries are the *mujtahids,* the interpreters of dogma who have been serving in the capacity of higher theologians.

Ismāʿīlis

It is important to note that Shīʿism opened the floodgates for the overwhelming majority of the splinter sects, no less than seventy-three according to tradition, that sprang into being in subsequent centuries. One sect that agrees with the Twelvers is the Ismāʿīli or "Seveners"; they honor the line of succession down to the sixth Imām, Jaʿfar al-Ṣādiq (d. 765), then regard his eldest son Ismāʿīl (d. 760) as the seventh (whence the appellation "Seveners") and last Imām.[1] He too in the eyes of his followers is the Imām-Mahdi who becomes the hidden leader and whose return they await.

Both in their cosmogony and in their religious beliefs generally, the Ismāʿīlis reflect a very pronounced influence derived from Greek philosophy in its primitive stage of development. The Pythagorean system with its stress on the number "seven" was consecrated by the Ismāʿīlis who have predicated all cosmic and historical developments on the number seven. Neo-Platonism imparted to them the conception of gnostic knowledge through emanation in seven stages: (1) God; (2) the universal mind (*ʿaql*); (3) the universal soul (*nafs*); (4) primeval matter; (5) space; (6) time; (7) the world of earth and man. The Ismāʿīlis acknowledge the prophet-legislator roles of seven prophets[2] who are considered founders; but the position of others, treated as "silent" legislators,[3] seven in between each set of two of the founders, is also respected. Next and parallel but at a lower level come the propagandizers (*ḥujjah*) and simple missionaries (sing. *dāʿi*).[4]

While Sunni Islam, with its emphasis on the fulfillment of the law (Sharīʿah) and of duties, was essentially non-proselytic, the non-Sunnis and especially the Ismāʿīlis actively labored to gain followers. They sent missionaries throughout the world of Islam to preach their esoteric (*bāṭini*)· doctrine, an activity which had a drastic effect on Islamic society and reflected one of the most pronounced facets of religio-political internecine conflict in Islam.

The esoteric of inner doctrine would look beyond the outward manifestation, insisting that the apparent (*ẓāhir*) is merely a camouflage of the true inner meaning which is purposely hidden from the non-initiates. Such an interpretation is quite familiar to the land where Gnosticism was first announced to the world. The Sunnis, on the other hand, pay strict attention to the literal pronouncements of the Qur'ān since to them it is the unembellished word of God. But the Ismāʿīlis and other sectarians subscribing to their views argue that one must look beyond the manifestations of expressed words and seek the inner meaning of the verses. This bold proposition is only one step removed from that sore spot of controversy among Muslims which revolved around the classical debate of whether the Qur'ān was or was not created.

Some historians[5] argue that behind this seemingly religious controversy lies a subtle political plot, an attempt by Persians overwhelmed in Islam to undermine Arab hegemony. ʿAbdullāh the son of Maymūn al-Qaddāḥ (d. ca. 874) of Ahwāz (Persia) not only perfected the Ismāʿīli religio-political system, but also used his religious doctrine to exploit Arab-Persian enmity in the hope of destroying the caliphate and gaining political hegemony for himself and his descendants. His pattern of scheming gave birth eventually to the Fāṭimid dynasty of Egypt and Tunisia; and one of his disciples, Ḥamdān Qarmaṭ, a peasant of Iraq, gave birth to the movement named after him, the Qarmaṭian.

Qarmaṭians

The Qarmaṭians appealed to native masses, both artisans and peasants, Persians and Arabs. The movement, bearing a sectarian coloring, appeared to revive the ancient feud between the townsman and the nomad. Admission to this predominantly communistic sect sharing in property and wives was by initiation. The Qarmaṭians made use of an allegorical catechism which derived principally from the Qur'ān but accommodated other creeds, appealing thereby to men of all races and castes. They insisted on tolerance and equality and organized the only well-disciplined guilds of tradesmen and artisans in Islam; indeed, some authorities believe that their concept and organization of the guilds within a fixed ceremonial and ritualistic structure led to the rise of Freemasonry, with its clear reflections of Arabo-Islamic influences, and the Medieval guild system.[6]

But the Qarmatians did not preserve their tolerance for long; indeed, in the subsequent century, they became militant and exceedingly violent, leaving behind them trails of blood in Syria and Iraq. They even raided Mecca in 930 and carried off the Black Stone from the Ka'bah, not to be returned until 951. Ultimately they fell, but their beliefs survived. The Fātimids of Egypt with their kindred doctrine fell heir to their domains and communicants.

Assassins

It is interesting to note here that the dreaded order of the Assassins of Alamūt and Syria, the scourge of many a Crusader or Muslim earmarked for death, were neo-Ismā'īlites. The founder of the order, Ḥasan ibn-al-Ṣabbāḥ was a native of Persia who had returned from Egypt as a Fāṭimid missionary. He seized the strategic natural fortress of Alamūt in 1090. Then in his capacity as the grand master (*dā'i al-du'āh:* missionary in chief) of the order, he found himself in a strong position to raid all around northern Persia with impunity. His emissaries, after being keyed up with *Hashīsh* (dope), could execute anyone marked for death anywhere. They cultivated the art of "daggermanship" and were so successful that relics of their success survive even in our Western vocabulary with the term "assassination." This was perhaps their only notable bid for immortality.

The Assassins spread terror everywhere, and for nearly two centuries all efforts to suppress them by force failed. It was only with the advent of the Mongols who attacked and destroyed their strongholds in 1256 on their way to destroy Baghdad that their menace subsided.

Their organization and doctrinal beliefs were modeled on Ismā'īli antecedents. They purposely minimized religious instruction, attached little significance to the role of the prophets, but actively labored to encourage daringness in the young initiates.[7] At the head of the order was the *Dā'i al-Kubīr* (grand preacher) followed by the grand priors, each of whom was in charge of a specific territory, and at the bottom of the hierarchy next to the ordinary propagandists stood the *fidā'i* (self-sacrificer). The fidā'i was ever ready at the command of the chief to execute orders blindly, with visions of an earthly paradise exciting his soul. The gardens surrounding the castle at Alamūt were not only filled with beautiful shrubbery but graced beside by the presence of real live black-eyed hūris to the delight of the Assassin whose vision of Paradise was made real on earth.

The Mongol's assault on Alamūt dealt the order a mortal blow. But the end came at the hands of the Mamlūk Sultan Baybars who in 1272 destroyed their Syrian strongholds at Maṣyād, where Rāshid al-Din Sinān (d. 1192), the "old man of the mountain" to the Crusaders, resided and whence he had continued the order's policy of spreading terror.

The survivors of the order, about 150,000 today, are known as Khojas or Mawlas. They are located principally in the Bombay area of India, with a sprinkling of them in northern Syria and Iran as well as Oman and Zanzibar. Their acknowledged titular head is the Agha Khan, whose headquarters are supposed to be in Bombay. But these alleged descendants of the last grand master of Alamūt find Paris and Switzerland more suitable for the exercise of their spiritual leadership.

Druzes

Another Fāṭimid missionary by the name of al-Darazi (d. 1019), appointed by the caliph al-Ḥākim (d. 1021), began to spread the Ismā'īli doctrine in the hamlets and vales of the southern slopes of the Lebanon among a conglomeration of indigenous Aramaeans, infiltrating Persians, and Arabs of the desert. The ground had been prepared by the presence there of adherents to the Shīʿah and Ismāʿīli doctrines. The preaching of al-Darazi centered on the notion that the mentally deranged caliph al-Ḥākim, notorious for his persecution of Jews, Christians, and orthodox Muslims, represented the last in a series of incarnations of the one and only God. Other extremist Shīʿah had also been preaching that ʿAli and his descendants were such incarnations. The general tendency of Shīʿah sects was to preach methods of bridging the gap between God and man. This is also the aim of mystics, as it has been throughout human history.

When the master al-Ḥākim died prematurely, victim of a conspiracy headed by the caliph's own sister whose chastity he had questioned, the faithful followers denied that he was dead, arguing that he had gone into a state of temporary occultation whence he will re-emerge when the time comes.

Al-Darazi himself, narrowly escaping with his life, headed north, and in the remote Taym valley at the foot of Mt. Hermon he began to preach the new doctrine named after him, the "Durzi" or "Druze" way. His ministry was cut short and he fell in battle two years later. Many of those who believed in his message preferred to call themselves "*Muwaḥḥidūn*" (unitarians) rather than "Durzis." Indeed, the doctrine formulator of Druzism, Ḥamzah al-Labbād, a Persian like al-Darazi, denounced him. He too, however, was killed, in Cairo, by an infuriated mob incited by orthodox Fāṭimid theologians.

The most important features of Druzism were enunciated in the middle of the eleventh century. It was to be a *bāṭini* religion, since prudence decreed secrecy; thus did an important principle of the religion come into being, namely, that in the "absence" of al-Ḥākim no part of his religion was to be made public. Access to the sacred handbooks was to be limited only to the initiated; these constituted a few of the *ʿUqqāl* (sing. *ʿāqil*: wise, intelligent).

The ʿUqqāl are highly selected individuals who must subscribe to a very rigorous ethical code after surviving the ordeals of a protracted period of trial and probation in which they must prove themselves trustworthy and able to keep secret. Following the ceremonial rite of induction, the initiates must conduct themselves with decorum and dignity and abstain from such vices as wine, tobacco, and abusive language. The most pious, called *ajāwīd* (godly), go so far as to abstain from partaking of food even at high levels of entertainment in the fear that it may have been acquired by illegitimate means. Women can also be initiated if they qualify. The Druzes observe strictly monogamous marriages. They hold their religious meetings on Thursday evenings in unostentatious secluded places known as *khalwahs,* usually located on hill tops overlooking their villages.[8]

Spreading northward, mostly into the southern mountains of Lebanon, Druzism gained converts among the Arab tribes roaming the area. These tribes supplied them with the families like the Maʿns, Tanūkhs, and Shihābs, who subsequently became their leaders and feudal lords in subsequent centuries.

Nuṣayris

The Nuṣayris, some three hundred thousand strong, are another surviving Ismāʿīli sect, located largely in northern Syria. They take their name from Muḥammad ibn-Nuṣayr who preached at the end of the ninth century. Ibn-Nuṣayr favored the eleventh Imām, al-Ḥasan al-ʿAskari (d. 874).

The members of this sect believe ʿAli to be the incarnation of the deity and are known consequently as "ʿAlawites." Their religion is more secretive than that of the Druzes. They have a liturgy altogether their own; and they observe a number of festivals distinctly Christian in nature, such as Christmas and Easter. Since they are alleged to have passed directly from Paganism into Ismāʿīlism without the salutary intermediacy of orthodox Islam, they have not cast off all their pagan beliefs.

Other Extremist Sects

The Shīʿah of Lebanon and Syria are known as *Matāwilah* (partisans of ʿAli) and subscribe to the standard beliefs of other

Shīʿah's, namely, that ʿAli, Muḥammad's son-in-law and his descendants are his only legitimate successors and that all those who preceded or followed ʿAli were usurpers. Instead of referring to them as "caliphs," they preferred to call them "imāms."

While the Sunnis looked upon the caliph as the secular head only of the Muslim community, the Shīʿah consider the Imām both the secular and spiritual head with his authority derived directly from God and not from the consent of the people.

The extremists (*Ghulāh*) would even compromise the divinity of God and disregard the finality of Muḥammad's prophethood in favor of ʿAli. Certain sects among them have gone so far as to argue that Gabriel when he was first seeking a spokesman for Allah mistook Muḥammad for ʿAli. The ʿAli-Ilāhis (ʿAli deifiers), mostly in Persia and Turkistan, simply look upon ʿAli as the incarnation of Allah. Quite closely related to this group are the Qizil-bāsh[9] (red-heads) of eastern Anatolia and the Bektāshis of Turkey and Albania.

At the opposite end of the Ismāʿīli sects are the Zaydis of al-Yaman (Yemen) who took their name from Zayd, the grandson of Ḥusayn. Zayd was not in the main line of the imāmate, but in the eyes of his followers he is the founder of their sect. Of all the Shīʿah offshoots, this group is closest in beliefs to the Sunnis and the most tolerant of the lot. They do not believe in any hidden imām, do not subscribe to *mutʿah* (temporary marriages), and practice no *taqīyah*. Like the other Shīʿahs, however, they are opposed to mysticism, or Ṣūfism as it is commonly known in Islam.

Sunnism

The main body of Islam is known as *Ahl al-Sunnah wa 'l-Ḥadīth,* or followers in the path laid out by the Prophet himself and believers in his *sayings.* The source of primary religious authority to them is the Qurʾān and the *sunnah* (path) and *ḥadīth* (sayings) of the Prophet. *Sunnah* and *ḥadīth* together constitute the *Tradition.*

That this body of semi-sacred text should figure prominently as a source of religious and legal guidance is the logical outcome of Muḥammad's function as God's spokesman. Surely he who was selected to transmit the sacred word of God could not be less inspired in his sayings concerning the trivia of daily life. To establish the hallowedness of such trivia is important in the eyes of the jurists who often find more need for the Tradition than for the Qur'ān as a source of official guidance to meet the requirements of imparting legality to decisions.

In the first few decades the Tradition was circulated orally, first by the Companions of the Prophet, then by those who heard it from them. This method of transmission opened the gates to a flood of fabrication, and within a few generations the sayings of Muḥammad appeared to transcend all logical bounds.

For more than a century *ḥadīth* passed from mouth to mouth because attempts to write them down had been discouraged. Had the narrators of *ḥadīth* been all pious men, the continuation of oral transmission might have been tolerated. But there were those who wanted to appear pious when they were not at the expense of inventing *ḥadīth* to justify their manner of life or dogmatic views. Invented *ḥadīth* played an important role in the rise of the sects and the justification of their own non-orthodox teachings. With the spread of forged *ḥadīth*, religious opinion tended to become confused.

The Corpus of Tradition

Finally, in the second half of the eighth century encouragement was given to the compilation and verification of a corpus of traditions, and the first surviving result was the *Muwaṭṭa'* of Mālik ibn-Anas of Medina. His compilation can not be classified as strictly religious since it is more in the nature of a *corpus juris;* Mālik recorded every tradition that had been used to give effect to a legal decision.

The relation of law to religion in Islam is here clearly illustrated. This law was revealed to Muḥammad as the will of God for the benefit of worshipers. God *is* the sole head and legislator of the community. Muḥammad is His agent, not vicar. "Consequently, to violate the law, or even to neglect the law, is not simply to infringe a rule of social order—it is an act of religious disobedience, a sin, and involves a religious penalty."[10]

The actual work of sorting out the thousands of traditions that sprang into being, eliminating the dubious ones and arranging those verified by a careful system of authentication, was not undertaken until the latter part of the third Islamic century. In the period between 815 and 912 traditions were sifted and reclassified according to their relation to the various aspects of religious life and practice.

During this same period the jurisprudents compiled all six collections which later were canonized by the Sunni Muslims. Leading among them is the *Ṣaḥīḥ* (The Verified) of al-Bukhāri who had spent sixteen years journeying through Muslim lands to collect upward of 600,000 ḥadīths; of these he included only 4,000 in his work.[11] Of the other five compendia,[12] only the *Ṣaḥīḥ* of Muslim (817-875)[13] compares with Bukhāri's in importance.

Ijmāʿ

When the orthodox community was confronted by a situation wherein neither the Qurʾān nor the acknowledged body of Ḥadīth provided adequate guidance, theologians applied the principle of *ijmāʿ* (consensus). *Ijmāʿ* was invoked to support religious observances and was explicitly sanctioned by prevailing canon law. This is as close as Muslims could come to agree on a principle of innovation by universal consent.

Ijmāʿ became a very important principle for the justification of religious beliefs or practices not specifically sanctioned by the Qurʾān and the Tradition. Much of these antedated the Islamic era, deriving from customs and norms of the Jāhilīyah period. While they were present all along, it was not until after three hundred years of Islam that their presence was detected. By then it was too difficult to uproot them from the lives of men. Since it was not easy to find traditions that would abrogate the practices of pre-Islamic days, the next logical alternative was to acknowledge their legality by means of *ijmāʿ*.

What is worth noting here is that not all Muslims accepting *ijmāʿ* as a means of legislation understood it in the same context. In Medina, for instance, *ijmāʿ* simply meant the consensus of the citizens of Medina, not of the whole Muslim community which was neither solicited nor recognized. Under the ʿAbbāsids *ijmāʿ* was applied much more widely as a means of gaining fealty for the caliphs. It was used also to win legal recognition for the six canonical books as sources of authoritative information on the sunnah and *ḥadīth* of Muḥammad.

The more conservative interpreters of religious law in Islam would restrict ijmāʿ to the early teachers of the law, *fuqahāʾ* (sing. *faqīh:* jurisprudent), also known as *mujtahidūn* (sing. *mujtahid:* interpreter of canon law), or to those who apply themselves to the proper interpretation and application of what orthodox Islam sanctions. In terms of time this would confine its development to the earliest period, a period which could not take in the decisions of mujtahidūn belonging to a generation not contemporary with Muḥammad. The Shīʿahs pay special deference to the principle of *ijmāʿ*, and have not ceased to apply it until the present time, even though the exercise of *ijmāʿ* is restricted to the religious class of ulema (*ʿulamāʾ*).

Qiyās

The next most widely recognized source of authoritative support of religious beliefs and practices among the orthodox Muslims is that embodied in the principle of *Qiyās* or analogical deduction. Qiyās simply is the way a belief or practice gains official credence and support on the grounds that it is similar to a practice or belief clearly embodied in the Qurʾān, *Sunnah,* or *ijmāʿ*. Before *qiyās* was officially recognized, Muslim interpreters of the *Sharīʿah* had exercised *raʾy,* private opinion, in the teaching of doctrine. Indeed, it was in an attempt to curb the widespread use of *raʾy* in a delicate area of religion that *qiyās* came into being as a more acceptable alternative.

The use of *qiyās*, however, was not free of controversy. Muslim theologians debated earnestly and almost continuously the extent and range of its application. Some argued that *qiyās* should be restricted to the area of "material similarity"; others advocated its use also in the not-so-well defined area of similarity in motive or cause. What enabled the principle of *ra'y* to gain acceptance in limited quarters, although it was merely the product of *ijtihād* (individual interpretation), was the lack of agreement among the *mujtahids*, who preferred the device of individual interpretation. In spite of its obvious shortcoming in purporting to achieve a uniform consensus, *qiyās* was one way of maintaining the progressive development of the community of Islam in conformity with the religious sanctification needed.

But as political upheavals within the community and the assault of the barbarians from without tore away at their political unity, which was mostly nominal by the thirteenth century when the Mongols made their appearance, the great majority of Muslim jurists and theologians determined to salvage what they could to preserve the uniformity of religious conceptions and beliefs by "closing the gate of *ijtihād*" (*sadd bāb al-ijtihād*). This meant that however erudite a Muslim may be in his knowledge of the *Sharī'ah*, *Sunnah*, and *Ḥadīth*, he could no longer officially function as a mujtahid, or an authoritative interpreter of the canon law. Logical formalism set in; no possibility of *bid'a,* questioning an accepted decision based on *ijmā'* or "innovation" would be tolerated.

This was a very significant development for Islam and for its capacity to adapt to changing needs and circumstances. With the "closing of the gate," no new interpretations, no matter how desperately desirable they were, could gain general acceptability or support. With the closing of the gate of ijmā', the panic-stricken ulema opened wide the gate of the "Dark Ages," or the "Medieval Era," in Islam, an era that stretched over five hundred years. Only in our century has there been some attempt to pull Islam out of its dark ages and usher in its "Renaissance" and "Reformation."

Madhāhib

The *madhāhib* (sing. *madhhab*: juridical-religious rite) were responsible for reducing the *Sunnah* to practical use. Where *ijtihād* may have served to keep Islam abreast of political and social upheavals, the emergence of the accepted juridical-religious rites tended to keep the faithful on the proper path of fulfilling their religious and non-religious obligations as members of one broad socio religious entity. The actual administration of law was the prerogative of civil and military officials of the caliphs. The *dhimmi*, or protected non-Muslim communities, were subject to their own administrative and judicial procedures, provided they paid the *jizyah* and remained loyal to the caliph.

These laws, predominantly secular in nature, varied from province to province as they had been heavily influenced by local laws; in Syria by Syro-Byzantine laws which the Umayyads did not hesitate early in their caliphate to adapt to their needs as they arose; in lands once dominated by Persia, by relics of the Sasānid laws, which again were not completely wiped out with the Islamic conquest. Even in Jāhilīyah Arabia customary and legal practices, managed to survive in Islam where the *Sharīʿah* did not provide specific alternatives.

During the first century and a half of Islam, what may be termed religious-scholastic, or *Sharʿi*[14] law, took on form outside the purview or demands of secular needs in the Islamic community. With the ʿAbbāsid caliphate, which came to power by proclaiming the return of the pietistic religious devotions reportedly neglected by the Umayyads, the *fuqahāʾ* were encouraged to set forth the principles that might be adopted in the fulfillment of religious obligations quasi-juridical in nature.

Sometime in the course of the third Muslim century, the principles for observing religious obligations jelled into certain categories or classifications. Categorization tended towards one of four *madhāhib*, each bearing the stamp of the norms prevalent in the geographical region where the *madhhab* gained its widest following. It is important to note that these four rites are in agreement on all points vital to Islam as a socio-religious force; all acknowledge the authority of the Qur'ān and *Ḥadīth* as sources of ultimate law for Islam, and all Sunnis who adhere to one of the four "ways," as they must, do not compromise their orthodoxy in so doing.

Ḥanafite

The earliest madhhab formed was that of Abu-Ḥanīfah (d. 767), known as the "Ḥanafi" rite or juridical school. It reflects the views of the jurists of Iraq much more than do other rites; manifesting considerable toleration in the use of *ra'y*. In many respects it is less rigid in its doctrinal interpretations of all four *madhāhib*. The school still prevails today in Turkey, the Arab countries of the Fertile Crescent region, Lower Egypt, and India.

Mālikite

The next school in order of time is that founded by Mālik ibn-Anas (d. 795) of Medina. As expected, it reflected strongly the views of the jurists and the practices associated with that city. Mālik was appointed judge in Medina and while serving in this capacity he gathered together his decisions into the corpus called *al-Muwaṭṭa'* (the Levelled Path). Like the jurists of Iraq, those of Medina preferred to depend more on the traditions associated with the Companions of Muḥammad than with the Prophet himself. When it came to conflicting traditions, Mālik and his followers after him simply made an arbitrary choice.

The time factor figured prominently. If for instance the conflict was between a tradition attributed to the Prophet and another to one of his Companions, they chose the Companion's. Two of Abu-Ḥanīfa's disciples, Abu-Yūsuf and Muḥammad Shaybāni, became responsible for solidifying the views of their master; unlike him, however, they did not decline to serve in judicial posts in Iraq. They shared with their Medinan counterparts, followers of Mālik, the view that it is safer to stay with the traditions that were generally known and less prone to conflict than to accept the irregular ones, however significant they might appear to be. They too attached more importance to the companions' traditions on the grounds that these could not have existed without knowledge of the Prophet's *ḥadīth* and *sunnah*. They sought harmony, even if it meant resorting to arbitrary choices, and rejected prophetic traditions contradictory to the Qurʾān. They regarded the traditions associated with the companions' successors as equal in importance to those of the companions themselves. Adherents of this rite are strong in North Africa, particularly Algeria.

A juridical school, strong in Syria-Palestine, but of very limited range, that of al-Awzāʿi (d. 774) developed an attitude similar to the Iraqi-Medinan, stressing perhaps a little more the Prophet's sunnah but still seeking to interpret it in the light of the companions' traditions. As this school differed little from the other two, it disappeared from the scene very early.

Shāfiʿite

The third important school in time was that founded by al-Shāfiʿi (d. 820), who had been a disciple of Mālik. More than any other jurisprudent he left the most telling impact on the development of Islamic jurisprudence on the basis of the Qurʾān and Ḥadīth.

While Mālikis and Ḥanafis were prepared to accept as binding the traditions of companions and their Followers (*al-Tābiʿūn*) if they accorded with the observances prevalent in the community, al-Shāfiʿi would not accept such traditions as legally valid if they did not sustain the Prophet's authority. Al-Shāfiʿi was well versed in his knowledge of the Qurʾān and the *Sunnah*. It was he who defined the components of Sharʿi law as consisting of: (1) Qurʾān, (2) *Sunnah*, (3) *Ijmāʿ*, and (4) *Qiyās* and reduced the use of ra'y to secondary importance even though it was at that time the method of decision most popular in the principal cities of Islam. He established furthermore the principle that no tradition directly received from the Prophet himself and properly authenticated could be superseded. Indeed, from his point of reference, an authenticated tradition automatically rendered invalid any tradition attributed to a Companion or Follower (*Tābiʿ*) that conflicted with it. If there was a conflict between two traditions authenticated as the Prophet's, then the one closer to the Qurʾān and the sunnah of Muḥammad himself was to be preferred.

It was al-Shāfiʿi who elevated the authority of the Ḥadīth to its position of pre-eminence, if indeed he did not give it a higher authority than the Qurʿān itself by making it the authoritative interpretation of Allah's sacred words as enshrined therein. "God had made obedience to the prophet incumbent on all believers, and therefore what he said came from God as the Qurʾān did." [15]

By giving more weight to the authority of the *Ḥadīth*, al-Shāfiʿi strengthened the trend making for rigidity in the adaptability of canonical law. Had his doctrines been strictly observed, Islam would have lost much of its dynamism and its capacity for adjustment to change. Indeed, in the period of "medievalism" in Islam, from the thirteenth until the present century, the influence of this doctrine was very strongly felt.

When al-Shāfiʿi predicated the validity of an act on conformity with Ḥadīth, a corpus limited in its development to the exigencies of Muḥammad's Meccan-Medinan world of two decades of preaching, he *ipso facto* circumscribed its applicability to the needs of an expanded Islamic community in an increasingly complex world. To decree that the sanction of the *Sunnah* and the Qurʾān is necessary for the sustenance of progressive measures may be desirable, but by narrowing the means of interpretation the Shāfiʿite paved the way for *bidʿa*. Where there was a strong determination to pursue progressive measures, even if they did not appear to conform to the letter of the *Ḥadīth*, the blessing of authoritative sanction could be gained by the would-be innovator's simply inventing a suitable tradition together with a convincing *isnād* (a verifiable chain of transmission) traceable right to the Prophet himself.

Al-Shāfiʿi may have been a man of strong integrity, but successors yearning for "new things" did not always resist temptation. In this regard the Māliki-Ḥanafi approach was more flexible: simply to take the tradition that best suits a situation, never mind whether it is the Prophet's, a Companion's, or a Follower's.

Besides, did not Muḥammad in his capacity as spokesman for himself prove to be quite adaptable to changing circumstances? Indeed, did not even Allah come to his rescue at a moment of crisis or serious confrontation with the proper *āyah*, His brand of "*ḥadīth*"?

This stress on prophetic confirmation of a ḥadīth contributed to the widespread fabrication of isnād to give validity to a spurious tradition, which made the task of the compilers like Bukhāri, Muslim, Ibn-Māja, and others who sought to sort out hundreds of thousands of ḥadīth for the purpose of authentication laborious if not impossible.

When the Sharīʿah was being fixed and defined in the third century of the Hijrah, purportedly for all time, the doctrine of al-Shāfiʿi left the strongest imprint thereon. The formula was to identify the sunnah with the contents of ḥadīth known to be from the Prophet, then to give it the blessed approval of the ijmāʿ of the *ʿulamāʾ*. The line was henceforth drawn: on the side governed by the Sharīʿah was orthodoxy; on the other, heterodoxy maybe, but heresy nevertheless. It was in this century, the third, that the *ʿulamāʾ* finally agreed on the acceptance and interpretation of ḥadīth; there was no more room for criticism and emendation. The last word had been spoken. The individual mujtahid could apply his personal judgment (*raʾy*) only on questions of detail not already defined but not on substance.

Al-Shāfiʿi, a forceful thinker who had a unique grasp of principles, a clear understanding of the problems, and the singular ability to muster forth persuading arguments, stands above other Muslim jurisprudents in terms of the impact he left on the *Sharīʿah*. The school of jurisprudence founded by him is strong in Lower Egypt, Syria, India, and especially Indonesia.

Ḥanbalite

The fourth school is that associated with Aḥmad ibn-Ḥanbal (d. 855), known as the Ḥanbali. Aḥmad himself did not establish a separate school; this was rather the work of his followers, strong in Iraq and Syria. The resultant madhhab was the most conservative of the four. Its intolerant and rigid views caused its eclipse during the Ottoman conquest in the sixteenth century, the Turks being more favorably disposed to the Ḥanafi rite.

But Ḥanbalism was revived again in the eighteenth century with the rise of Wahhābism in Arabia. The triumph of the Suʿūd (Saud) dynasty and its strict espousal of the Ḥanbali doctrine gave the Ḥanbalis new vitality. Their almost exclusive support is confined largely to Central and Northern Arabia.

The Ḥanbalis adhere almost to the literal injunctions of the Qurʾān and Ḥadīth and are least compromising on matters pertaining to prophetic traditions, with a fanatical insistence on the strict fulfillment of religious duties and responsibilities exactly as defined by the *Sharīʿah.* Being concerned with matters that can be classified under the category of religious or canonical law, they are independent of caliphal and secular authority. Neither sultan nor caliph could interfere with the decisions they made; indeed, it was the duty of the ruler rather to support and enforce such decisions by providing for the appointment of the *qāḍis.*

Owing to the concept that law in the Islamic community is essentially indivisible and the fact that in reality the caliph, sultan, or amīr governed the community according to the tenets of the *Sharīʿah,* there did not develop a corpus of genuine secular law until very recent times; nor was there anything that could be termed "secular" legislation. Adjudication of wrongs (*maẓālims*) was on an ad hoc basis in judicial sessions. When a question of "constitutionality" or "legality" arose, a summary was submitted to a juriconsult, called a *mufti* versed in the rules of the madhhab of the litigants. The opinion he gave was in the form of a *fatwa* and it might or might not be honored.

Until the rise of Ottoman hegemony in the Muslim world, these muftis were men of no definite official status in the community and were independent of the secular side of the administration. In the Ottoman Empire they were graded in an officially recognized and operative hierarchy headed by a chief mufti in Istanbul known as *Shaykh al-Islām* (chief of Islam).

It is in these various fatwas that we are able to perceive how the madhāhib were able to put into force their views and principles. In these we can also detect the impact of doctrinaire interpretations regarding the *Sharīʿah* on local customs, resistances to them, and the extent such local customs have been assimilated in orthodox Islam.

Far from compromising the powerful unifying appeal of the Sharīʿah—indeed, far from even lending it flexibility—the madhāhib did not detract from the orthodoxy of canonical law ordained by it. Despite the spread of heterodoxy, the spirit of the *Sharīʿah* continued to permeate all facets of the community's social, political, religious, and even literary life. It is "the epitome of the true Islamic spirit, the most decisive expression of Islamic thought, the essential kernel of Islam."[16]

CHAPTER 10

Formalism and Free Expression

THE SIMPLE DOCTRINES of Islam deriving from the injunctions of the Qur'ān, supplemented by the *ḥadīth* and *Sunnah* of Muḥammad, formalized in the *Sharīʿah* as a coherent entity and put into practice by one of the four madhāhib, would have served the Muslim community's needs well and long if it had remained in the world of Mecca-Medina. But when a small community develops into a world empire, the simple puritanical and coherent doctrines formalized for the original Islamic community could not remain unquestioned or unchallenged.

Outside Influences

The challenge came from the quarter of "free thought" and "free expression," qualities very strongly imbedded in Arabia and dear to the Arab's heart long before the Greeks provided him with the vehicles for systematic expression: logic and reason. Powerful stimuli came also from contact with non-Muslim Arabs and non-Arabs following the first two stages of expansion, 634-642 and 700-732. The Umayyad caliphs were particularly tolerant of non-religious views and of non-Muslim religions as well. Their court at Damascus was worldly and relatively tolerant from the point of view of Islam's religious interests. Being concerned primarily with worldly gain, the Umayyads strove after dominion (*mulk*), made no attempt to propagate Islam, and favored Christians like the renowned al-Akhṭal, the poet, and John of Damascus, the celebrated Church father who served also as a high ranking official in the administration of the Arabo-Islamic empire.

In the atmosphere of tolerance and free exchange (680-750) fostered by the Umayyads a general intellectual fermentation began to take place. The lands newly acquired by the quick-minded sons of the desert were impregnated with all sorts of theological and philosophical concepts dating back to man's beginning in time. Even before the impact of Hellenism was felt, following Alexander's conquest of the Middle East, the area was rife with religious and philosophical literature. The dualistic philosophy of Persia penetrated Islam as it had previously permeated the doctrines of Christianity. Logical and metaphysical speculations originating in India and the dialectism of the Christian fathers also left an impact on the molding of Islamic beliefs.

Greek knowledge found its way into Islam partly through the heritage of the Near East, and more directly in the second century of the Hijrah when Greek learning became attractive to Muslim thinkers.

In the early stages, such non-conformist Christian sects as the Jacobites or Monophysites contributed their share of Neo-Platonic speculation and mysticism. The Nestorians have been regarded as the earliest teachers of the Muslims, particularly in the area of Medicine. The Muslims were in contact with the center of Zoroastrian and Neo-Platonic learning at Jundi-shāpūr, with the pagan stronghold at Ḥarrān where strong Neo-Pythagorean as well as Neo-Platonic schools thrived, and also with the Jews first in and later out of Arabia. The general Christian debate over doctrine at the time of Islam's emergence appears also to have contributed to Muslim theological and philosophical debates, particularly in the realm of dogmatics.

Earliest interests in the logical writings of Aristotle were fostered by the translations of the priest-physician Probus of Antioch as early as the first half of the fifth Christian century, almost a century before the rise of Islam in Arabia. Jacob of Edessa (640-708) had undertaken an extensive translation of Greek theological writings into Syriac, the intermediate step before Arabic. The Syrian thinkers were interested in Pythagorean and Platonic wisdom and in their moralizing collection of aphorisms, also in Aristotle's logic which was directed towards the end of elevating knowledge above faith, a very important point of departure for later Muslim Aristotelians and a great stimulant for Muslim thinkers such as Ibn-Rushd (Averroës). That aspect of Platonic philosophy which treats of the soul's consciousness of its own inner essence had not as much significance as the trend towards Aristotelian logic. Thus in Islam were galvanized these two important trends characteristic of Plato and Aristotle.

The early Muslim thinkers took up philosophy where the Greeks left off (as did the great Medieval thinkers of Christiandom continue the dialogue where the Muslims left off). The aim of Muslim thinkers was to reconcile such Platonic concepts as the creation of the world, the substantiality of things spiritual, and the immortality of the soul with the more popular Aristotelian emphasis on reason and the consequent subordination of the spiritual and ethical to the rational process. The stress was on the *virtue of knowing,* which served to buttress the cause of dialectics among Muslim thinkers and to play up the importance of *intelligence* (*ʿaql*) as the next most important "determiner" after God.

As Aristotle's thinking was suited to the Syro-Arab conceptual approach to philosophical thinking, his teachings emerge as a source of reference to them. They were especially interested in his principle: *all that exists, including the soul itself, exists by intelligence.* This formula proved itself to be quite attractive to the Arab mentality which stressed the approach of *knowing things as they really are.* Thus in Aristotle Muslim thinkers found the great guide; to them he became the "first teacher."

Having accepted this a priori, Muslim philosophy as it evolved in subsequent centuries merely chose to *continue* in this vein and to enlarge on Aristotle rather than to innovate. It chose the course of eclecticism, seeking *to assimilate* rather than *to generate,* with a conscious striving to adapt the results of Greek thinking to Muslim philosophical conceptions, but with a much greater comprehensiveness than was achieved in early Christian dogmatics, which were similarly influenced by Greek thinking.

Among the earliest to take an active interest in Aristotelian logic were the Muslim grammarians and mathematicians in the eighth and ninth centuries who resided mostly at Basra in Iraq. Basra was also the home of the jurists who developed the principle of qiyās as a tool of canonical legislation and who also acquired, on account of it, the title "the people of Logic." Its influence was felt equally in a broader segment of the Muslim doctrinal system.

The Qur'ān, as we observed, was understood to provide *precepts* but not doctrine and the *Ḥadīth*, guidance, but again no doctrine. In the evolution of a Muslim doctrinal system, Christian Orthodox and Monophysitic influences, mostly in Damascus, left a determining imprint; as did the Gnostic and Nestorian theories in Basra and Baghdad.

Among the first doctrines to come under the attack of logic was that of "freedom of the will," already accepted by the Christians of the East and through them by the rationalist Muslims. The orthodox theologians who resisted the application of pure logic to matters of doctrine countered with dialectism (*kalām*) to suppress what they termed a "violent innovation."

The "science of reasoning," however, had been accepted as a medium of exposition; the jurisprudent and the theologian began to apply it in their deductions. The result was a form of categorization of methods. The *exoteric* method made use of "free thinking" to scrutinize accepted beliefs for rational truths regarding the fundamental problems of the universe pertaining to the concepts of God and the Soul, irrespective of whether they conformed or did not conform to established doctrines. The dialectical method, on the other hand, favored the attainment of so-called "truths" in a way compatible with the established beliefs of Islam.

Such categorization was the natural product of the clash between two basic approaches to the same issues. Those who preferred the traditional approach, namely, the orthodox spokesmen, insisted on respecting the way of the Sunnah as established by the Sharīʿah. They were for the most part descendants of the early Arab believers. The "rationalists," on the other hand, derived largely from the new converts, descendants mostly of Byzantine and Persian elements steeped in Hellenic and Zoroastrian theological and philosophical traditions.

In the early stages of the clash, the debate may have been looked upon as academic, or an experiment in logic; with the passing of time and the persistence of the debate, the theologians decided to fight the rationalists with their own weapons. They began to employ logic in affirming religious principles and thus took to the path of scholasticism. Europe in the upper Middle Ages became the beneficiary of the Muslim experience; the scholastic thinkers of the Church followed in the steps of their Muslim counterparts and, like them, sought to reconcile religious dogma with the dictates of reason.

Classification of Schools of Thought

The orthodox Muslim writers on the schools of thought in Islam and the sects attempted to classify them into certain recognizable categories. Al-Shahrastāni, a principal authority on the sects, had listed seventy-three; and because his predecessors who had dwelt on the subject made unclear differentiations among them, he himself endeavored to distinguish between them on the basis of how they reacted to the principal areas of controversy over religious doctrine.

For a premise in distinguishing between the schools and classifying them, he chose the position each adopted regarding points of contention in doctrinal interpretation, namely, the matter of: (1) predestination and free will; (2) the divine attributes of God; (3) promises and threats, faith and error; and

(4) revelation, reason, and the imāmate or leadership. On this basis, al-Shahrastāni was able to classify the contenders into the following schools: Qadarites, Ṣifatites, Khārijites, and Shīʿites. He also classified the opposing schools or those who held divergent views. The Qadarites, for instance, stressed the doctrine of free will, while the Jabrites denied it; the Ṣifatites argued for the eternal nature of the attributes of God, while the Muʿtazilites denied they were eternal; the Murji'ites stressed that human actions must not be subject to human judgment, while their opponents, the Waʿdites, insisted on the condemnation of man in this life, before the Day of Judgment; the Khārijites played down the importance of the role of secular leadership, i.e., the caliphate which they considered merely a human institution, while the Shīʿites went so far as to consider their imām as divine.

This categorization of positions on doctrinal views into factions, represented by Muʿtazilites, Jabrites, Ṣifatites, Khārijites, Murji'ites, and Shīʿites, accounts for the principal schools of thought that have endeavored to interpret Islamic doctrine, often to justify positions which did not always accord with the prevailing orthodox view.

Murji'ites versus Qadarites

In outlining the range and tenor of doctrinal conflict in Islam, one would have to make mention of two schools which had been influenced by Greco-Christian theologians: the Murji'ite and Qadarite. The Murji'ites, or "postponers," acquired their title from the doctrine they preached, namely, that judgment of human actions should be postponed until the Day of Judgment as promised in the Qur'ān. They were less concerned with the question of rule in Islam and were willing to tolerate the Umayyad rulers when the pious looked upon them as usurpers. But in the realm of religious belief (*īmān*), they clung tenaciously to belief only in the unity of God and in the Prophet Muḥammad and to no other basic concept. They were genuinely convinced that no one who adhered to this position could actually perish even though he were a sinner. This was quite in contrast with the doctrine of the earliest dissenters, the Khārijites, who insisted that the unrepentant sinner was destined for Hell even though he had professed Islam.

The Qadarites, believers in divine decree, championed "free will"; they opposed the Jabrites (Necessitarians) who denied free will to man and argued that God only had all power to arbitrate. Among the earliest protagonists of free will was Ḥasan al-Baṣri, who is also regarded as one of the first systematic theologians as well as mystics of Islam. He stood above others for his orthodox views and personal piety.

The Qadarites insisted that man had power over his own deeds even though the fate of man had been preordained. Their concepts stemmed somewhat from the resignation of the Muslim to his fate in the war on the heathens. Muslims went into battle convinced that God held full power over their destinies and that if death or life were predetermined they were powerless to escape God's will. If they should fall in battle, however, they would be transported directly to Paradise. Hence "Kismet" was the logical outcome of such rationalization.

But in the sophisticated environments of the city where most Muslim thinkers functioned and found themselves in disputation with the Christians, they were confronted with the problem of having to reconcile this philosophy of predestination, that had grown out of necessity and common belief without much intellectual support, with the Qur'ān's specific appeal to man's own self-determination to good, to courage, and to actions that would please God.

The Qadarites' espousal of the doctrine that man is responsible for his actions was eventually held to be a heresy because the preaching and teaching of predestination had gained too strong a hold on Muslims to be displaced. As early as 699. Maʿbad al-Juhani, one of the first teachers of free will, was executed for his doctrine.[1]

In the period that saw the execution of al-Juhani, Medina was the center of intellectual life. In the city of the Prophet and the pious caliphs, free thought in religion had little chance to assert itself. The primary preoccupation of intellectual striving was the study of the Qurʾān and the collection of *Ḥadīth*.

Muʿtazilite

Though rationalization in an Aristotelian sense had no chance in Medina, it gained a following in Iraq among the students of Ḥasan al-Baṣri. One such student, Wāṣil ibn-ʿAṭāʾ, seceded (*iʿtazala*) from the councils of his master; and all those who shared his views and followed suit were henceforth known as *Muʿtazilah* or Muʿtazilites. They were par excellence the protagonists of rationalism and the doctrine of free will; among their supporters at one time they counted leading Muslim thinkers and caliphs, like al-Maʾmūn.

With the Muʿtazilites, rationalism reached its peak; theirs was an important breakthrough, for up until Umayyad times the prevailing theological view was that "reason" should not apply to the revelations of God. The barrier to the rational interpretation of Muslim theology was now removed; and what agitated Muslim minds was more than the issue of predestination versus free will. Among the important issues now subjected to rational analysis was the question of whether God's attributes (*ṣifāt*)—all ninety-nine of them—constitute an integral part of His essence, as the theologians had argued, or are qualities independent of His essence and not co-existing with Him, as the Muʿtazilites now had the boldness to proclaim. The Muʿtazilites insisted on God's divine unity, and received for their tenacious view the further appellation by which they became known: *ahl al-tawḥīd wa-'l-ʿadl* (the people of unity and justice).

Those who had hitherto argued that the Qurʾān was the uncreated word of God were now disputed by the Muʿtazilites, who insisted that the Qurʾān was created in time. The idea of the uncreated word of God, an important principle of Christian theology—"in the beginning was the word and the word was with God"—was perhaps behind the Muslim Traditionist's insistence on the Qurʾān, the word of God, being by similar reasoning also uncreated. These Muslim theologians could have been influenced by St. John of Damascus (d. ca. 748).

While the Muʿtazilah endeavored to respect this view, they nevertheless went on preaching that the Qurʾān was created and sent down to man. They were persecuted for this type of reasoning and dubbed heretics; it was not until the caliphate of al-Maʾmūn (813-833) that they gained reprieve and official support.

Theirs was the "thinking" class view and they drew the line between *reason* and *revelation.* They asserted the supremacy of reason as distinct from faith and resorted to reason as the deciding factor between good and evil. The creation of the Qurʾān was officially proclaimed by al-Maʾmūn, as were other Muʿtazilite doctrines later. The once persecuted Muʿtazilites were appointed to official posts by the caliph; indeed, he went so far as to sanction an inquisition (*Miḥna*) for the purpose of enforcing their doctrine.

Some of the leading spokesmen of Muʿtazilism included al-ʿAllāf (d. 841) who taught that God's very essence consists of knowledge. His reference to "creation" as an intermediary between the Eternal Creator and the transient "created" world betrays Platonic influence. He made distinctions between the absolute world of creation and the accidental world of revelation. He also challenged the orthodox theological view of a physical resurrection of the body and considered human actions as natural and moral. Al-Jāhiẓ (d. 869) insisted that man by the exercise of reason is capable of knowing the Creator and in comprehending the need of a prophetic revelation.

It is interesting to note that the four orthodox rites came into being almost simultaneously with the prevalence of Muʿtazilism, patronized not only by al-Maʾmūn but also by his immediate successors until the caliphate of al-Mutawakkil (842-847). When the renowned *qāḍi* ibn-Dāʾūd, who had espoused Muʿtazilism, served as "chief justice" for the empire he used the office to propagate their doctrine.

Their success however was relatively short-lived; the orthodox theologians, and others victimized by the *Miḥna* for having rejected the notion of a theology based on reason, found a vocal leader in Aḥmad ibn-Ḥanbal, a strong traditionalist. Through the support of the conservative caliph al-Mutawakkil they gained ascendancy with the view that the Qur'ān is uncreated. The restoration of orthodoxy followed soon after the official proclamation.

Ashʿarism

While Muʿtazilism left a dent on the prevailing orthodox conception of religious tenets and their application, the compromise within the orthodox body in terms of the acceptance of the rational approach to the religion of Islam was also very important for the process of adaptation and readjustment. The Ashʿari movement which legitimized the scholastic interpretation of religious dogma was by far the greatest single force working for such adaptation.

The most articulate spokesman of the anti-Muʿtazilite school was al-Ashʿari (873-935). For forty years he was one of them but chose to break away and revert to orthodoxy. This gave him the extraordinary advantage of having assimilated their views and all they had to teach; he had mastered their logic, philosophy, and science of reasoning and now sought to apply their weapons in support of the orthodox view. His aim as an independent agent was to reconcile their position with that of the Traditionists, known also as Ṣifatites.

Al-Ashʿari's was an open approach; his contemporary the mystic al-Junayd (d. 910) had followed the same method, but only in quiet preaching and secret teaching to a few followers. Thus for the first time the methods of scholastic philosophy were being systematically applied. They reached perfection with the *qāḍḍi* Abu-Bakr al-Bāqillāni (d. 1012). Scholastic Ashʿarism's greatest following was in the environs of Baghdad. Elsewhere it was suspected and often counfounded with Muʿtazilism.

With the advent of the Seljuk Turks in the middle of the tenth century, the Sunni caliph was freed from his subservience to the local Shīʿite dynasty, the Buwayhid, which they destroyed.

The Buwayhids actually had favored the Ashʿari system and had endeavored to propagate its teachings following the death of the founder. While the Seljuks subscribed to Sunni Islam, less than a century later, the Seljuk ruler Tughril Beg (d. ca. 1053) persecuted the well-known Ashʿarite teacher al-Juwayni[2] (d. 1085) and even exiled him. But Tughril's successor Alp Arslan had a very wise and knowledgeable vizier, Niẓām al-Mulk, who not only subscribed to the Ashʿarite view but even founded a theological school named after him, the renowned Niẓāmīyah, for the purpose of perpetuating the Ashʿarite system. Al-Juwayni was then restored to favor.

Far from Baghdad in Andalusia, the noted rationalist ibn-Ḥazm fiercely opposed the Ashʿarite view; but then came al-Ghazāli, a teacher at the Niẓāmīyah, to establish its orthodoxy and to promote its dicta as the universal creed of Islam.

Gradually Ashʿarism spread from Iraq eastward to Persia and southward to Syria and Egypt during the critical century of the Crusades and the ascendancy of the strong Sunni dynasties: the Kurdish Ayyūbids and their successors, the Circassian Mamlūks. It spread westward into North Africa, to be accepted by the fiercely unitarian and Ṣūfi-inclined ibn-Tūmart (d. 1130) and his Almohad (*al-Muwaḥḥidūn*) dynasty, which for a while controlled most of the Maghrib and Muslim Spain.

The Ashʿari system of theological reference has continued to be the predominating influence in Islam. The only rival to cross its path is the Māturīdīyah of al-Māturīdi of Samarqand (d. 944), a contemporary of al-Ashʿari, who belonged to the Ḥanafite *madhhab* and whose stronghold was among Muslim Turks. His creed was an important source of reference for Muslim theology since he attempted to steer a middle course between materialistic teachings on one hand and ideas associated with pure speculative philosophy on the other. His chief complaint against the Muʿtazilah was that their doctrine was too abstract to be understood by the Muslim public. It would seem that he was seeking to make what he approved of their views more platable to the partisans of the orthodox comception. His was the medial path and his system was built on reconciliation of views and compromise.

Al-Ashʿari sought, for instance, a compromise between the Muʿtazilah views of the attributes of God and those of the Ṣifatites; he admitted the existence of these attributes but did not liken them unto human attributes and conceded their eternity with the Deity. As pertains to God's visibility, al-Ashʿari argued that he can be seen independent of the limitations of human sight. As to the important question of free will, he denied that man had power over his will but affirmed that man did have control over his responsibilities even though they were willed by God.

Al-Ashʿari treated all the important doctrinal points of contention pertaining to God, the Qurʾān, the question of sin, the role of intercession, and other matters, articulated his views thereon, and produced for the first time in Islam a systematic theology. He held firmly to the belief that one can not apply rational knowledge to divine things outside the provision and sanction of the Qurʾān. He argued that one may know God by the application of reason, which was consonant with, if not derived from, the divine revelation as embodied in the Qurʾān.

Everything that exists is due to the will of the Supreme Intelligence, God. One can not account for nature by reference to nature's forces, but rather through the medium of some divine creative act. In this regard, al-Ashʿari showed strong kinship with the Greek Atomist theory as it relates to Greek natural philosophy.

It would appear that al-Ashʿari's supreme effort was directed towards the reconciliation of *Reason* and *Revelation,* and to do so he resorted to *kalām* or "scholastic theology." Thus did he turn their own weapons against them, and thus did he defeat the Muʿtazilites.

His doctrine was formalized by a disciple, al-Nasafi (d. 1310), who placed less stress on formalism and more emphasis on the importance of rationalism in establishing religious truth.

From the time of its establishment onward, the Ashʿarite system prevailed among Sunni theologians following a strong boost in the twelfth century from al-Ghazāli (d. 1111). From the tenth century to the present, only twice was there a breach in the quiet realm of theological life dominated by the Ashʿari system: once by the Wahhābis of Arabia in the eighteenth century and once by the Bābis of Persia in the nineteenth century.

Ṣūfism

There was one area where both orthodox and non-orthodox Muslims eventually found a common religious ground. This was *Ṣūfism,* or the Islamic version of asceticism and mysticism. The whole underlying philosophy of Ṣūfism was to interject a *personal* element in the otherwise impersonal legalistic approach to the fulfillment of religious devotions. The result was the introduction of asceticism into religious practice and of mysticism into religious thought. While it is not considered a distinct sect of Islam, Ṣūfism certainly can be looked upon as a pattern of religious contention which found a lasting place in the body of Islam.

The protagonists of asceticism and mysticism, like all other diverters, traced the development of their movement to Muḥammad, the Qurʾān, and Ḥadīth. Muḥammad was known to have had much respect for the Christian ascetics, especially the legendary monk Baḥīra. The Prophet's night journey (Miʿrāj) had a certain ascetic flavor to it. The striving to achieve in deed as well as theory the "unity of existence" provided much incentive for Ṣūfi efforts. The attention paid in early Islam to the joys and punishments of the future life led to self-denial and simple living in this life. The rightly-guided first four caliphs were noted for their simplicity of living and for their pious approach to the affairs of this world out of consideration for the promises of the next. Early Muslims, inspired by their example of austere living, went even further and gave up all concern for the affairs of this world, preferring to live in poverty, in wanderings, and in retirement from the material comforts of this world.

The attitude in the first Islamic century was predominantly ascetic and not so much mystical. It became increasingly mystical in the second century under the dual influence of Greek and Christian stimuli. The monastic attitude in Christianity was by then well established in the lands where Islam became dominant. The Christian preoccupation with the idea of "purifying the human soul" must have spilled over into Islam where the pious Muslim became inclined in the same direction. This type of mysticism in the early stage of development was more practiced than defined. Its gradual evolution and subsequent movement from speculative mysticism to theosophy was bolstered by the strong impeti it received from the Hellenistic legacy.

By the tenth century, and under the inducements of Indo-Iranian concepts, it became theosophical. The continuous striving of the devout Muslim to identify himself with the cause of all being culminated with the execution of one such devotee, Manṣūr al-Ḥallāj (d. 922), for having audibly proclaimed *ana al-Ḥaqq* (lit. "I am the Truth"). This was his way of identifying himself mystically with the Creator, a pattern of mystical expression familiar to the old Persian Gnostics but baneful to the orthodox Muslims.

Among the earlier Ṣūfis who articulated the path to mystical union with God was Ḥallāj's master, Junayd. In his writings Junayd endeavored to show that man's supreme effort in this life is to fulfill his covenant with the Creator as ordained in the Qur'ān; he argued that it is man's duty to return to his primeval state, and to Junayd the mystical path of achieving ecstatic union with God is the only way.

During the early period of its development the spokesmen of mysticism came mostly from the class of orthodox teachers. By the time of Junayd, however, they began to derive from Muslims who were not brought up in the traditional religious disciplines but represented rather the artisan classes of the towns where the Aramaic and Persian ethnic groups were strong. In certain instances the espousal of the Ṣūfi doctrine was a sort of protest against the social and political abuses engendered in the early schisms, i.e., Khārijite, Shī'ite, and the like. They hoped to achieve this type of reform by appealing to the religious consciousness of the Muslim and inculcating him with some sort of spirituality not awakened by the legalistic stress of orthodox doctrine on prescribed acts of devotional expression.

This in turn had its impact on the social structure of the Islamic community. Not only did the Ṣūfis strive hard to make converts among their fellow non-mystics, but they became actively engaged also in missionary-type activities and propagandistic preachings in most of the lands of Islam, particularly in the safer confines of the periphery where the persecuting arm of the orthodox theologian could not reach them. They were suspect to the orthodox teachers from the start. The Shīʿah divines were equally suspicious and outrightly hostile to them.

Ṣūfi concepts and practices drew them further apart from the orthodox doctrine, especially when Ṣūfi leaders began to publicize the underlying philosophy of their mysticism and to gain a larger following. The Ṣūfi appeal and ". . . strength lay in the satisfaction which it gave to the religious instincts of the people, instincts which were to some extent chilled and starved by the abstract and impersonal teachings of the orthodox and found relief in the more directly personal and emotional religious approach of the Ṣūfis." [3]

Clearly, the growth of Ṣūfism was in reaction to the intellectualism of orthodox Islam and to the legalistic injunctions of the Qurʾān, devoid as they were of the natural and personal impulses for man to contemplate his Creator in the intimacy of his soul and mind.

The three essential ingredients of Ṣūfi philosophy are *light, knowledge, love,* the means by which a strong direct consciousness of divine presence is experienced. There is no acceptance of the idea of an incarnate God as in Christianity. The Ṣūfi looks upon man as an incarnation of God, but he does not believe in the savior principle or in any sort of intermediation between man and God. He has a highly unitarian conception of the Deity. What the Ṣūfi aims for is a glimpse of immortality while he is still entrapped by life in this world.

To achieve personal unity with their creator, the Ṣūfis laid out the "path" (*ṭarīqah*) that would lead to gnosis (*maʿrifah*) or mystic knowledge of the Lord. The "path" of ascension to divine union (*tawḥīd*) with God passes through stages known commonly as "stations" or "states"; the last stage is that of *fanā'*, or passing away in God, which is the ultimate desire of a successful mystic. The Ṣūfi at this point ceases to be aware of his physical identity even though he continues to exist as an individual. Ḥallāj expressed the mystic's sentiment most eloquently at the moment fanā' is achieved when he uttered:

I am He whom I love, and He whom I love is I.
We are two spirits dwelling in one body.
When thou seest me thou seest Him,
And when thou seest Him, thou seest us both.[4]

It is not surprising that the Ṣūfi attitude should provide a bridge between Islam and Christianity. Ṣūfis and Christians share the conception of God as love; both regard man as having been created in God's own image out of love for man, that man might behold the image of God in himself and attain the desired union with Him. The difference is in ends: the Ṣūfi seeks union with God in *this* life, while the Christian expects it in the life to come. The Ṣūfi's equivalent of Christian notions of incarnation is *ḥulūl,* the stage of indwelling with God.

As the mystic was seriously convinced of the presence of divine truth in him through his ability to attain direct communion with the Creator, it is little wonder that he should gloat over his alleged superiority to the prophets whose communication with God is looked upon as more formal than personal.

But to believe in the divine presence in you is one matter; to proclaim your identity with the "Truth," which identity is reserved by the highly unitarian orthodox theologians to God and God alone, is to commit the kabīrah, or the major unpardonable sin; this is shirk of the highest order because the Ṣūfi is associating a partner, in himself, with Him who "hath not partners."

The one salutary byproduct of Ṣūfi theory is the stress on the meeting of the spiritual and physical world in man, placing him thus at the center of the universe.

The Ṣūfis were persecuted as heretics. This led to discretion in public utterances and to the expression of mystic yearning in such metaphors as wine and love. Their language therefore became veiled and allusive, if not secretive; and only those who were apprised of the secrets could grasp the inner meaning of the wealth of Ṣūfi poetic literature that sprung into being.

Their audacity in certain instances made discretion a matter of prudence. Abu-Saʿīd (d. 1049), a Persian Ṣūfi, went so far as to argue that the *Sharīʿah* was unnecessary for those who had reached the end of the "path." Such *Sharīʿah* ordained that religious observances such as the pilgrimage to Mecca or praying when the call to prayer is sounded—particularly when the initiates are already engaged in ritual dance—should not be obeyed.

In the fourth and fifth centuries the Ṣūfis grew in numbers and commensurately in strength. They began to take on peculiarly distinguishing features. The *dhikr,* for example, previously served to concentrate the mind on God; now in the later period the Ṣūfi dhikr began to embrace clear liturgical tendencies marked by the recitation of chants and litanies. The orthodox theologians feared, and rightly so, that the Ṣūfi dhikr sessions would weaken the significance of the mosque as the place of congregation. They were angered with the Ṣūfis for rejecting the *Sharʿī* path to religious truth on the ground that knowledge of theology and law does not lead to knowledge of God, as was zealously maintained by the theologians. Not this rational and second-hand knowledge of the *ʿulamāʾ* but rather the direct personal experience of the devoted Muslim, the *maʿrifah* that culminates in absorption into the Godhead, was posited as the only way to attain religious truth and satisfaction.

While the orthodox view condemned celibacy, as Christian asceticism condemned marriage, the Ṣūfis equivocated on the subject; but the prevalent trend among them by the fifth century of Islam was to refrain from marriage.[5] It was not so much their practice of celibacy that contramanded the orthodox doctrine as it was their increasing veneration of their shaykhs, to the point that they made saints out of them. This indeed ran contrary to the grain of the fundamental notion of Islam, namely, that nothing should distract from the uncompromising devotion to God.

The decrees of the *corpus sancta*, Qur'ān and *Ḥadīth*, as interpreted by the theologians, regarded the invocation of other than God in supplicatory prayer as tantamount to passing into polytheism.

In popular Islam, however, encompassing the rank and file of Muslims on the fringe of the Islamic heartland, there was much closer contact with the religious practices of Christians; the rank and file Muslims evolved as a consequence a sort of "folk religion" version of Islam, and they were not readily distracted from their non-orthodox approach to God by the thundering threats of orthodox theologians.

A rather extreme departure from the orthodox norm, touching almost on shirk, is the strong devotion accorded the shaykh or leader in some Ṣūfi orders. An important Muslim authority on the subject regards the posture of the Ṣūfis on this issue as one of the fundamental tenets of their beliefs. The posture is predicated on the theory that knowledge of God can be achieved through the intercession of saints. In this regard they show a strong affinity with concepts deriving from Gnostic and Christian sources. Indeed, the Ṣūfis went so far as to institute a hierarchy of saints topped by the *Quṭb*, pole of the world, assisted by a host of deputies and superintendents on earth.

Acceptance by Orthodoxy

That this type of approach to God should gain ascendancy among the rank and file of Muslims is due considerably to the myopic dogmatism of the orthodox theologians and their undue stress on pedantry arising from rigid legalism or formalism. The performance of the prescribed acts of worship did little to quench the soul of the Ṣūfi who yearned for a more personal identification with God.

The gains of the Ṣūfis became more explicit in the eleventh century when they won over to their cause some of the ablest thinkers of Islam. Their persistent defiance of the orthodox view culminated in the great compromise which gained for Ṣūfism official recognition and acceptance from their adversaries. The credit belongs to the respected theologian al-Qushayri (d. 1072) who urged his colleagues to acknowledge the Ṣūfi doctrine of mystical communion with God. But the real architect of Ṣūfism's triumph was the celebrated Abu-Ḥāmid al-Ghazāli (d. 1111). His impact on orthodox Islam is no less comparable in magnitude than Augustine's and Luther's on traditional Christianity.

Like Augustine six centuries before, al-Ghazāli felt the torments on his soul of the relentless personal search for a satisfying experience of the divine. He had explored the avenues that lay open before him: the speculative, metaphysical, and doctrinaire, but to no avail. He found no religious truth in the philosophies of the day familiar to him. He refused to take the path stretched out before him because the tormented spirit within him was crying out for a type of fulfillment which he could not realize by the traditional method. So he abandoned his professorship at the renowned Niẓāmīyah school of theology at Baghdad and went about his search with great determination to explore more fully the existing theological systems; but again he could find none of the satisfaction he yearned for. Neither the orthodox nor the Shīʿī systems had any alternatives to offer him. Out of despair he turned at last to the mystical path, and it was through it that he found the personal contentment he had been seeking.

It is indeed to the glory and enhancement of Islam that al-Ghazāli did not stop at his discovery of personal contentment. He chose to announce the results of his discovery to all Muslims and wrote as a consequence his own "Confessions." [6]

In this classical autobiography al-Ghazāli discusses how he found religious truth in the Ṣūfi *dhikr* which materialized when he abandoned all the corruptive influences of the flesh and rid himself of "evil thoughts" and desires. He shared with the Ṣūfis, whose works he had thoroughly imbibed, the basic credo that the path to God can not be intellectually delineated, but lies rather in a mystical experience. Like St. Francis of Assisi, al-Ghazāli abandoned the wealth and prestige of his professional standing, also his wife and family, and set out on extensive wanderings to tell others of his great triumph over himself in attaining closer communion with God.

The beliefs of al-Ghazāli are set forth in such of his important writings as *The Revivification of the Religious Sciences,* the *Folly of the Philosophers,* and the *Niche of the Lights.*

His services to Ṣūfism and Islam were well summed up by a leading Western authority on Islamic theology[7] who pointed out that al-Ghazāli revolutionized the interpretation of religious dogma resting on the Qurʾān, Sunnah, and exegesis so as to bring it into a closer awareness of personal experience. The same can be said of his efforts in making philosophy and theological rationalism more palatable and understandable to the average Muslim. In leading theologians to work less on the scholastic and more on the historical precepts of Islam's development, he made it possible for those who hitherto resisted the ascetic trend now to accept it. In so doing Ṣūfism gained acceptance and respectability in the eyes of its erstwhile distractors. While Ṣūfism did not attain to full orthodoxy, at least it succeeded in making orthodoxy more mystical.[8]

Al-Ghazāli was the great mystic of eastern Islam. His counterpart in western Islam was the Hispano-Arab ibn-al-ʿArabi (d. 1240). Ibn-al-ʿArabi evolved a sort of Logos doctrine which bears strong kinship with the Neo-Platonic school. The "idea" he concerned himself with is that which represents the creative or rational principle behind the universe, the "first intellect." Muḥammad the Prophet to ibn-al-ʿArabi is the first reality because in his opinion he stands for the perfect man. "Every prophet is a Logos whose individual Logoi are united in the idea of Muḥammad, the perfect man is he in whom all the attributes of the macrocosm are reflected. The reality of Muḥammad is the creative principle of the universe, and the perfect man is its cause."[9]

While ibn-al-ʿArabi is difficult to decipher, and his writings more enigmatical than understandable, his views tend towards the Ṣūfi aim to achieve a closer experience of the divine. What he appears to have accomplished is to project his interpretation of the perfect man "as the visible aspect of God in relation to the world."[10] He speaks of Muḥammad "Lord . . . the source of all mysteries, and the cause of all phenomena." In his *waḥdat al-wujūd* (unity of existence), he projects the doctrine "that things pre-exist as ideas in the knowledge of God, whence they emanate and whither they return." [10] The world is merely the outer aspect of God.

Ṣūfi Organization and Orders

The Ṣūfis became organized in the twelfth century when they saw the need for hierarchical discipline. There came into being about twelve major orders. The rallying center was usually where a saint resided. To organize was the logical extension of their extreme reverence for and pride in their shaykhs whom they often beatified. The need for organization resulted also from the increasing number of novices and disciples who had to have some formal and definable position among the senior devotees. With organization, converts became linked in a widespread number of brotherhoods; and in such organized brotherhoods we have the only type of ecclesiastical organization in Islam.

A member of the brotherhood was known as a *faqīr* (fakir) or *darwīsh* (dervish). He joined the order after submitting to a solemn rite of initiation and receiving the symbol of investiture, namely a special frock (*khirqah*). Following his formal acceptance into the order, the novice associated himself closely with the shaykh until he rose to the status of a leader.

The Ṣūfi fraternities extended over the whole length and breadth of the Muslim empire. Their elaborate code of ascetic moral discipline stressed (in a manner suggestive of the Christian way to salvation) repentance, abstinence, renunciation, poverty, patience, satisfaction, and trust in God.[11]

The diffusion of the *Epistles* of the Brethren of Purity (*Ikhwān al-Ṣafā᾽*), an encyclopaedic compendium with strong Neo-Platonic impulses that had a material influence on the development of the esoteric Ismāʿīli sect, contributed to the crystallization of the orders' organization and philosophy.

The impulse to organize received also a great boost from the monistic and pantheistic philosophy of ibn-al-ʿArabi. In the mystical interpretation of Islamic doctrine, which ibn-al-ʿArabi claimed was revealed to him as the "Seal of Saints," he set himself up as a rival of the orthodox theologians. His views were particularly appealing to the Muslims in the Persian and Turkish zones of Islam. Under the influence of his views the mystical schools became gradually closed circles of initiates.

It is important to note that the mystical approach to God, even at the zenith of its development, did not gain a large following among the Muslims. Perhaps the aberrations to which it became susceptible from the point of view of the orthodox believers account to some extent for its relatively unpopular appeal. The Ṣūfis, we noted, tended to clothe their expressed yearning for the divine in their writings, particularly in odes and poetry, in terms that the neutral observer found very difficult to comprehend outside their Ṣūfi context. The use of "love" and other rather mundane if not sensuous terminology to conceal Ṣūfi metaphors was too real not to be taken at face value. He who reads the poems of the famous Persian poet Ḥāfiẓ finds it difficult to determine from them what is in reference to the divine and what may easily be taken as expressions of worldly love. Love and wine figured prominently as metaphors in the allegedly mystical verses of Ḥāfiẓ which together with Saʿdi's attained a stylistic perfection foreign to earlier verse. The outstanding poet of the Ṣūfis, Jalāl-al-Dīn al-Rūmi (d. 1273), is less prone to such bewildering interpretations. Indeed, in his deeply moving verses lies the acme of mystical expression. In his poetry embodied in the *Mathnawi* (Mesnevi) we discover that al-Rūmi has expressed all that is to be said on mysticism. Jāmi (d. 1492), another Persian mystic poet, wedded romance to his mystical writings.

Among the important orders that were established, mention should be made of the Qādirīyah, named after ʿAbd-al-Qādir al-Jīlāni (d. 1166), once a preacher with powerful appeal to his listeners in Baghdad. Al-Jīlāni stressed tolerance, piety, and philanthropy. His followers built for him a *ribāṭ* (monastery) outside of Baghdad and continued in his path. His numerous descendants were responsible for a number of offshoots of the Qādirīyah order, some of which, like the Rifāʿīyah, were not nearly as tolerant as the parent organization. Another, the Badawīyah[12] located primarily in Egypt, acquired notoriety for their orgies centered around the founder's tomb at Tanta in the Nile Delta.

The Ṣūfi movement gained a stronger foothold in the Maghrib on account of its strong political links with the ascendant Mahdi ibn-Tūmart and the Almohad dynasty in the twelfth century. The Almohads from the start were closely affiliated with the Ṣūfi movement. Through this association the Berbers who were not deeply inclined to Islam became more intimately involved with the religion of the Arab conquerors. Ṣūfi Islam attracted the Berber because it tolerated his animistic proclivities. To the Berber convert the *shaykh* was not much unlike his "holy man" who was alleged to possess magical powers.

The strong foothold of Ṣūfism in western Islam enabled it to influence the eastern wing firstly through ibn-al-ʿArabi who hailed from Murcia in Spain and secondly through al-Shādhili (d. 1258) who studied in Fez but settled in Alexandria, Egypt.

Most of al-Shādhili's disciples were artisans who were discouraged from an all-out mystical living. While he favored no organization or Ṭarīqah, not much later than a generation following his death a Ṭarīqah did evolve; it was named al-Shādhilīyah, after him. The order developed a ritual that transcended the Qādirīyah's in elaborateness. Its offshoots were more numerous than theirs. The two extremes were represented; one by the Isawīyah, noted for their swordslashing ritual, and at the opposite end by the Darqāwa of Morocco and Western Algeria.

The Turks and Mongols were no less susceptible to Ṣūfi influences, among whom, as with the Berbers, the *Ṭarīqahs* developed from a substratum of Shamanism or animism. The oldest order, in which women unveiled participated in the dhikr, was the Yesevīya. The next order of consequence came in among the Osmanli Turks of Anatolia under the name of Bektāshi. Some say it was the product of the Yesevīya.

The Bektāshis were much more syncretistic, enjoying connections with esoteric Shīʿism on one side, folk Christianity and Gnosticism on the other. They were much more extreme than other Ṣūfi orders in their discarding the ceremonies enjoined by the *Sharīʿah.* Their rituals betrayed strong analogies with the cultic observances of Christian communities next to whom they lived. The Bektāshis at one time were a powerful order because of their close association with the Ottoman Janissaries up to the time they were suppressed in 1826.

The urban Turks favored the Mevlevi (Mawlawi) order, founded by the mystical Persian poet Jalāl-al-Dīn al-Rūmi. The dhikr of the Mevlevis revolved around the pirouetting of the initiates which accounts for their being termed the "whirling dervishes." Like the Bektāshis, the Mevlevis suffered loss in strength when the secular modern Turkish republic came into being in the 1920's. They still have a few *tekkes,* however, in some of the larger cities of the Middle East.

Another well-known order is the Naqshbandi, which was first started in Central Asia by al-Bukhāri but managed to work its way westward through India until it found for itself a wide following in Western Asia and Egypt. One can see more clearly the mystical appeal to the divine in a prayer of the Naqshbandis recited at the end of the dhikr:

> Oh God bless and preserve our Prophet Muḥammad in the beginning. Bless and preserve our Prophet Muḥammad at all time. Bless and preserve our Prophet Muḥammad in the High Heavens till the Day of Judgment. Bless and preserve all the prophets and messengers, the angels and the righteous worshipers of thee from amongst the dwellers of the heavens and earth. May Allah, the Merciful and Exalted be graciously pleased with our Lords, the possessors of high esteem Abu Bakr, ʿUmar, ʿUthmān, ʿAli (the Orthodox Caliphs), their (righteous) predecessors, Thy devotees and Thy followers till the Day of Judgment. Gather us unto Thy mercy, Oh Most Merciful, Oh God, Oh Living, Oh Creator. There is no god but Thee, Oh God, Oh our Lord, Oh Most Forgiving, Oh Most Merciful, O God, Amen.[13]

The literature of the Ṣūfis is rich and revealing of their unselfish mystical search for God. Indeed, Islam's Ṣūfis have left us a most heavily endowed body of devotional literature, enough to evoke the envy of all those who have dedicated themselves to the worship of the one God.

A more lasting impression on the orthodox body of Islam was felt during the seventeenth and eighteenth centuries when a number of outstanding orthodox scholars strove to restate the bases of Islamic theology independent of the set dogmatism and formalism enshrined in the orthodox manuals of religion. These scholars attempted to place more emphasis on the psychological and ethical elements in religion.

The Ṣūfi influence in the Shīʿah world was persistent, albeit circumscribed. Here Ṣūfi doctrine and Shīʿah "orthodoxy" fused in the work of Mulla Ṣadra (d. 1640) and Shaykh Aḥmad al-Aḥsāʾi (d. 1826), the systematizer of Ṣadra's beliefs into a heterodoxy termed Shaykhīyah. Their chief doctrine stressed the necessity of having an open channel of communication with the "Hidden Imām" of the Shīʿah. It is this one concept that gave rise almost immediately to the Bābi movement and its offshoot Bahāʾism.

CHAPTER 11

"Medievalism" and the Dawn of "Renaissance"

THE TRIUMPH OF Ashʿari orthodoxy represented the first significant religious development of any consequence down to present times. Several factors may account for this subsequent dearth of theological agitation. The political dislocations in the body politic resulting from the Crusades, the split of the ʿAbbāsid empire at the seams and the Mongol invasions, the rise of multiple dynasties, and the disappearance of caliphal authority as a force symbolizing spiritual unity, the deterioration of commerce and sources of wealth, the stepped up incursions of Tartar and other Turkic invaders, all contributed to a widespread spirit of uncertainty.

In the atmosphere of mounting social and political insecurity, the doctors of Islamic law and the theologians deemed it essential to the religious survival of Islam that further theological agitation or the application of *ijtihād* to dogma should cease. It was agreed that further efforts to interpret doctrine when coupled with the assault of the rationalists and philosophers on the bastions of the theologians would only serve to widen the areas of disagreement and loosen the bonds of unity essential for the preservation of

Islam as a vital religious element in the troubled political society of the believers when they were left with hardly much of the material comforts of life to fall back on.

The "Medieval" Era

And so the Islamic world marked time, as if it had come to a standstill, for the next seven centuries. The only upheavals of any consequence were political: the rise of the Ottoman Turks and the extension of their political control over much of West Asia and North Africa from the sixteenth century to the twentieth. Being subscribers to the Sunni view, the orthodox doctors of law and the *Sharīʿah* asserted themselves under the Ottoman hegemony.

Political turmoil in Persia enabled a new dynastic family steeped in Ṣūfi traditions, whence their name "Safawi," to come to power at the beginning of the sixteenth century; and with its triumph, the forceful conversion of Iran from Sunni orthodoxy to Shīʿah heterodoxy took place. Still no stimulus for any rethinking or adaptation of religious doctrine was deemed essential. There was no felt need for it, because the Islamic world was still wallowing in its self-styled superiority over the lands of the infidel, and for good reason. Had not the Muslim Turks beat back the combined forces of Europe in the Crusades? Did not the sons of Osman with their mighty and seemingly invincible armies sweep all before them right to the walls of Vienna? The Islam they experienced appeared to meet their needs. The world of Islam was sufficient unto itself; so was the prevalent credo of the faith.

The turning point came when "infidel" Europe began to assert the superiority of its own arms over the leading Islamic power, the Ottoman. This was brought home to the Arab portions of the Islamic world when Napoleon invaded Egypt and gave a visible demonstration of modern know-how. The once confident Muslims, at least of Egypt, now vividly witnessed for themselves the product of the West's material advancement. The West, it would seem, had raced past the Islamic world in the push towards the future. The nineteenth and twentieth centuries with all their revolutionary social, political, and intellectual accomplishments gave the inquiring Muslim much to ponder, much to rethink. The dawn of a new era had arrived.

Muslim intellectuals concerned with the fate of their inherited faith began to apply themselves to the task of adapting this faith to the exigences of a modern world propelled by great scientific and technological achievements. Behind them now trailed the traditional forces of religion. The tenets of the faith as then observed seemed insufficient to bolster a sagging Islamic society in confrontation with a revitalized and materially advancing Western society, a society with sufficient force and dynamism to impose itself as if at will on a prostrate tradition-riddled Muslim world. The West moved against the Muslim East with full impunity not only by the power of arms and conquest, but more importantly by the weight of its appealing intellectual stimuli laden with revolutionary ideas.

The fundamental problem now confronting Islam was not how to bring about a "Reformation" in the religion, because the orthodox body was not at war with itself, but how to effect a much needed "Renaissance."

The triumph of scholastic theology and its perseverance had occasioned none of the abuses which brought about the Protestant revolt in Europe. Islam had no clergy to dictate to it. The ʿulamāʾ, theologians and jurisprudents, never attempted to enlarge on the Qurʾānic conception of how the faithful must gain salvation. The Ṣūfis already had pointed a way. Their movement gave those seeking a more flexible experience of religious contentment the means for it. They were careful not to cross swords with the orthodox theologians. Islam consequently achieved a sort of inner harmony and serenity which Christianity in the Europe of the sixteenth century, shaken by the aftermaths of the Reformation and Counter-Reformation, may well have envied.

But the bridge which al-Ghazāli had built between Ṣūfism and orthodoxy did not last. Ṣūfism gradually drifted towards pantheism while orthodoxy kept moving towards greater transcendence. Ordinary Muslims simply followed a middle path. When we hear of fatalism in Islam, less attention is paid to the fact that it was the result of ignorance and poverty, which became widespread with the deterioration of trade in the Near East from the fifteenth century onward, than it was occasioned by the dictates of theology or belief in predestination.

In the centuries following the prevalence of Ashʿari theology, there was but one abrupt and short-lived fundamentalist reaction directed largely against the Ṣūfis. It took place in the fourteenth century when the Ḥanbalite ibn-Taymīyah (d. 1328) and his disciples attempted to rid orthodoxy of Ṣūfism. When tensions relaxed in the subsequent centuries, a sort of equilibrium was worked out between both sides: the Ṣūfis steered clear of interference in orthodox theology and the orthodox theologians felt freer to join Ṣūfi orders. The participation of theologians had the sobering effect of preventing Ṣūfism from degenerating into outright pantheism, but aberrations were not altogether eliminated.

The Ḥanbali fundamentalists, however, did not give up the hope of reintroducing puritanism; and nearly four and a half centuries later they were in a position to assert once again their puritanical views. By the middle of the eighteenth century it was evident that the orthodox theologians had not succeeded in keeping the Ṣūfi system from eliminating the aberrations which they were accused of harboring. Sunni theology in the meanwhile seemed to be compromised by the theologians giving in more and more to Ṣūfi demands. A general downgrading appeared to be in progress. Reaction was bound to come from the more doctrinaire, and in this instance fundamentalist, theologians.

Wahhābism

The founder of the reactionary movement around 1774 was a central Arabian by the name of Muḥammad ibn-ʿAbd-al-Wahhāb, who gave his name to it. Wahhābism was clearly inspired by the puritanical Ḥanbalite madhhab whose most recent vocalist was ibn-Taymīyah. Wahhāb struck up an alliance with the dispossessed house of Suʿūd (Saud), and when the Suʿūdis achieved their miraculous triumph in Arabia the Wahhābis who had hitched their fortunes to the Suʿūdi chariot triumphed with them; but their system of theology did not become ensconced until the second quarter of the twentieth century.

The Wahhābis were not modernists; they were rather traditionalists who attacked innovations such as those of the Ṣūfis, which they treated as heresy. They also attacked the other orthodox rites for compromising with the Ṣūfis and tolerating their "perversions." They were puritans fired with the zeal to purify not only the religion of what they deemed infidelities but also corruption in manners and religious practices in Arabia which they attributed to laxity in enforcing religious injunctions.

Incited by Wahhābi zeal the Suʿūd family not only took to the conquest of Central and Eastern Arabia, but attacked also Arab settlements in Iraq, destroying the sacred shrine of the Shīʿah at Karbalāʾ (Kerbala) in 1802. They warred on the hereditary Sharīfs of Mecca in the Ḥijāz and succeeded in capturing and "purifying" the sacred city in 1806. Both the Ottoman sultan in Istanbul and Muḥammad ʿAli, governor of Egypt, were challenged by the bold defiance of the Wahhābis and compelled to strike back twice in 1812–13 and 1816–18 breaking momentarily Wahhābi power. The Suʿūd family's political power was reduced and their erstwhile vassals, the Rashīds, now governed in their place. But a century later the well publicized king ʿAbd-al-ʿAzīz ibn-Suʿūd succeeded in reconquering Arabia. Both the Sharīfs of Mecca and the Rashīds of Shammār were uprooted altogether and permanently from Arabia. Once more Wahhābism was triumphant and so it has remained in Saudi Arabia.

What is significant for Islam is the fact that Wahhābism provided important stimuli to Muslim elements outside Arabia not contented with the status quo of their religion. Motivated by the same zeal to emulate the puritanical revival abetted by Wahhābi successes, like-minded Muslims in India and West Africa at the beginning of the nineteenth century began to follow suit. Their stronghanded methods evoked the resentment and earned the condemnation of the Muslim public, as had the Wahhābis for similar extremist and violent deeds. In their zealous attempts to impose their creed, they conducted themselves no differently than did the ill-fated Khārijites, the earliest puritans at the beginning of Islam. As their violent intolerance of those who disagreed with them began to subside, the Wahhābis went about the task of reasserting the unmitigated monotheism of the early Muslims. The drive for greater observance of the monistic principle was at the expense of the partisans of transcendentalism among whom the Ṣūfis had played an important role.

What is of significance also is the fact that the reassertion of uncompromising monotheism started in Arabia where the orthodox faith was launched nearly twelve centuries earlier. It would seem that Ḥanbali puritanism was in accordance with the inclination of the Arab, particularly when we note that in the post-Ghazāli period the transcendentalists were predominantly non-Arab: Berber, Turk and Persian. One can not assume from such a deduction that the choice of creed was motivated by preference deriving mostly from ethnic instinct, or that with the rise of Ṣūfism to eminence, the *Mathnawī* of Rūmi had come to replace the Traditions in importance; yet for many Persians and Turks the gains of transcendentalism symbolized to them a sort of revolt of the "nationalities" against the idea of the Arab ascendancy in Islam. Rather, one may attribute this to the inherently divergent conception of how to reach the Deity among the Semitic Arabs and the non-Semitic nationalities. Was it not in the Indo-Aryan World that the notions of transcendentalism were formally articulated —Gnosticism in Persia, Platonism in Greece?

When the needs for reform became more obvious to the enlightened disciples of the *Sharīʿah*, the motivation came from the orthodox reaction against the growing deterioration which seemed to lead to animism (*jinn* worship) and pantheism rather than from pressures by the Western world. The tensions built up in Islam between the orthodox and the Ṣūfis generated the urge for reform.

Challenge to Reform

The call for the reinterpretation of the tenets of Islam was somewhat sporadic but clearly evident in certain parts of the

Islamic world. Not all of the impeti can be construed as religious in nature, neither was the approach to reform necessarily novel. Al-Murtada al-Zabidi (d. 1790) of the Yemen found al-Ghazāli's theories suitable for his interpretations, and the end result of his efforts was the reassertion of the Ghazāli type of orthodoxy. With the spread of the printing press in the nineteenth century, a great number of medieval theological works were printed and circulated from Egypt. The increasing interest of European scholars in Islam, manifest in a variety of their publications on the subject, also served to bring out the contrasts between the earlier and later conceptions of the religion.

The probe went deeper and new issues were interjected. Modern scholarship and its stress on textual criticism brought out the distinctions between the pure Qur'ānic text and the mass of accretions accumulated over a span of several centuries which heavily weighted Islam and precluded a more adaptive view of it. A great deal of opposition to reassessing the tenets of the faith in the light of modern needs resulted from myopic interests. Hosts of spokesmen, *ʿulamāʾ*, muftis, *qāḍis*, custodians of and propagandists for the Sharīʿah, stood to lose their sources of gain were they to be exposed for having promoted unduly a vast body of "guiding precepts" that might now be proved irrelevant, if not un-Islamic, from the point of view of the Muslim's needs in a progressing society, a need that could enjoy the circumspection of Islam by the application of pure Qur'anic sanction.

A reformation based on reading into the spirit when the letter of the Qurʾān does not satisfy is needed. Europe in the Reformation and Counter-Reformation periods faced up to the problem albeit reluctantly, and not without agonizing reappraisals of dogma accompanied often by violence. The Muslim world is on the verge of facing up to the same problem. It should be easier because there is no entrenched religious institution to oppose the reformers.

Islam throughout the nineteenth and present centuries has been poignantly challenged by "modernism" and technological advancement. The theocratic spirit permeating all facets of the Muslim's life was found to be restricted. When the Christian

West had been similarly confronted by material progress, it responded to the confrontation by distinguishing clearly between "what is Caesar's" and "what is Christ's."

The need to separate what can be regarded *secular* from what may be treated as *spiritual* has been no less evident in the lands of Islam than it had been in the world of Christianity. The rising generations of Muslims eager to preserve their faith but willing to enjoy the fruits of the secular modern world have experienced the need more than those who claim to be non-interested in the material promises of our new era, which is guided by science and machine technology. Those among them who favor modernization have applied themselves to the task of revaluating the fundamental tenets of their religion in the light of modern needs. They have labored to find compatibility between their spiritual loyalties and their desire for the material offerings of a rapidly advancing world.

Once more the rational force has come into play, and a host of modern "Muʿtazilahs" have set themselves to the task of rethinking their religion on the basis of the premises they inherited with Islam. They find much they can strip it of, namely the deadweight of medieval accretions, without in any way compromising their fundamental religious beliefs.

Efforts expended in this direction to date have been sporadic and widely scattered, stretching from India to the Maghrib; and often the impetus to reinterpret Islam is the product of a local need. That there should be no wide-scale deliberate approach to reform is the logical consequence of the absence of an organized ecclesiastical system to take charge of the situation. In recent times the great theological institution of higher learning, the Azhar of Egypt, has been serving in a self-styled fashion as the ultimate recourse for the doctrinal reinterpretation of orthodox Islam. Because of the Azhar's conservative orthodox views, the modernists have not always been able to look to it for encouragement and support. Indeed, not until very recent years did this bastion of traditional orthodoxy begin to expand its teaching curricula to include the secular sciences. Further liberalization is indicated, but it appears to be still at the inception stage.

"Modernism"

The first serious dent on Azhar thinking was made by the modern Egyptian reformer Muḥammad ʿAbduh (d. 1905), whose main target of reform was the purification of Islam from its corrupting influences and practices, *not* the revision of established orthodoxy. ʿAbduh felt the change could be achieved with the reform of Islam's higher education, which in his times was heavily governed by theological precepts. Educational reform to ʿAbduh was the *sine qua non* for the reform of Islam. He sought a readjustment of Islamic doctrine to accommodate modern thought. One way to achieve this adjustment is to eliminate *bidʿa* (unorthodox innovations). By introducing reform along these lines, ʿAbduh believed he could supply the means for checking the encroachment of Western ideas laden with Christian polemics which he felt were undermining the bases of Islam.

For precedents ʿAbduh reverted to the period in Islam's development that anteceded the formulation of the orthodox doctrine, the period before the principal madhāhib were established. His antagonists, foremost among them being the Wahhābis, chose to harken to the puritanical doctrine of ibn-Taymīyah instead. ʿAbduh by contrast may be considered a modernist. The results of his broad preachings fostered not only a modernist school of thought but also a reformed traditionalist school, the Salafīyah, spearheaded by Riḍa, a student of ʿAbḍuh.

ʿAbduh's reforms were aimed at Muslim higher education at the pinnacle of which stood the Azhar. When ʿAbduh began to advocate reform, there had been in existence for some time a secular system of primary and secondary education, but no institution of secular higher learning. ʿAbduh sought the establishment of this type of institution in order to insure the separation of secular and religious education. Then the religious reformists, it was argued, would be able to update the Azhar upon which institution the reform of Islam depended, particularly since the Azhar had long since become the center of Islam and had come to exercise a determining influence on issues affecting religious beliefs.

Beside the establishment of a secular system of education, other tangible reforms included higher salaries for instructors, larger allowances and better care for students, more liberal library holdings, closer exchanges with provincial mosque schools, and the revival of the Arabic language in its pure classical form as the medium of print for the great theological works of medieval Islam.

The printing of classical treatises led to a literary revival which stressed the employment of classical Arabic as the vehicle of expression. Was not Arabic after all the language of the angels, the Qur'ān and Islam! In 1900 ʿAbduh spearheaded a society specifically for the purpose of reviving the Arabic sciences.

The most eloquent testimony of ʿAbduh's religious views is embodied in his classical treatise *Risālat al-Tawḥīd (The Epistle on the Unity* [*of God*]),[1] which is the principal exposition of his basic theology. In it ʿAbduh stresses the need to purge Islam of its superstition, to correct the Muslim's conception of the articles of his faith, and to eliminate the errors that had crept into Islam on account of the misinterpretation of its texts. He insisted that the exegesis of the Qur'ān should be simplified and modernized.

Early in his life ʿAbduh was enthusiastic about pure philosophy, but later on he reached the conclusion that it was not in the best interest of Islam. Yet he still made use of logic, arguing that the science of reason is not the possession of philosophy. With the use of reason he intended to establish a rational interpretation of Qur'ānic text so as to adapt it to the modern needs of a society anxious to maintain the spiritual ties enjoined by the sacred book.

The exercise of reason in matters of faith ran contrary to the Ḥanbali form of exegesis, which remained faithful to the literal interpretation of the revelations contained in the Qur'ān, tailored as they may have been to the needs of the community's forebears over twelve centuries earlier. This was indeed a form of blind following, a *taqlīd* (imitation), of the precedents set by *ʿulamā'* who could not believe that the word of Allah might be construed differently if necessary to make it conform to the requirements of man and the vicissitude of his motions in time and space.

What is significant and meritorious in ʿAbduh's reassessment of Islam's capacity for adaptation to modern needs was his insistence on the need for *ijtihād*. He argued for the reestablishment of *ijtihād* as a tool for reinterpreting the tenets of the faith, and insisted that it must be made the right of all generations of Muslims to apply these tenets as the circumstances called for it. ʿAbduh preached tolerance of other sects and enjoined that others do the same. He sought to soothe the anxieties of his religiously minded listeners by stating that they need not fear any non-reasonable conflict between science and the precepts of their faith. Applying reason to bring about changes that would conform to the demands of a modernizing society could not be un-Islamic.

ʿAbduh's ideas of reform were evident in his unfinished commentary on the Qurʾān. His modernist views lie mostly in his advocacy of measures which he believed were in conformity with the fundamental precepts of Islam. While he was no innovator or synthesist in the tradition of the great medieval reformer al-Ghazāli, by stressing the need to apply reason to faith he loosened the iron grip of immobility on the religion of Islam after lifting it from its medieval setting, and made possible the reformulating of doctrinal concepts in a modern context.

The legacy of ʿAbduh lies chiefly in the modernist revival which he launched, aiming, as we have seen, at introducing the changes that would make the religion adaptable to a rapidly transforming world. He preached the return to the simplest and most essential forms of the religion. In so doing the *ʿulamāʾ* would provide the common basis on which Muslims of varying sectarian affiliation could agree. In the modern tendency to cast aspersion on the religion that was alleged to sanction polygamy, easy divorce, even slavery, ʿAbduh countered by discourses to show that such practices did not belong to the essentials of Islam but were rather subject to change.

ʿAbduh's concepts and preachings of reform yielded two continuous trends. One trend persisted in a secular vein, abetted by

Western notions of modernism, but without attempting to abandon the dogmas of the faith. The other trend was towards evoking the support of the ancestral tradition and the *Salafīyah* (the founding fathers), whence the name of the movement.

The secular modernists thought in terms of separating Church and State, confining *Sharīʿah* provisions to the religion and adopting Western-style laws for the state. In Turkey we have an extreme example of secularization, one that has been followed in the last decade by Nasser in Egypt. With Nasser as with Ataturk before him, there is an all-out effort to secularize and modernize without regard to theological sanction. Often this has amounted to rejecting the theocratic edifice of law, government, and society erected by the medieval doctors of Islamic *Sharʿī* law.

The Salafīyah on the other hand, while upholding the faith of the Orthodox Caliphs and the Companions of Muḥammad, did not hesitate to join the modernists in rejecting the authority of the medieval conceptions of Islam. Like the modernists they placed their trust in the Qurʾān and *Sunnah* for guidance in a modern world. But unlike them, the Salafīyah would not make use of Western-type ideas like realism and rationalism for guidance in reforming Islamic society outside the pale of religion and its traditional precepts of organization.

Reformed "Traditionalism"

Since the reinterpretation of the Qurʾān was essential for the success of both the modernist and Salafīyah trends, Muḥammad ʿAbduh's unfinished commentary on the Qurʾān was continued upon his death by one of his disciples and the architect of the Salafīyah movement, namely the Syrian Rashīd Riḍa (d. 1935).

Besides serving as editor of the Qurʾān commentary begun by ʿAbduh, Riḍa founded the *Manār* (Lighthouse), a journal publicizing the Salafīyah notions of reform. The *Manār* gained a wide audience and following from Morocco to Indonesia.

Riḍa like ʿAbduh treated the modernists with caution and did not hesitate to condemn the extremist measures directed against Islam by the followers of Ataturk in Turkey. When pushed, the

Salafis would adopt a fundamental approach which tended to draw them closer to the Wahhābis but without their sharing the latter's strong sectarian mood.

The Salafīyah have been dubbed as "Neo-Ḥanbalites," a group of conservatives who favored the reopening of the gate of ijtihād so it could be applied to issues of law and theology. This stems from the fact that Riḍa and his followers harkened back to the puritanical doctrine of the ibn-Taymīyah (d. 1328) and one of his followers ibn-al-Qayyim al Jawzīyah (d. 1355). At one time, before modern Turkish secularists broke with Islam, Riḍa favored the pan-Islamic ideas of the fiery mostly political reformer Jamāl-al-Dīn al-Afghāni. Afghāni had preached political revitalization and reunification of the Islamic world under the leadership of the sultan-caliph in Istanbul. His intense conviction and zeal of preachings tended to scare not only the modernists, but also many conservatives even in their own homelands.

Al-Afghāni's checkered career took him to all parts of the Islamic world. He was born and raised in Persia, but in his preachings he was transported to India (1869) where he was first exposed to Western ideas and ways. Next he journeyed to Istanbul (1870) to address students, but was compelled to leave (1871) by the *Shaykh al-Islām* (Chief Spokesman of Islam) who had official status in the Ottoman Empire. He entered Egypt but was expelled (1879) by the Khedive because of his agitations against British involvements in Egypt. He returned to India and from there journeyed to Paris where he founded and edited the nationalistic periodical *al-ʿUrwah al-Wuthqa* (the firm bond) designed to serve as the mouthpiece of a revitalized Islam. Later (1884) he was joined by ʿAbduh when he too was expelled from Egypt because of his ties with the Egyptian nationalists. Al-Afghāni returned to Persia (1889) to become prime minister where he rallied around him a core of revolutionaries and disciples. A year later (1890) he was arrested and taken to Turkey, but he managed to get away, this time traveling to London (1892). He returned again to Istanbul where he died in 1897.

The strong impact of al-Afghāni on the political destinies of the Islamic countries that felt the fiery eloquence of his nationalistic preachings was evident in the 1881 Egyptian show of force against the British in Egypt, the 1906 revolutionary movement in Persia, and the 1908 Young Turk revolt in Turkey.

The legacy of al-Afghāni as a reformer lies chiefly in his political preachings. He awakened the conscience of his audiences to the need of ideological and political unity in the Islamic world if it were to resist the political and ideological encroachments of the West. This he hoped to achieve through reforming Islam and making it a vital force for unity by adapting it to modern conditions. He advocated force and revolution if needed to bring about Islamic unity. There was no doubt in his mind that Islam had the capacity to make the necessary adjustments. He went so far as to envision a unity between Shīʿah and Sunnis. He was not able, however, to penetrate the conservative shield of the ʿulamāʾ to reach the mass of Muslims. His converts, as a consequence, derived mostly from the "efendi" class that thrived on the status quo and had no particular interest in seeing it overturned. The success of his preachings was contingent on purging the minds of the masses from foolish notions and superstitions, but the ʿulamāʾ were in his way. Al-Afghāni had confidence in Islam's capacity to survive the "purge" because Islam inspires freedom of religious belief, permitting everyone to reach perfection just short of prophecy. He shared with the modernists the view that reason can serve the ends of religion and that a revised program of education can serve to update the thinking of the ordinary Muslim and train his morals.

In his *Manār* Riḍa continued the trend fostered by al-Afghāni's *ʿUrwah* which aimed at promoting social and economic as well as religious reforms on the premise that Islam is suitable for modern life and exigences. The Sharīʿah was held to be sufficient for providing adequate precepts of government to Muslim rulers if encumbrances deemed un-Islamic could be eliminated. Riḍa also believed that tolerance among the various sects of Islam could be achieved. He too advocated the use in schools of common text material in order to insure uniformity of religious education.

The Salafīyah through the *Manār* called for the establishment of an Islamic society (*al-Jamʿīyah al-Islāmīyah*) to watch over reform. It was to have its headquarters at Mecca with branches in all Muslim countries and enjoy the patronage of the caliph.

The Salafīyah opposed secular nationalism in its radical extreme, the nationalism represented by Kemal Ataturk and his new Turkey, which strove consciously to break with its Islamic traditions. The brand of nationalism preached by Muṣṭafa Kāmil of Egypt and his *Liwāʾ* Party in 1908 was equally repugnant to them, for this group was no more interested in religious reform than Kemal of Turkey. The *Manār* on the other hand supported the Wahhābis of Arabia, as militantly traditionalistic as they were, because of their religious puritanism. The *Manār* attacked the Ṣūfis and bidʿa as much as the *ʿulamāʾ* who would substitute human for divine law. The *Manār* sought to simplify Islam by stripping it down to its pure tenets and practices as they were observed in the days of the Prophet and the first four caliphs. It proposed the reduction of the madhāhib to one and recommended flexible civil laws, provided they are based on the Qurʾān and the Sunnah. The Salafīyah like the modernists believed that Muslims should build schools not mosques. They were not satisfied with just preaching; they sponsored missionary activity among Muslims with the establishment of the *Jamʿīyat al-Daʿwa wa-'l-Irshād* (the Society for Propagation and Guidance).

The scope of the Salafīyah's work ranged into the political field where again the reformist ideas of Afghāni were more clearly continued. The aim, like Afghāni's, was to evoke a Muslim nationalism that would infuse the Muslim world with sufficient dynamism to withstand, then turn back the colonial assaults of the Western world. Socially, they probed for norms from the folds of Islam that would make available to the devout Muslim the niceties of modern life without jeopardizing the religious requirements of Islamic society.

The intellectual fermentation engendered by the modernists and Salafīyah has had a lasting and far-reaching effect not only on religion but also on the genre of Arabic literature in the twentieth century. The range and nature of this influence lies beyond our present study. But it may be noted that much of the literature typified by the Egyptian school of Ṭaha Ḥusayn, Tawfīq al-

Ḥakīm, Maḥmud ʿAbbās al-ʿAqqād, Aḥmad Amīn, and others has been influenced either by the secular modernists or the Salafīyah. The theme and content of their writings often reflect the conviction that modernism is not incompatible with their religion.

The Indian Reformist Movement

The challenge of modern ideas to Islam did not elicit a consistent pattern of response. The reaction of the Egyptian thinkers spearheaded by the *Manār* followers is but one of several. Another school of modernizers is the Indo-Pakistani, which is less traditionalistic than the Syro-Egyptian. Like the Arab modernizers they believed Islam could be subjected to rationalism without jeopardy to the authority of the Qurʾān and the *Ḥadīth.* They were to test, however, the validity of traditions which had been accumulated over a protracted period of time outside the requirements of the Qurʾān and *Ḥadīth.* Such accretions, it was believed, tended to load the faith with a body of spurious dogmas and injunctions that contributed little to the enhancement of Islam but prevented it rather from adjusting to the demands of modern life.

In India, and later in Pakistan when the split took place in 1947, enlightened Muslim thinkers led by Sir Sayyid Aḥmad Khān (d. 1898) actively labored to accommodate what was suitable of Western knowledge to their conception of a modernized Islam. Perceiving the role of modern education in the accomplishment of their goal, they founded a system of higher education, today known as ʿAligarh Muslim University. The system introduced Western knowledge into the curriculum on the assumption that Islam is in conformity with science and similar studies.

The social ramifications of a modern approach to the study of man in present-day society were noticeable when educated Muslims began to question some of the social practices rooted in the religious tradition, such as plural marriages, "easy divorces," and slavery. With a new bold and critical view towards the increments of the past in the face of strong opposition from the *ʿulamāʾ*, these modernists challenged not only their inherited way of life but also the authority on which it rested, which meant the body of religious practices passed on from generation to generation with all its un-Islamic features.

The trend set by Sayyid Aḥmad was continued by another Indian, a Shīʿite Muslim by the name of Sayyid Amīr ʿAli, whose noted work *The Spirit of Islam*[2] embodies his eloquent testimony concerning the powers of Islam to adjust to modern life. Like other reformers he advocated return to the simple unadulterated texts of the Qurʾān and the verified sayings of the Prophet. He condemned on the authority of the Qurʾān what came to be regarded as evil practices: polygamy, divorce, purdah, and the like. In his judgment Islam can eliminate the blight into which it had fallen by breaking the stranglehold of the past and by reopening the gate of ijtihād, or independent judgment, and vesting it in the ʿulamāʾ.

Amīr ʿAli went much further in his radical departure from the past by declaring openly that the Qurʾān was the work of the Prophet Muḥammad. In the view of a modern writer, this position is defensible "because the doctrine that the Qurʾān is 'uncreated,' i.e., literally the word of God, was not finally established until the third century of the *hijra*."[3]

The Indo-Pakistani School leaned towards apologetics. Apparently it was more concerned with a defense of Islam than with outlining a feasible program of reform. The Persian poet-philosopher Sir Muḥammad Iqbāl (d. 1938) belonged to this school. Like other Eastern intellectuals he had studied in the West, in England and Germany. He took up law, as did Mahatma Gandhi, to acquire financial self-sufficiency in order to pursue his intellectual interests unencumbered by the need to gain. While his poetry in Persian and Urdu is widely read by scores of dedicated followers who have all but immortalized his name in Pakistan, it is in his English writings that we must search for his views on the revitalization of Islam.

In 1928 Iqbāl delivered a series of lectures, entitled *Six Lectures on the Reconstruction of Religious Thought in Islam*.[4] "These present the first . . . thoroughgoing attempt to restate the theology of Islam in modern immantist terms."[5] Like other Muslim modernists, he called on his followers to adopt the principles of vitalization that made Western societies strong and allowed them to leave the once dominant Islamic world far in its trail. Modern science to him was a chief reason. He stressed rather strongly the compatibility of science with Islam. "The knowledge of Nature," he argued, "is the knowledge of God's behavior. In our observation of Nature we are virtually seeking a kind of intimacy with the Absolute Ego; and this is only another form of Worship." [6]

Iqbāl was also deeply inclined to Ṣūfism; perhaps he was enmeshed in what the orthodox *ʿulamāʾ* would construe as a "hopeless tangle of thought." Evidence of this "hopeless tangle" is often betrayed in his writings, which may help explain the rather elusive character of his views.

The writings of Iqbāl provide an index to diverse currents in the religious, social, and political thinking of Indian Muslims, as each and all could find a source of reliance, if not succor, in his expressed poetic and philosophical views. He approached the problems confronting Islam on such a high plane of philosophical interpretation that the speculator, political agitator, or a young Muslim inclined to Marxism can find what he seeks of comfort in Iqbāl's works.

Iqbāl's approach to Islam rested on the belief that its tenets and sacred texts must be rethought and reinterpreted allegorically. He began from the premise that the Muslims possessed the free will to reinterpret. Such doctrines as pertain, for instance, to immortality have both ethical and biological bases. Hence the Islamic conceptions of heaven and hell may be treated as reflections of a state of mind.

He resorts to Qurʾānic revelations in order to prove that humans possess the freedom to interpret in a creative sense. The Fall of Adam "is an allegorical reflection of man's rise from a primitive state of instructive appetite to the conscious possession of a free self capable of doubt and disobedience," also "the emergence of a finite ego which has the power to choose." He condemns the traditional conception of fatalism as morally degrading, an "invention of men with little grasp of philosophical truth" who have perpetuated it out of self-interest.

The basic supposition of Iqbāl, like those of the Muslim modernists of Egypt and Syria, is that religious reforms can be achieved without the need to sever connections with the social institutions of Islam, in contrast to the strong advocates of a thoroughgoing secularism like the Kemalist Turks who set themselves to the task of achieving it. Again the compelling factor was the need for preserving Islamic solidarity as a counterpoise to the aggressive intents of a materially superior West.

In this regard, reformers concede that the initiative for change must rest with the religious element of Islam. Iqbāl undertakes to project interpretations that could easily be branded heretical by the pious without providing his disciples with concrete methods to achieve the needed transformation. On specifics he is precise, but on fundamentals he withdraws to the comforts of the Ṣūfi realm of retreat.

Radical Departures

The fermentation of thought resulting from probings for a reform of Islam has resulted sometimes in a radical departure from the basic Islamic norm, and has given rise to splinter movements that can be scarcely termed Islamic. Yet they have quoted the Qurʾān to justify their existence; and they have also taken the initiative to reconstitute Islam in a manner suitable for their treatment of the Qurʾān and *Ḥadīth* to provide, as they were convinced it would, the cornerstone of Islam's "modernization."

The problem lies in the fact that these popular movements tended towards the realization more of political and social than religious reforms. Indeed, they are not altogether devoid of nationalist sentiments, the preachings of al-Afghāni being a case in point.

The secular trend has not served to cement the bonds uniting Muslims because it has encouraged *ethnic nationalism* rather than *communal universalism* among them. The architects of modern Turkey, nominal Muslims that they are, may well have attempted to uproot the concept of universalism altogether from the social life of the nation, had they not encountered resistance from the Turkish folk.

Another radical departure is the policy of modern secular leaders in predominantly Muslim countries ranging from Egypt to

Pakistan to Indonesia, a policy which uses the principle of communalism in Islam as a political weapon against imperial encroachments on their lands, as it was used decades ago to confront the physical occupation of their countries and the presence of foreign troops on their soil. Until very recent times, even after independence was gained, young Muslim nationalists, however minimal a role religion played in their personal lives, have not hesitated to marshal the forces of Islam to combat "the foreigner" and show that they will not be influenced by decisions contrary to their likings or political ambitions. These nationalists have been operating on the premise that they can answer the West by brandishing against it the sword of Islam in a modern form of *jihād* when secular measures fail. This type of solidarity, known half a century ago as "Pan-Islamism," has lost much of its luster and was never an effective weapon, as the recent history of Muslim countries attests, because of the predominance of secular nationalism whenever confrontation of the two took place. Religious solidarity had been weakened; how could it sustain the political arm of Islam? Until religious solidarity is reestablished with reform, all other facets of Islam are likely to suffer.

The Trend Towards Eclecticism

Numerous societies, movements, and ideologies bearing the stamp of modernism have sprung into being during the past century in response to a variety of urges emanating from Islam. Most of these, like *al-Ikhwān al-Muslimūn* (The Muslim Brethren), have had more of a socio-political than a religious orientation and therefore do not concern us in this study. What is relevant can be deduced from a brief account of certain movements that have responded to the call for a modern approach, namely, the Aḥmadīyah of India and the Bābi with its offshoot the Bahā'i of Perisa. The former has attempted to preserve an Islamic identity, while the latter has shown every evidence of losing a distinguishing Islamic character. Both sprung from Islam, yet both have chosen the course of eclecticism and syncreticism in their beliefs and preachings to the point of risking their Islamism for heresy in the eyes of their orthodox coreligionists.

The Aḥmadīyah

The Aḥmadīyah movement was founded by one Mirza Ghulām Aḥmad Qādiyāni (d. 1908) who launched his career with the proclamation that he was divinely charged with the mission to reinterpret Islam in the light of the requirements of the modern age. He moved cautiously and in his doctrinal pronouncements he deviated but little from the posture of the moderate orthodox reformers.

As his followers grew in numbers and his pretensions grew commensurately, he proclaimed himself the "Promised Messiah of the Christians," a prophet and the "Mahdi of Islam," as well as the "return of the Krishna for the Hindus." He was soon branded a "heretic." When his first successor (***khalīfah***) died in 1914, the followers, now dubbed Aḥmadīyah after the founder, split into two groups. The majority elected Aḥmad's son Maḥmūd as their ***khalīfah***; but a minority bolted and withdrew to Lahore, now in Pakistan. The majority, or Qādiyāni, stood by the founder's claim to prophethood and continued to recognize Maḥmūd as the *khalīfah;* the minority, or seceders, discarded both and organized themselves into a "society for the propagation of Islam" with a new leader. They then endeavored to become reconciled with orthodox or Sunni Islam, but the *ʿulamāʾ* have been reluctant to accept them.

Both branches of the Aḥmadīyah launched extensive missionary activities with sub-Sahara Africa becoming the chief target of their syncretistic preachings. Here, as in the East Indies, they ran into considerable rivalry from Christian missions operating in the same areas; yet their ranks were steadily swelled by African converts until they number today over a million followers. Their missionary activities have extended even into England and America.

Over seventy years old now, the movement does not seem to suffer from its preachings on the fringe of orthodox doctrine. In many instances converts gained to Islam through Aḥmadīyah efforts often are won over to the Sunni doctrine through the subtleties of the orthodox fathers using the Azhar as a lure. Every year several thousand African students are enrolled in the theological and related programs offered by the Azhar. They return to their homelands more deeply imbued with the Sunni doctrines of Islam.

From the point of view of doctrinal interpretation the Aḥmadis depart slightly from the basic orthodox position. What is significant in their interpretation is the notion that prophecy did not end with Muḥammad, hence their justification for Ghulām's role; also their conviction that the Qur'ān is open to "inexhaustible meanings"; and as "each succeeding age discovers fresh properties and new virtues, the same is the case with the Word of God, so that there may be no disparity between God's Work and His Word." [7]

The Aḥmadis are convinced of the Qur'ān's superiority over other non-Muslim sacred texts, which accounts for their zeal to spread it. When the alleged superiority of the Qur'ān is coupled with a non-doctrinaire attitude towards the role of Muḥammad as not having ended, the Aḥmadi arms himself with the motivation to expound his version of Islam's function in the modern age. As long as he does not defile the honor of the Prophet, the Qur'ān, and himself in his preachings, he is at liberty to interpret the tenets of his faith to meet the challenge of any given situation. His belief in continued revelation from God tends to strengthen the Aḥmadi conceptions of Qur'ānic text. His strong mystical orientation abets such an understanding; "the deeper truths of the Qur'ān are the result of divine assistance; the light of the reason unaided by God is too dim to bring those truths into view." [8]

The Aḥmadīyah claim to modernism lies principally in a liberal interpretation of the Qur'ān, which is translated and disseminated as part of their zeal to spread Islam, in their increasing reliance on reason, and in their willingness to accept modern science. The secret of their success is their willingness to adapt to any given need, even to the point of inconsistency, to gain credence for their doctrine.

At first, "reason" was suspect; Ghulām Aḥmad did not believe that Islam should be championed through rationalism, but rather through the authentication made possible by revelation and divine assistance. The Egyptian reformer Muḥammad ʿAbduh on the other hand advocated the "precedence of reason over the literal meaning of the Divine Law in case of conflict between them." [9] Later on, when Aḥmadi missionaries were confronted by Christian rivals in search of converts, they did not hesitate to resort to reason, arguing that "objections raised against Islam are due either to a lack of serious reflection or because passion is allowed to prevail over reason." [10]

The Aḥmadi stand on science countenances the important premise that Islam encourages the study and use of science, as proven historically when Muslims in medieval times made basic contributions to the sciences. If the spirit or text of the Qur᾿ān is used as a measure, there can be no contradiction; indeed, science is more incompatible with Christianity, it is argued, than it is with Islam.

Similarly the Aḥmadis find Ṣūfism perfectly Islamic on the grounds that "the leaders of thought among them [the Ṣūfis], never diverged a hair's breadth from the path chalked out for them by Islam." Furthermore "they have been the true expounders of Islam, and during the decline of the Muslims it is they who held aloft the beacons of true Islamism." In continuing their defense of the Ṣūfis the Aḥmadis argued that "There was never any question of their departing from the Holy Qurān [*sic*] or the traditions of the Holy Prophet." What the orthodox termed as "Ṣūfi aberrations" the Aḥmadis defended by denial, holding that the Ṣūfis "put down all those beliefs or practices that savoured of asceticism, monasticism or esotericism as un-Islamic [*sic*] and wholly foreign to their own convictions." [11]

Bābism and Bahā᾿ism

Bābism originated not from Sunnism but from Shīʿism. Like the Aḥmadīyah, this earlier movement was also eclectic. In the earlier centuries we witnessed the rise of equally eclectic and syncretistic movements: the Nuṣayri, Druze, Yazīdi, a number of Shīʿah sects, then later, in the Turkish period of ascendancy, of the Bektāshi order.

The founder of the Bābi sect is Sayyid ʿAli Muḥammad of

Shīrāz who had been an adherent of the Shaykhi school of philosophical thought among the Shīʿahs. The sect's name derived from the symbolic name "Bāb" (gateway) by which Sayyid ʿAli called himself in reference to the "gateway" through which divine truth is said to be revealed unto the believers. It was on May 23, 1844 that Sayyid ʿAli, "moved by the Spirit of God," officially proclaimed his mission to the Persians, in the city of Shīrāz where there had gathered together "eighteen spiritually prepared souls, men of religious wisdom to whom it had been given to understand divine realities." [12]

The core of Bābi teachings lies in Sayyid ʿAli's belief that he had been divinely commissioned to warn his listeners of the coming of the "great promised One," "Him-whom-God-shall-manifest,"—the "Latter-Day Revelator," "The Lord of Hosts" promised in the revealed sacred writings of the past, who would establish soon the Kingdom of God on earth.

The Bāb preached a peculiar mixture of liberal religious doctrine reinforced by a heavy dose of Gnosticism which actually yielded little success. His followers were few and scattered throughout Persia. Persian officials, not to mention the Shīʿah fathers, did not take too kindly to Sayyid ʿAli's personal and doctrinal claims. By inciting his listeners the Bāb compelled Persian authorities to arrest him and, following an uprising of his followers, to execute him as a common criminal in 1850.

But the movement established by the Bāb did not die out as the Persian authorities had hoped. It merely changed form and proceeded to grow and spread, mostly outside Persia. Instrumental in the further spread of the beliefs established by Sayyid ʿAli was a disciple, Bahāʾullāh (d. 1892) who had taken charge of the majority of the Bābis following the split that ensued upon the death of the founder.

Bahāʾullāh continued to elaborate on the doctrine of the Bāb in such radical terms that he and his successors managed to draw it outside the religious fold of Islam. Since then the original doctrine based on Islam has taken on the trappings of a universal religion resting on two sustaining principles: *pacifism* and *humanitarianism.*

The movement was driven out of Persia largely because of the intense persecution to which its adherents were subjected. Bahā'ullāh himself spent four months in a prison in Tehran. Scores of Bābis were turned over by Persian officials to the orthodox Shī'i fathers to be tortured and slain for their heresy. Bahā'ullāh was exiled to Baghdad, then under Ottoman rule, in the hope of discouraging his followers and confining Bābi preachings to limited circles. But he continued his preachings in Baghdad and in the fury of ensuing orthodox reaction he sought refuge in the mountain fastness of Kurdistan. Next he was exiled to Istanbul, thence under military surveillance to Edirne where he lived and preached for five years. These setbacks notwithstanding, his small group of followers continued to see in Bahā'ullāh "Him-whom-God-shall-manifest."

Trouble still followed him wherever he went because of the anger of the Sunni Muslims, who were provoked by his radical preachings. Finally in the summer of 1863 he was led to the fortress prison of Acre on the Mediterranean coast together with about seventy men, women, and children who constituted his following at that time. Privation and suffering accompanied him and his followers until his death. A shrine was later erected over his burial place on Mt. Carmel near Haifa. Today it serves as a place of worship and prayer, visited annually by those who call themselves "Bahā'is."

His missionary activities were continued by his son 'Abd-al-Bahā' who styled himself "The Center of the Covenant." He carried Bahā'i teachings first into Egypt, then into Europe, and later to America where he resided for eight months in 1912. While in America 'Abd-al-Bahā' traveled extensively from coast to coast and delivered addresses to various churches, synagogues, university and civic organizations. During the period of World War I he confined his efforts to humanitarian activities in Palestine and was knighted after the war by the British Crown for these services. When he died in 1921, he was entombed next to the Bāb in the Bahā'i shrine on Mt. Carmel.

The core of Bahā'i teaching lies in the collective writings of the founder, the Bāb, known as *The Bayān* (Expositor) with its stress on awaiting "Him-whom-God-shall-manifest." In the period of "awaiting," the devotees are exhorted to prepare themselves spiritually for meeting Bahā'ullāh. What is significant about Bahā'ullāh's teachings is their source: Torah, Bible, Qur'ān, which makes the movement highly eclectic and imparts to it the basis for a universalistic appeal.

Bahā'ism utilizes a sophisticated approach founded on the premise that man can not achieve a higher spiritual status if he does not perfect the powers latent in his body and soul; training the body, it is said, provides man the organism to manifest his spiritual side. Education, according to the "world teacher" (Bahā'ullāh), plays an important role in summoning all of mankind to one spiritual world-consciousness.

The Bahā'i view is that Muḥammad arose at a time when people in Arabia were submerged in ignorance and superstition, and that he changed the situation by calling to the worship of one God and inculcating his followers with high moral standards through a code of laws and ordinances suitable to the spiritual and material needs of his day. The Muslim "church," however, soon departed from the real spirit of Muḥammad's teachings. But Muḥammad had taken the precaution of preparing his people for the "great latter-day Bahā'i revelation," as witnessed in the Ḥadīth. The time of the spiritual awakening, equated with resurrection, was to be accompanied by signs mentioned also in the Bible, that is when religious faith has decayed and general demoralization set in.

So the early converts to Bahā'ism accepted the new calling with the understanding that the Bāb is the promised Mahdi and Bahā'ullāh the Christ (spirit), as both seem faithfully to have met the prophesied condition and time of appearance.

The Bahā'i Revelation is held to confirm also the Hindu truth of religion as well as the Buddhist expectation of "Maitreya," i.e., "He-whose-name-is-Kindness," or Bahā'ullāh. Thus he becomes to the Buddhists the return of their promised Buddha. The Zoroastrians had looked upon fire as the great cleanser; the Bahā'is say this really signifies spiritual purity, "for it is through the spiritual fire of the love of God that men's souls are purified and quickened into eternal life." The Zoroastrians also have similar ideas concerning the resurrection or spiritual judgment. The end of the Zoroastrian dispensation, as foretold in their sacred writings, is contingent also on the prevalence of spiritual impurity which would necessitate another "Manifestation" to bring the divine fire of purification, or love of God, back to earth. Their latter-day prophet, "Shah Bahram," is again the bearer of the Bahā'i Revelation, which accounts for the Zoroastrians of India and Persia—known today as Parsees—accepting the message of Bahā'ullāh. This is indeed an attempt at the broadest possible symbiosis, with Bahā'i Revelation being equated with the long-awaited one of Muslims, Christians, Buddhists, Hindus, and Zoroastrians.

The Bahā'is evolved a liberal cult conforming to the essential ingredients of other faiths—temple worship, fasting, prayer, good deeds to supplement creed and dogma, separation of state and church, and the unification of mankind through common institutions acceptable to all, such as what Bahā'ullāh represents, based not on separation of church and state but on the union of religion and state.

The Bahā'i modernist outlook stems from the conception that peace is desirable and can be achieved in the federation of all small and large nations and the establishment of a universal governing body supervised by one system of adjudication. Bahā'ism teaches co-operation in all affairs, between capital and labor, East and West. Co-operation materially and spiritually will make of various peoples one harmonious world-family.

There is no conflict between the divine and the natural; there exists rather, it is stated, scientific harmony between the two and perfect accord throughout the whole of creation. Indeed, natural science in the view of the Bahā'is "teaches man how to live properly upon a human plane." Man can discover and utilize the laws of nature; but the laws of God are revealed unto man only through His mediators: Christ, Muḥammad, the other prophets, and Bahā'ullāh.

The near-avid interest in modern thinking by the Bahā'is bespeaks their respect for it as an aid to religious fulfillment. "This general and widespread spirit of modern thought," they argue, "has been as a plough which has prepared the religious ground of the world to receive the spiritual seeds of universal religious ideals."[13] Bahā'is regard themselves as being in perfect harmony with modern trends on the grounds that "the modernists of all religions are teaching many of the same principles as held by the followers of the Bahā'i Cause."[14] Conflicts in the past between science and theology are attributed to "imaginations and superstitions" which religions had accumulated over the centuries to make them unacceptable to science. Since these are held to be outside the realm of the actual teachings of the great prophets like Jesus and Muḥammad, dispensing with such unhealthy accretions in no way compromises the basic teachings of these religions. And by eliminating them there would remain no area of conflict between theology and science.

What makes the Bahā'is modernists in their outlook is the conviction that their doctrine and teachings are free from the superstitions of the past and are compatible with modern science.

The Role of Extra-Sharīʿah Legislation

Such radical movements typified by the Aḥmadīyah and Bahā'īyah are symptomatic of the impact of modern thinking on traditional beliefs and organizational concepts in Islam. The trend towards creeping change and readjustment may not be fully delineated as of the moment; but there is no denying that the motions already in process tend clearly in that direction, and not even the *Sharīʿah* will be spared further scrutiny.

Revisions of the *Sharīʿah* started tangentially with a variety of Ottoman decrees in the nineteenth century and more directly with the secular laws enacted by Muslim leaders in the twentieth. There are definite attempts in the Arab countries today, excluding perhaps Saudi Arabia, consciously to adapt *Sharīʿah* legislation to the needs of modern life and to a more liberal conception of human views. The resulting reforms betray careful thinking, stemming from the search and utilization of precedents in the *Sharīʿah* that are best suited for the realization of such reforms without encroaching on the spirit and intrinsic philosophy underlying it. There is no outright innovation, but the trend towards an eclectic system of legislating for modern needs within the more broadly interpreted tenets of the canon law is clearly in evidence.

Muslim heads of state and legislators today may seem to be resorting to a form of *ijtihād*, justified by the argument that it is their prerogative to override a traditional canonical principle if the interests of the modern public demand it. Invariably they resort to the argument that they are not innovating outrightly but simply choosing from the opinions of accepted, albeit rival, jurists. They have circumvented *Ijmāʿ* with the argument that it can not be established how encompassing public consensus really was when resorted to in the past. They have also drawn a line between the *compulsive* and *permissive* nature of canonical decrees on the grounds that by exploiting the permissiveness of a decree they are committing an act of conscience which they are willing to risk should they be called upon to account for it on the Day of Judgment. One of their stronger arguments, however, is that a divine ordinance can not be binding for all time when the condition and circumstance of its promulgation have changed.

What has encouraged the trend towards extra-*Sharīah* legislation in recent times is the insistence of the innovators that even in the earlier centuries caliphs and local rulers did not hesitate to make use of customary law (*ʿādāt*) and set aside the *Sharīʿah* where specific issues not fully treated therein were involved; these related often to the areas of commerce and crime.

In the nineteenth century under the political impact of the West, the Ottoman Porte began to give in to demands for formal legislation outside the purview of *Sharīʿah* specification. A good example is the introduction in the early 1800's of commercial and penal codes reflecting Western prototypes; a civil code along the lines established by the Code Napoleon was promulgated in Egypt in the 1870's.

At the turn of the century, also in Egypt, secular courts besides those decreed by the *Sharīʿah* were established; and in more recent times these courts have nearly taken over adjudication of issues formally reserved to the *Shar īah* courts, namely those related to personal matters and family affairs. Even courts of appeal, unheard of in the earlier Islamic periods ruled by the *Sharīʿah*, have been introduced. New court procedures designed to bypass the *Sharīʿah* have operated side by side of the traditional with the aim of eventually supplanting the latter altogether.

Modern legislation has even invaded the privacy of family relationships which formally were understood to belong strictly to the domain of the *Sharīʿah*. The Law of Family Rights, promulgated by the Ottomans in 1917, is largely in force still in the Lebanon; while in Syria and Jordan it has been replaced by even more progressive codes.

The trend in Arab countries is towards more and more secular codes which are designed at first to operate alongside the Sharʿī with all the attending overlap, unavoidable in many areas, and to enjoy equal validity with them until they can replace them. The choice of court for purposes of litigation is left up to the citizens to make. Often the aim of secular enactments is the amelioration of *Sharīah* decrees, particularly in the areas of family affairs and women's rights, granting them more privileges than previously they enjoyed.

Laws passed in recent years in most Arab countries have raised the marriage age to eighteen for a boy, seventeen for a girl; in earlier times child marriages had been very common. Marriage contracts specify often the terms which the wife can dictate beforehand and have enforced afterwards. In Iraq such innovations have been slower to come, owing to Shīʿah-Sunni differences over such matters. In Saudi Arabia the *Sharʿīah* remain almost unchallenged.

The same type of mitigation is evidenced also in testamentary bequests; the aim is to broaden the base so as to enable the testator to bequeath property to other than legitimate heirs.

Mortmain (*waqf*) was hitherto under strictly *Sharīʿah* procedures. The system was highly abused; land set aside for philanthropic purposes was often taken out of cultivation and in recent times converted to private use. What was to be a pious benefaction had become a private benefaction. Reform of the waqf system started with Muḥammad ʿAli in Egypt when in the opening decades of the nineteenth century he confiscated all of the land. The system survived separately until 1924 when the Ministry of Waqfs was placed under parliamentary control. There were further modifications in 1946 which permitted Sharīʿah courts to pass on all proposed waqfs; but with the 1952 revolution private waqf was abolished altogether. Syria in 1949 prohibited the creation of family waqfs and sought to liquidate those in existence. The Lebanon in recent decades followed suit.

Such are samples of the type of change that has been stimulated by increasing contacts with the West. Self criticism among the educated is becoming rapidly more evident in Muslim lands. This new generation, educated for the most part in Western institutions and sciences, is convinced of the necessity of adaptation to modern needs. A good number of them are prepared to push through the barriers to social readjustment erected by traditional Sharʿīah decrees, not all of which can be shown to enjoy the full sanctity of Qurʾānic injunctions. The power of the *ʿulamāʾ* and mullas is on the wane.

The organization al-Ikhwān al-Muslimūn came into being in 1928 for the express aim of applying the tenets of Islam in a purer context to the needs of a modern industrial Muslim society. To them and other like-minded Muslims it was the means towards erecting a modern traditionally oriented society. Nearly wiped out of Egypt in 1954-55 and suffering definite setbacks since then elsewhere, this type of a lay religious attempt at a revival of traditional religious zeal with a strong nationalistic spirit apparently can not meet the challenges confronting the modern Muslim state. The Ikhwān's opposition to purely secular governments on the grounds that Western-style democratic institutions are irreconcilable with Islam has found little popular appeal. The organization's belief that only by reviving the theocracy can Islam progress attracted much less attention. Their zealous "Calvinistic spirit" proved to be their undoing.

The route to salvation lies in a gradual reinterpretation of Islam with greater recourse to the spirit rather than the letter of the earliest Islamic canonical decrees, and above all the Qurʾān. In the heyday of its accomplishments Islam demonstrated a remarkable capacity to absorb a variety of seemingly incompatible philosophies and contradictory religious conceptions. The same spirit of liberalism motivating Islam then can, and probably will, be revived again. The trends are clearly in that direction. The liberal forces which had given direction to Islam in its glorious past can serve the same ends again, as they appear to possess still some of that moving power. The two forces, one making for "puritanism" and the other for "innovation" have always been present. What is needed is that the catholic tendency in Islam that permitted the need of reinterpretation when called for in the past assert itself again in the present, and that it tolerate the interplay of non-orthodox views if the great compromises that previously yielded such principles of legislation as *Ijmāʿ* and *Qiyās* are to materialize once more.

CHAPTER 12

Resilience and Dynamism

MEDIEVAL ARRESTATIONS and sporadic attempts at revitalization notwithstanding, Islam's capacity for survival and expansion in the face of strong detractions appears to have gone on unencumbered. This may be attributed to the resilience and dynamism latent in the religion and readily activated when warranted. The same forces of attraction that gained a large following for Islam in the first century continued to attract even when the polity ceased to function as an adjunct of religion. Nearly one half of those who regard themselves as Muslims today came into the faith from among peoples who had never been subjected to the political domination of Islam, and at times when the luster of Islam's imperial power had long ceased to shine.

Neither the sword nor the work of an ecclesiastical order can account for Islam's continuous gains in new following. The phenomenon of growth, therefore, must be attributed in the last analysis to its powers of appeal and ability to meet the spiritual and material needs of peoples adhering to cultures totally alien to the founders, the desert Arabians, but at a level of religious and socio-political development familiar to them at the time of their conversion. Continued growth can be explained also in terms of Islam's willingness to tolerate views and practices stemming from alien cultural norms brought into Islam by the converts which a more rigid system of religion would not countenance. Flexibility at this, the crucial stage, of conversion is an important factor contributing to Islam's success. What would ordinarily be deemed heretical at the instance of conversion inevitably drifts or is lured towards orthodoxy. The spread of Islam into Southeast Asia and sub-Saharan Africa presents a vivid example of its dynamism while its ability to survive in areas dominated by Communism is a testimony to its remarkable resilience.

Resilience in Asia

One of the earliest examples of mass conversion was that of the Bulgar Khan along the Volga around 900 which resulted in the Islamization of the region known later as Kazan. The emigration of Turkic peoples into Islamic lands following the conquest of Central Asia by the Arabs in the early eighth century had resulted in their mass conversion to Islam. The conversion of native inhabitants in Java, Sumatra, the Celebes, Burma, Malaya, Thailand, Indo-China, China, and the Philippines was the product largely of persuasion, the work of Arab mariners and merchants from the twelfth to the sixteenth centuries. Much of the success resulted usually from the initial conversion of a local reigning prince who was followed into the faith by his subjects. In most instances such conversions were the result of individual initiative and not of any large-scale deliberate missionary activities as pursued by various Christian missionary societies, often competing in the same areas. Success is also the result of lack of immediate insistence on the full Islamization of the convert.

In Indonesia, for instance, Islam was blended with a mixture of animistic and pantheistic concepts of very old vintage. There is no full-fledged rule of Qur'ān, *fiqh*, and Muslim traditions in Indonesian societies even though the influence of Islam has penetrated every facet of life and cultural norm. This is evident in Indonesian laws, rules of conduct, ethical conceptions, and esthetic ideals which Islam permeated to the extent that it has furnished these societies with an important base for political and social action in the development of the country.[1]

The interplay of Islam with indigenous customs and norms resulted in a curious cultural dichotomy; and while their observation of cultic rites may not be entirely orthodox, the faithfulness of carrying out religious obligation attests to the power of Islam's grip over the lives of Indonesians. In view of the heterogeneity of Indonesian cultural and social structures, Islam to the Indonesian becomes a unifying and durable cultural ideal, the realization of which gives him social status and prestige. It is the element of prestige associated with adherence to Islam, here as elsewhere in Africa and America, which accounts for its successes in Indonesia.

Islam reached Malaya even earlier, in the eighth century, again largely through the efforts of Arab traders. The process of Islamization there pursued the same pattern as in Indonesia, and in many of its traits it betrays strong resemblances to it, particularly in the importance attached by Malayan Muslims to the pilgrimage to Mecca.

The Muslims constitute a 55 per cent majority in the Federation as a whole, but in the important city of Singapore they form only 12 per cent of the total, a distinct minority to the Chinese there.

In Thailand the Muslims number about 600,000. In their cultural and religious adaptation to Islam, the Thais betray strong Malaysian influences. The same influences have also penetrated about 100,000 Cambodians, established mostly on the coast and at river entries.

In Vietnam there are but some 5,000 Muslims concentrated mostly in the coastal zone south of Nha Trang. Their cultic practices are in sharp contrast with those of their Hindu neighbors. Because of their protracted isolation from the mainstream of Islam, their conception of Islamic theology is tenuous; their religious spokesmen, for instance, ignore Arabic, language of the Qur'ān, and read the sacred book without comprehending the text. Their vision of Allah and Muḥammad in the scheme of their faith is blurred. They invoke ʿAli, whom they consider the "Son of God," in their prayers.

Their very incomplete knowledge of Islam is partly the result of little indoctrination and the syncretistic and pantheistic influences of the religious climate in the Far East. This syncretistic evidence can be seen, for example, in their mosques which are less Islamic and more Oriental; the miḥrāb of the mosques bears such Oriental imprints as dragons, flowers, bamboo shoots, and similar Chinese designs. Ramaḍān is observed for three days, and only by their religious spokesmen. The break of the fast follows a banquet served in the mosque itself; the food is usually prepared and offered by Cham Hindus of neighboring villages with whom they maintain good relations.

The nearly one million Muslims of the Philippines again are the product of Malayan influence; indeed, they are in part Malayan and in part Tagal, Islamized towards the end of the fourteenth century by a preacher from the Malayan peninsula at the time when the Tagal were engaged in a strong war of resistance with Spanish invaders. Most of the Muslims, less than 20 per cent of the population, are concentrated in Mindanao and the Soulou archipelago. Their faith has been sustained since 1932 in a sort of jihād against their neighbors, starting with the Houkbalahop rebellion which affected them very slightly.

The fate of Islam here as in other regions of Southeast Asia is very much linked to the national struggles engulfing these lands in recent times. Muslims in these countries are above all nationalists like the rest of their agitated counterparts; further gains for Islam here are contingent on the same powers of persuasion and appeal to indigenous culture groups as Islam manifested in the early stages of its development. They are also dependent on how strong a challenge a foreign ideology like Communism is capable of mounting, as is evident in China and the Soviet Union where the Muslims are much more numerous.

Survival in China

According to available statistics Muslims in China number between 10 and 25 million. They provide us with an example of Islam's capactiy to survive in the face of overwhelming odds favoring the destruction of all organized religion. Whether the resilience exhibited by Chinese Islam can hold up under the power of the totalitarian Communist monolith bent on its subversion and eventual elimination is a matter of conjecture.

To speak of continuing dynamism here would be to belabor the issue; but to deduce through a brief perusal of Islam's development in China the qualities that enabled it to withstand the organized powers of the Communist State should help us gain some appreciation of Islam's capacity for survival, a tribute to its powers of resilience.

Islam reached China at a very early date. When exactly, no one knows. Inhabitants of Northwest China had had long overland contact with ancient Arabia. Arab traders plied between Arabia and ports in south and southeast China. Some settled in Canton in the early period of the T'ang Dynasty.[2] Muslim Arab mercenaries had been employed by the T'ang to quell uprisings, and many stayed on in China.

The Yuan Dynasty gave official posts to foreigners in an effort to create a counterforce to the scholar-gentry class. There were many Muslims among them who served as governors of provinces, and in the central government. They held high positions also in areas of intellectual endeavor like literature, medicine, astronomy, and in the field of military affairs.

Up to the Ch'ing Dynasty (1644-1911) Chinese Muslims enjoyed a high degree of religious freedom even though the ideology of the state was Confucianism. Henceforth, however, they began to experience serious reverses; the Manchus were hostile, stirring up the Han Chinese against them. Repressive measures led to rebellions in Kansu Province, Yunnan, and the Northwest from the seventeenth to the nineteenth centuries.

The Nationalist government of the twentieth century followed a policy of minority assimilation, but it did not pursue an anti-religious campaign. Clashes complicated by U.S.S.R. involvements in Mongolia, Manchuria, and Sinkiang resulted from Nationalists' attempts to strengthen their control over these provinces. The war with Japan brought on a lenient policy towards minorities; and in February of 1939, upon the petition of the Chinese Islamic National Salvation Federation, the study of Islamic culture was formally inducted into the curriculum of Chinese universities.

The Chinese Muslims have clung to peculiarly Muslim customs: marriage, burial rites, the dietary laws, religious celebrations, circumcision, adoption of Qur'ānic names, and they have even maintained Muslim dress like turbans; they still use Arabic and Persian expressions, and they tend to prefer military to civil posts.

Communism finds in religion a repugnant competitor for loyalties. The Marxist-Leninists have argued that religion is a distorted and fallacious expression of natural sociological forces. Religious beliefs, attendant rites and organizations are not considered permanent institutions; they came into being in response to certain historical conditions and will vanish when they are removed. When people find themselves helpless in a class society where "exploitation" prevails, belief in miracles and the blissful life after death provides them with a consoling diversion. So if socialism can eliminate the material conditions favoring religion, religion itself will automatically disappear.

Yet how do we account for the constitutional guarantees, in the Soviet Union as well as in China, for religious freedom? The Communist party is convinced that with proper scientifically rationalized theories they can point out to the masses the fallacy of religious conceptions and allow religion thereby to die a slow natural death. The object is to avoid modern-style martyrdoms upon which organized religion had built in the past. With the elimination of class oppression and vestiges thereof, religion should disappear. So the Chinese Communist rulers have tacitly endorsed freedom of religious belief while actually seeking the negation of this freedom.[3]

The Communists have been discreet in their treatment of

Islam because of political considerations; but their attitude towards this and other similar religions is unequivocal. Islam to the Communists is a device to consolidate the "feudalistic divine right state" established by the Arabs in the first century and a half of its existence. Islam demands blind obedience, they say, and incites in its followers enmity towards other religions. Islam, it is further argued, has allowed itself to become the tool of imperialist nations, like Turkey, England, and France in the nineteenth century. Pan-Islamism endorsed in the past by the "Imperialists" is a reactionary philosophy.

The policies of the official government in power, first non-Communists then Communists, have not succeeded in daunting the spirit of the Chinese Muslims in recent times. These Muslims have had a solid territorial base in the northwest and have succeeded in the past in exercising considerable autonomous political influence. The Muslim uprisings here and in Yunnan Province during the nineteenth century reflect a strong spirit of independence which the Communists respect. The consensus is that the Muslims in China, under the guise of a nationality rather than a religious minority, have received better treatment than some other religious groups.

Tolerance of Islam has its international significance for the Chinese Communists who are in competition with the Russians to win over powerful Islamic states like Indonesia and the Arab countries. If they are not lenient at home, they could hardly expect support from their national's coreligionists where China entertains political ambitions in Southeast Asia, the Middle East, and Africa.

When the land was being communized, the Muslims were singled out for special treatment in the Agrarian Reform Law of 1953. Land owned by mosques and imāms was to be retained with the consent of the Muslim community residing there. Imāms were to have the right to engage in production of the land as a form of livelihood "if they have no other means of making a living and are able and willing to engage in agricultural work." [4]

While allowing Muslims certain freedoms, Communist authorities launched campaigns with the aid of Muslim cadres to de-

Islamize them. Respected well-trained Muslim cadres were used in order to give the appearance that the initiative for the "unification," then the "transformation" was a spontaneous movement. Such organizations as the China Islamic Association and the China Hui (Chinese Muslims) Cultural Association were formed to carry out the Communist plan for control of the religious, social, economic, and political activities of the Muslims, and of all other minority group activities. Not only are these organizations instruments of the Communists in "reeducating" the Muslims, but they also serve to further their foreign policy objectives. The China Islamic Association, for instance, played a determining role in securing diplomatic recognition for the Chinese Communist government from the United Arab Republic, Syria, and Yemen.

The Association has served its benefactor well by acting as an agency for contact with Muslims abroad, sponsoring cultural missions, and translating Communist writings into Arabic, particularly Mao Tse-Tung's works.[5]

The China Islamic Association, the Communist front organization, was to promote love of the fatherland, assist the People's Government to implement its religious policy, and take part in the campaign to safeguard world peace. Muḥammad and the Qur'ān are called in to further the cause; as the chairman of the Association proclaimed:

> Sage Mohammed once said to a Moslem: 'If you love your Fatherland fervently, it is just like being faithful to your religion. . . . For the sake of our Fatherland and for the sake of our religion we certainly will stand on the same battle front with peoples of all other races in the country fighting to protect the People's Fatherland.'[6]

The Qur'ān was to be treated in the same light as other literature enlisted in the service of Marxism: the parts that could be used would be taught, the rest would be ignored. If need be, the Communist Party and Government were ready to extend a benevolent hand and provide leadership to "patriotic" and "law-abiding" Muslims.[7]

The Chinese Communists have their own subtle ways "to nibble away" at the institutions of Islam. In 1952 they published a translation of the Qur'ān in Chinese in order to make it possible for the "ordinary Hui People . . . to deeply understand the Koran . . ." and "basing themselves on the religious teaching of the Koran, to unite, mutually help each other, promote culture, develop production and render service to the people." [8]

The Communists have adapted the substance of the Qur'ān to their own schemes, and particularly to verify the "truth" of Marxism. For example dialectical materialism asserts that the "state of being determines ideas" or that truth is discovered and verified only through practice. They claim to find justification for this point in the Qur'ānic text: ". . . Allah brought you forth from the wombs of your mothers knowing nothing . . ." [9] The underlying assumption here is that knowledge comes from the outside world, and that "correct knowledge and knowledge that agrees with subjective facts come from actual practice." [10] The point of justification is the Qur'ānic verse: "Most of them follow naught but conjecture. Assuredly conjecture can by no means take the place of truth." [11]

To promote labor, the Qur'ān is cited as not providing for rest periods before or after the hour of congregation on Friday. The Qur'ān, it is further argued, speaks negatively of individualism and egoism and enjoins unity and co-operation. It frowns on prejudicial views and identifies those who dissent with the idol-worshipers. The love preached by Islam is for all good people. "As to those who are hostile to the people, although they may be intimate friends and close relatives, we must sever all connections with them and bring them to censure and justice." [12] If Communism can be identified with Allah's will and the work of the authorities with the mission of Muḥammad, then the verse of the Qur'ān they cite can apply to their schemes:

> Thou wilt not find folk who believe in Allah and the Last Day loving those who oppose Allah and His messenger, even though they be their fathers or their sons or their brethren or their clan.[13]

Their aim is the peaceful reform of the Muslims by convincing them that what they believed in is wrong, the result of their misinterpretation of the Qur'ān.

The Muslim Classics Institute was established in 1955 by the Communist regime to train imāms who have the "exalted qualities of fervent love for their Fatherland and fervent love for Socialism and can handle well the Arabic language, understand the principles of the Moslem faith . . ." [14] It is not an ordinary cadre they seek but a well-indoctrinated religious leader whose position would make his new interpretations of Islam authoritative and acceptable to the Muslim masses.

There is a deliberate curtailing of religious instruction in Islamic middle and primary schools, and in certain of the larger cities there is no instruction at all. It is permitted only in mosques. There is a lot of indoctrination, on the other hand, in the area of materialism. In the mosques it is not unusual to see devout Muslims absorbed in the study of social structure theories, Communist principles of economics, and the doctrines of Mao Tse-Tung.[15] There are subtle attempts to break down the fasting rites, dietary laws, and other institutional observances of Islam.

But the Muslims have been resisting, sometimes by passive methods—where they are few in numbers—and often by violent methods—where they are numerically strong. Independent-minded Muslims like the Pingliang in Kansu and the Kazakhs in Sinkiang resent the state's efforts to "reform" them. In 1952 an agrarian reform was carried out in Pingliang, and land belonging to a mosque was confiscated. The Muslims revolted and the rebellion became widespread with the Communists being compelled to move troops in to quell it. There was destruction of communication lines; public granaries were ransacked, and a number of areas in Kansu came under the control of the rebels. The Communists decided to pacify them through a "comforting delegation" sent for that purpose. The Kazakhs of Sinkiang frequently defy the Communists and have rebelled against them on more than one occasion, and the Communists have been obliged to adopt tactics of pacification and appeasement towards them also.

Islam in the Soviet Union

The twenty to thirty million Muslims in the Soviet Union are concentrated principally in the southern republics. They have been subject to the same Communist techniques of gradual subversion leading to complete transformation. There has been a deliberate policy of Russification, and in places like Kazakhistan the process of denomadization and collectivization has radically transformed the economic traditions of the Kazakhs and with them, their whole manner of existence. Russians settling in Muslim territories have been a factor in the ethnical disintegration of Muslim tribes. The more Slavs settle here, the more Russian cadres can be depended on to perform the task of breaking down nationality and institutionalized religion in schools, administrative posts, centers of cultural activities, and the like.

Only in areas where Muslims are densely settled and heavily outnumber non-Muslims are Islamic religious practices and institutions likely to survive.[16] This is particularly evident in Uzbekistan where Islam is a strong religious and cultural force, ardent and rich in a long past to which the Uzbeks cling fanatically. To be sure, the indirect technique of persuasion is at work here as elsewhere in the Communist world, but secular atheistic groups sponsored by the Communists have a great deal of work ahead of them. When called for early in the 1920's, Stalin and Lenin affirmed to the Muslims of Turkestan that "your beliefs and customs, your national and cultural institutions are henceforth free and inviolable." The Bolsheviks were then fighting for survival.

Resistance reduced tolerance in the later twenties on account of the war on feudalism and the radical social transformation preached by the Communists. Pan-Turanism, espoused by the mullas, brought on persecution. Communist authorities nevertheless labored to stress the common points of Islam and Marxism: "The Qur'ān is plainly in accord with the program of the Communist Party which can and should be construed as conforming with Islam."

World War II and the desperate struggle for survival against the invaders brought the state and religious institutions into closer rapport; a *modus vivendi* was worked out between state and church that has remained in force.

The secularization and modernization of the U.S.S.R. need not portend the destruction of Islam here anymore than it was destroyed by the same process introduced by Kemalist Turkey in the twenties.

Far from being interdicted, Islam in the U.S.S.R. appears to be surviving. On the religious plane the Muslim community is directed by four spiritual directories, each presided over by a mufti elected by the assembly of believers.[17] The overall head is the grand mufti of Russia, Shākir ibn-Shaykh al-Islām Khialed-dinov. Freedom of religion, however, is circumscribed by the exigencies of Communist policy interests. Moscow prefers to be in the place of Mecca, the *qibla* of Islam; hence not many Soviet Muslims are allowed to perform the annual pilgrimage unless it serves a policy end of the Soviet government. But other institutional observances, like prayer, fasting, religious instruction, religious celebrations, and sacrifices appear to go on without serious interruption or interdiction.

The important institution of waqf has been entrusted to the supervision of the state, but with the religious associations having a voice in the selection of the civil personnel directing it. In many cases these Muslim associations received priority for construction material and other scarce items.[18]

Notwithstanding the vicissitudes of its existence in the Soviet Union, Islam manages to conserve all that which has been rigorously indispensable to its existence. To be sure, its distrain of political, economic, and social life has been arrested; but as an expression of individual faith, Islam is allowed to persist.

Islam has lost some of its followers to Communism in the face of strong social and moral pressure but it continues to survive in spite of all subtle and open Communist manipulations to rationalize it out of existence. Again Islam has been able to hold its own and manifest strong powers of resilience through which it has staved off complete subversion, here as in China.

Islam in Africa

For thirteen centuries Islam has been the religion of Arab North Africa. The spread of Islam into sub-Saharan Africa at a time when numerous other ideologies ranging from local nationalisms to universal socialism have been contending with it for converts is one of the most important examples of its dynamism. Nearly one fourth of the inhabitants of this region today are Muslims, a testimony to the appeal and success of Islam.

When the Arab Muslim penetrated Africa in the earlier centuries, he was seeking to traffic with precious minerals and ivory, not to proselytize. The caravan trade from Cairo and the nomads of Upper Egypt extended their reaches to Chad and Kufra in the eleventh century. By the end of the twelfth, a Muslim kingdom had been established at Kanem. Other traders reached the Great Lakes and the Congo in east and east central Africa. But in the western extremity the Berbers and Zanātis rallied to the Arab conquerors, and soon the Sanhājas became the most vigorous agents of the new faith in its spread southward. Until the eleventh century the traffic north and south centered on the caravan trade. After penetrating Mauritania, these Muslim traders established themselves in the adjacent regions as far south as Ghana.

The credit for Islam's penetration south of the Sahara may be attributed to the Almoravids (*al-Murābiṭūn*) who in the eleventh century were its principal promulgators. Islam in this region thrived on the fluctuating fortunes of warring local societies. The steadfastness of the Muslim in conflicting situations proved a major source of appeal to the natives.

A new cycle of conversion was generated at the start of the thirteenth century through the aegis of the Mandingas, founders of the Mali Empire. It began with the conversion of a sovereign and his entourage. When a century and a half later the Songhay replaced them, Islam remained the religion of the bourgeois and lettered class who had formed a coherent element in the principal cities like Djenne and Timbuktu. The Songhay relit the torch of Islam on the Niger.

At the end of the fifteenth century the brilliant Askia dynasty was established by Sarakole chiefs. When Mamadou (Muḥammad) Touré went on a pilgrimage to Mecca the security of the important commercial route running through Muslim lands was assured, and with it the eastern and western currents of Islam running south into Africa converged. Mamadou came back from the pilgrimage with an investiture from the nominal caliph, a relic of the ʿAbbāsid line then located in Cairo, and he proceeded to model the organization of his kingdom along Islamic precedents. Islam was now firmly implanted in central Africa.

After seven centuries of effort Islam gained a solid position in the cities and won over important ethnical elements, but it was not yet firmly established among the masses. The concerted drive mounted by influential chieftains, vigorous nomadic groups, and the militant zeal of the Ṣūfi brethren like the Tijānīyah and Qādirīyah were not only reminiscent of the old Murābiṭ spirit but, when coupled with the Berber fervor, the drive was bound to keep Islam on the move.

Refreshed by Qādirīyah incentive, pastoral Muslims of the north penetrated from the west into the sedentary strongholds and often imposed themselves by the force of their arms on the peasantry, as in Hausa, a land already Islamized. They founded new kingdoms in what is today Nigeria, and their imperial sway lasted till the beginnings of the nineteenth century. A wandering Shaykh of Mecca, Muḥammad ʿUthmān Amīrghāni boosted the influence of Arabian Muslims in his extensive voyages; indeed, an order was established, named al-Amīrghānīyah after him, which played a significant part in furthering Islam. Parallel to the Amīrghānīyah drive, the predominantly Berber Tījānīyah penetrated as far as Hausa. These orders were responsible for imparting their characteristics to African Islam.[19]

The colonial onslaught on Africa, especially in the second half of the nineteenth century, caused considerable radical modification of the conditions abetting the spread of Islam. Paradoxically, both French and British colonial expansion tended to encourage the expansion of Islam.

Stepped up economic activity, the security of travel and communication, the development of cities, the free effulgence of Islamic culture in public places were the natural outcome of the peace imposed domestically in French and British dominated territories. These and similar factors played an important role in the propagation of Islam. The proselytism of merchants was now replaced by the proselytism of the soldier, and manifested itself in a variety of efficacious forms.

Often the native's identification with Islam was unconscious; he adopted the veneer of Muslim observances, customs, names, and the like because to him it was an entrée for identifying himself with prosperous commercial communities. A significant attraction for the convert was the opportunity to link himself with a prestigious group and enjoy the hospitality and solidarity of Islam, two precious advantages placed immediately at the disposition of the neophyte.

Interestingly enough during this later period of conversion to Islam, the process was not the work of Muslim traders astride the traditional caravan routes or in control of interior markets; the agents of Islam were now more varied, numerous, and powerful, situated in the port regions of the western coast. There were Shīʿahs from Lebanon, Sunnis from Syria, Aḥmadīyah, and Ismāʿīlis from India-Pakistan, many of whom were liberated repatriated slaves who had adopted Islam earlier and sought to preserve it following emancipation in order to avoid the reprisals of their former milieus.[20]

In Nigeria, for example, the British enlisted the support of the Muslim chieftains; and in co-operation with the latter, the Islamic way gained more following. The law of the Sharīʿah was increasingly applied to the land and became more widespread. The rigid adherence of the Fulānis to the laws of Islam experienced no parallel, with the exception perhaps of Wahhābi Arabia.[21]

The French administration contributed to the strengthening of Islam in West Africa by organizing the pilgrimage to Mecca, building mosques down to the village level, and depending on the aristocratic Muslim minorities in the towns and villages among whom they found competent administrators.[22] Often by design the French administration favored the Muslim expansion because to the administrators Islam was "a known quantity"; moreover, a generation of experience in administering Algeria where French rulers became familiar with Arab-Muslim bureaucratic practices provided an easy outlet for carrying out the same procedures in Black Africa. This entailed, for instance, in the Senegal, substituting Qur'ānic for African customary laws which hitherto had served merely as an adjunct of faith to the Muslim, not to the African community at large.

Favoritism extended to Muslim chieftains fostered a sort of pro-Islam snobbism. Non-Muslim chieftains assigned administrative positions found it important for the exercise of authority to give an Islamic base to their authority; such a religious base was regarded as indispensable to a society where command was looked upon as sacred in essence.

Notwithstanding certain negative reactions to its increasing presence in African societies, Islam in some parts of Africa wrought only superficial changes while in other parts it made deep inroads on indigenous cultures. Some say Islam made more progress in the seventy-five years of French dominion than in the nine previous centuries.[23]

Reasons for Gain

How can we explain the reasons for Islam's substantial gains deep in the heart of Africa? How do we account, moreover, for the gains acquired under the benevolent eyes of dominant "Christian" nations and in the face of an intensive rivalry for converts staged by Protestant and Catholic missions?

One good reason is the fact that Islam is free of the onus of identification with the "White devils" who extended their political dominance over the Blacks while Christianity is not. Secondly, while Christian Blacks felt restrained because of religious identification with the White man from rising against him, the Muslim Black experienced no such restraint; he readily joined demonstrations and outbursts directed against the White overlord. Islam gave vent to Black nationalism and gained favor in the eyes of nationalists when Christianity could not.

Of greater relevance for explaining the reason is the fact that Islam represents to the indigenous inhabitant a cultural force; by identifying himself with it, the African is lifting his morale, enhancing his social standing, and acquiring a new dimension of intellectual growth.[24]

Islam is strongly entrenched in Africa today. If it were at all looked upon as a measure of defense against the West, the growth of the religion in recent times suggests that the establishment of even the most cordial ties with European nations will hardly detract from Islam's continuing spread in the African continent. The advantages it enjoys in its growth stem from its minimum demands and maximum promises to the convert; also from its remarkable capacity first to absorb, then ultimately to purify and integrate norms of cultural response quite alien to the orthodox tenets of Islam.

Islam in Africa is capable of countenancing the "sacred" and the "sacrilegious," the spiritual and the secular, the political and the religious, and a variety of what may appear as non-spiritual criteria. An African may be regarded as a Muslim even if he has only a superficial knowledge of the faith and despite the fact that he may have brought into his laconic Muslim beliefs from his previous animistic affiliations a variety of local observances and usages.

To be sure, many pagan and superstitious practices survive in the Islam of sub-Saharan Africa. Many are the African Muslims who have not abandoned all their animistic beliefs and practices. There are certain African groups, particularly in the Senegal among whom the men subscribe to Islam while the wives continue their animistic practices.[25]

It is interesting to observe that the animism of Berber and Black in Africa comprises certain traits to which Islam can adjust here more readily than elsewhere, like Southeast Asia. In the Negro-African milieu, religion and society are looked upon as one and the same; so it is in the orthodox conception of Islam. In Negro cosmogony the world is in the process of continual creation and man is in harmony with his world of creation. Islamic theology conceives of this in similar tones: the world is the creation of God; man is also the creation of God; God's creation is perfect, so must man and the world be perfect. Departures from this norm in African animism and in Islam are due to the evil deeds of man. Both in Negro and Muslim interpretations, the community combines the religious and social functions and strives to enforce submission to the Deity so it will reflect the divine order in all of its terrestrial facets.

At a time when the African seemed to collapse under the burden of modern civilization and the social and religious system of animistic traditions, Islam comes to his rescue with an offer to reinstate himself within a new framework not entirely alien to him in its broad confines. The Negro's propensity for the symbolic, the esoteric, and the mystic renders him receptive to the Ṣūfi way. He is intrigued by the Ṣūfi path and is often lured into embracing Islam by it. He finds a certain compatibility between the animistic priestly and Muslim Ṣūfistic practices. Ṣūfism indeed has remained one of the great magnets for Islam in Africa.

Islam defines for the African in precise terms the concept of the divine which the Negro more or less had confused in his thinking. He looked upon God as creator, but he also regarded Him as the chief of a pantheon consisting of secondary deities. Islam could not tolerate such a conception; so the neophyte is taught strict monotheism, and not to associate partners with the Deity. He learns to appreciate a simpler and more forthright religion than he had previously experienced. In Islam he is an *equal* associate among those who do not attribute status levels even to their God.

The adherence of the Negro to Islam poses no special difficulty. The case of conversion is abetted by the reduction of the ritualistic formalities to a minimum; this is indeed one of the chief factors in Islam's rapid penetration of Black Africa. There is no need for a preliminary study of doctrine; all the convert needs is to have some knowledge of the fundamental principles of Islam and to accept them. By solemnly pronouncing the Shahādah before witnesses, he is formally introduced into Islam. Before long he is fully acquainted with the traditional largess of Muslim institutions. The Muslim community at large takes care of the matter of integrating the neophyte socially and inculcating him with the right amount of knowledge concerning dogma and ritual. He enjoys the privileges which result from his adherence to the global society of Islam and all its attending benefits.

Islam has the added advantage over Christianity today of being propagated by non-Westerners. At a time of strong nationalistic anti-West outbursts, this is a distinct advantage. Islam, if it chooses, can play on the emotions of agitated Africans and Black racists. It is not a strange antipathetic system of beliefs to the African because Asians and Africans who profess and preach Islam play down differences of color, language, and ethnical affiliation. Asians and Africans seem to control Islam which appears to the Negro as a typically Afro-Asian form of social and religious life. "In proclaiming himself a Muslim many a youth is not adhering to a religion (witness how many prefer the European way of life, aside from maintaining a certain façade), he is giving proof of his Africanism. He is asserting a dynamic sense of independence. There is today a vulgar infatuation for Islam."[26]

The prospect of being treated as an equal is a real incentive for the Negro to adopt Islam. Indeed, the Islamic stress on equality has been a powerful inducement for the popularization of Islam in Africa. Welcomed as an equal into the Islamic community, the neophyte delights in a newly acquired sentiment of social elevation. He finds himself suddenly in a milieu which does not discriminate between African or Asian, Black or White. The convert's whole moral attitude is radically transformed in Islam. Equality is manifested both in the family and in the community. Wherever he goes the Negro Muslim can expect equal treatment in the society of Islam; nowhere will he find himself without interlocutors or guarantors among fellow Muslims regardless of their ethnic and tribal backgrounds. He ceases to be alone; this is a godsend and welcome reprieve for an African who is usually made to feel out of his own element when deprived of the warmth of social belonging.

Race and color are not material to his Islamism. There is no feeling of inferiority; self-dignity and pride are accentuated through the stress on equality and brotherhood among all African Muslims. By adhering to Islam the African is not asked to abandon his strong national feelings, nor is he expected to undergo revolutionary social changes; family and social ties are strengthened not weakened, and loyalty to his people is not diminished.[27] There is the additional factor of common antipathy towards the West in both the Islamic and African predisposition.

An important factor in the popular appeal of Islam is its non-demanding attitude towards the convert: (1) no pressure to convert, (2) limiting Islamic education to the study of the Qur'ān and Arabic, (3) reduction of the role of women to household chores, and (4) no insistence on full conformity or uniformity since it is a rule of Islam to permit monotheists to safeguard their customs and laws within the circle of Islamic government.[28]

Islam can present itself as a unitarian force to the African while Christianity projects the image of a divided and disconcerting ideal. The simplicity-loving African is confronted with the Catholic version on the one hand and the numerous Protestant versions of Christianity on the other, much too complex for him to comprehend, let alone digest, the doctrinal points of Christianity. The paradox lies in the fact that the Muslims do not project any more of a uniform image of Islam than the Christians of Christianity, yet the appeal of Islam remains stronger.

There are not only the orthodox Sunni Muslims, but also the Berber Khārijites who have a strong foothold in the former "French Sudan" where their impact is felt even in the architecture of the area. In recent years the Shī'ites of south Lebanon have been entrenched on the western, Ismā'īlis from India and Pakistan on the eastern coast where they control much of the commercial traffic.

The Aḥamdīyah have specialized in missionary activities in

Ghana, Dahomey, the Upper-Volta, and especially Nigeria. Differences between the various sects however seem to escape the African, and the total missionary effort adds up to increasing converts for Islam and fewer for Christianity. The reason for this is that at the critical initial stage of conversion Islam tolerates indigenous concepts brought in by the neophyte more than Christianity, provided these concepts do not negate the basic dogma of Islam: There is no god whatsoever but God.

The African proclivity for the mystical way is abetted by the Muslim Ṣūfis, which would explain why the two principal orders of Tījānīyah and Qādirīyah have been successful in the propagation of Islam in Africa. Here the grounds have been adequately prepared by animism, which has succeeded in preserving an attachment to a transforming society.

Islam in a broader context seems to lend itself to a civilization that favors an admixture of the temporal and the supernatural. The simple practical ritual offered the African by Islam is attractive to him; and he responds readily because in it he sees a manifestation of the universality of Islam. He is pleased moreover by the fact that Islam allows him to preserve under an Islamic guise the magical-medicinal objects of his former animistic ritual. Besides, mystical communication with God and its attending fetish touches a sensitive familiar chord in the African's heart. All the Ṣūfis insist on is the profession of divine unity and leaves to the African his pantheistic inclinations. Islam does not insist on the full performance of the ritualistic observances defined by orthodoxy. If he chooses, the African may pray three instead of five times a day, and he may simplify the ritual if it suits him better.

Islam in America

Islam in America is comparatively a very recent phenomenon. Muslim immigrants from Arab countries, India, Malaya, Yugoslavia, and Albania form small enclaves located mostly in the larger cities, although it is not uncommon to find them in the smaller cities as well.

These Muslim immigrants and their descendants are representative of the numerous sects of Islam: Sunni, Druzes, Shīʿites, Aḥmadīyah, Bahāʾi. They have organized themselves into numerous societies which reflect their ethnical derivation supplemented by all types of women's and youth's auxiliary groups.

American Muslims have endeavored to observe the tenets of their faith as best as they can determine them. Besides the Islamic mosque and institute in the capital, which caters principally to the diplomatic corps representing Muslim states, there are only a few other mosques in places like Chicago, Detroit, Toledo, and Cedar Rapids. It is difficult to ascertain the number of immigrant Muslims in America because statistics are incomplete. An educated guess would point to about ten thousand. They are mostly withdrawn into themselves and have no active interest in propagating Islam in America. They have their Islamic culture centers in New York, Washington, and San Francisco where the Sunni view predominates. These centers are open to all those interested in learning about Islam.

The Qādiyāni Aḥmadīyah and Bahāʾis are, on the other hand, quite active in disseminating their respective versions of Islam. The Sunni elements lose no time, however, in discrediting their claims to Islam wherever and whenever the opportunity presents itself. Yet both have well organized missionary activities and are willing to spend to spread their beliefs; this type of zeal is lacking among the orthodox Muslim groups.

"Black Muslims"

The group popularly known today as the "Black Muslims" is worth watching because it is less concerned with the religious than it is with the social dynamism latent to Islam. Its leaders have identified themselves with the main body of Islam. ". . . we here in America who are under the Divine Leadership of the Honorable Elijah Muḥammad, are an integral part of the vast World of Islam that stretches from the China Seas to the sunny shores of Africa." [29]

In the 1950's regular Muslims were quick to denounce the

movement as un-Islamic; but no such denunciation has been heard in recent years. Negro leaders despairing of attaining full civil rights and equality within the traditional framework of American society have seized upon Islam as the vehicle for achieving social and political ends. Islam has become their weapon of resisting the suppressive measures in American Society that have prevented the Negro from realizing his human and legal rights under the American Constitution.

Under the guise of an Islam little understood by most of the Negro adherents, a doctrine of Black supremacy is being preached, based on hatred of the White man for having oppressed the Black man: God's creation in His own image, whence his superiority over the White man whom Negro Muslim leaders argue was created in the "devil's image." God is near, not a spirit beyond reach. Heaven and Hell are two states of existence, and the Resurrection perpetuated by Christianity is designed to make the Black man wait until the next life for social justice.

Islam is giving the Negro the dignity and pride of belonging which his Christian environment failed to secure for him. Allah not Jehovah is responding to the Negro's appeals. It is highly probable that Islam will become eventually the religion of the Negro in America if present trends continue. While the membership today is estimated anywhere from seven thousand to a quarter of a million, the rate of conversion to Islam, "the religion of the Black man," is increasing very rapidly.

Under the banner of Islam the Negro, like other downtrodden peoples, i.e., the dispossessed dwellers of Mecca when the Prophet began to preach, are not only regaining their human dignity, but also for the first time they are exhibiting the moral qualities identified with practicing Muslims: abstinence from smoking and drinking, fidelity, and above all, discipline and solidarity with fellow Muslims. Indeed, the movement today led by Elijah Muḥammad, son of a former Baptist minister, and the offshoot led until his assassination by Malcolm X, also the son of a former Baptist minister, both seem to favor a separate identity and a separate existence for the Black man. It seeks to establish "the Nation of Islam" with its own flag, state, and discerning symbols.

That Islam has provided them with the motivation Christianity apparently could not is evident in the serious transformations it brought into their personal and social lives. The Negro Muslim has become thrifty and industrious; he is taught to depend on himself not on others; to become active in agricultural and manufacturing pursuits, and to lead an exacting regimented life. The Muslims observe the dietary laws of Islam and avoid contacts with Whites as much as possible. Strict discipline is observed at home; the respective functions of man and wife in the family are clearly defined. The children are taught the essentials of the faith at home. The Fruit of Islam, which is a supervising body responsible for the enforcement of discipline, reaches right into the home. The male Muslim must engage in gainful work; if he undertakes a small business enterprise, he is assured the patronage and support of fellow Muslims.

The center of his socio-religious life is the temple and the temple restaurant where many meals are taken in common. While regular Islam insists on one congregational prayer a week, the Negro Muslims conduct up to three such prayer sessions per week.

Discipline among Muslim women is strongly manifest. They are schooled in the need and art of homemaking and taught to take back seats to their husbands, never to talk to strangers, nor wear make-up and fancy dress.

While they are mostly a male oriented society, stature is achieved when the initiate is inducted into The Fruit of Islam, the functional and disciplinary arm of the movement headed by Elijah's son-in-law, Raymond Sharieff, whose responsibility it is to enforce brotherhood and protect the leaders at public functions.

Formal training centers are open for young women known as the MGT (Muslim Girls Training). The Muslims have their own schools, the University of Islam in Chicago, where they learn Arabic, among other subjects, their supposed native tongue before slavery. Religious and secular subjects are taught with emphasis on Islam, their religion, and the history of the Black man, their ancestor.

To dismiss Black Islam as a passing phase is to underestimate the full impact of Islam on the adherent. The Negro may gain his constitutional rights, but once a Muslim always a Muslim. The historical record attests to it. There is no recognized apostasy in Islam. Islam's grip on the true believer is strong. Evidence to date suggests that Islam has wrought deep changes, permanent changes, not only on the Negro individual, but on his society as well.

> Black Muslims were a catharsis for us, purging our innards of the bile brought on by slavery and segregation [30]

The relation of the Black Muslim to orthodox Islam is important because the validity of his Islamism rests on its being accepted by the main body of Islam. The movement has been fortunate in one respect: by concentrating on socio-political ends, not enough interpretation or "misinterpretation" was done to the Message of Muḥammad and the Qurʾān. The movement has been free of theological disputations and subscribes to no doctrinaire stand. Negro Muslims are contented to accept orthodox Islam as is. Hence the danger of Black Islam pursuing the path of eclecticism like Bahāʾism and Qādiyāni Aḥmadīyism in America is quite remote.

Both Elijah Muḥammad and Malcolm X have performed the pilgrimage to Mecca, returning with inflated pride and prestige. They acquired a more direct appreciation of the true nature of Islam, namely, that it is the White man's and not only the Black man's religion; that it does not encourage the establishment of "separate states" for Black men and White men; that Islam does not preach violence except in self-defense; that Islam preaches love and brotherhood among all races, and that the Messenger of Allah died in 632.

At first the official Muslim organization in the United States and Canada, the Federation of Islamic Associations, would have no traffic with Black Islam because of its strong racist views. Since the mid-1950's, however, there has been a major change of attitude. Orthodox Muslims in America and the Islamic East are quietly and actively laboring to place the Black Muslim ship on an even keel in the turbulent sea of the fight for recognition and equality.

It is evident that the movement is tending towards a sober and more realistic policy, particularly under the leadership of Wallace Muḥammed, Elijah's son. More and more Black Muslims are now studying at the Azhar in Cairo, the famous Islamic theological university and center of orthodox Islam. Graduates now beginning to return, including Elijah's son Akbar, have less of a somber attitude towards the fate of the Blacks in a White Society. They are preaching unity among all Negro factions, Christian and Muslim, cheek-turners and cheek-slappers. The new generation of Muslims trained in Egypt and elsewhere in the Muslim world will reflect more of traditional Islam and its preachings concerning tolerance, solidarity, and charity than hitherto manifested by the movement. There are fewer factors to distract the Black Muslim from a meaningful and constructive appreciation of Islamic concepts. Understanding and applying such concepts would dull much of the cutting edge of the knife wielded by the extremists among them whose main motive is revenge on the White man's "oppression of the Black."

We may conclude with the observation that Islam is a leading force today in World affairs. It has had more success in withstanding the onslaught of materialistic ideologies than the lay observer might suspect. Hundreds of millions of formerly Christian peoples have succumbed to atheistic Communism in East Europe where the authoritarian grip of the institutionalized church has been replaced by the equally strong grip of the "proletariat's dictatorship." Perhaps it is a blessing in disguise that the gains for Islam from among the rank of the socially and economically dissatisfied is robbing Communism of that many potential converts.

Western-style freedom and democracy appear to hold less attraction to the masses of humanity seeking the better life. Christianity has offered much less of an alternative because it has not projected an image of unity and strength desperately sought by Africa today, the real testing ground of the ideological struggle for dominance. Only very recently has Christianity considered steps for healing the deep wounds opened by centuries of internecine struggle. But in the meanwhile Christianity has been deprived of much of its dynamism. It has failed to stand up to the challenge of the present day world and its contrasting ideologies, in Africa as elsewhere.

Where Muslims in China and the Soviet Union have been subjected to strong pressures to give up their traditional beliefs, they seem to hold up; evidence of Islam's resilience. Where Islam, as in Africa, has had an opportunity to compete with other ideologies, it appears to outdistance its rivals in gains: evidence of its dynamism.

Islam's potential for growth in a troubled world searching for closer ties and firmer direction is a reality worth heeding.

Its recent resurgence in Iran as a dynamic political force under the leadership of Shiʿite Mullas and Ayatollah Khomeini is fresh evidence of its appeal in situations where other alternatives are inadequate.

Footnotes

1. An Introduction to Islam

1. *Mohammedanism,* cited by C. Snouck Hurgronje (New York: G. P. Putnam's Sons, 1916), pp. 20-21.

2. G. Weil, *Mohammed der Prophet, sein Leben und seine Lehre* (Muḥammad the Prophet, his Life and his Teachings), Stuttgart, 1843.

2. The Setting in Arabia

1. ᶜAbd-al-Malik ibn-Hishām, *Sīrat Rasūl Allāh,* trans. Alfred Guillaume: *The Life of Muḥammad* (London: Oxford University Press, 1956), p. 41.

2. From the Arabic root *"ghaza:* to conduct a foray" through the French.

3. Literally "the days of the Arabians," more immediately in reference to the intertribal wars ensuing from anywhere a personal insult to dispute over cattle and water holes or the sportiness of it.

4. Muḥammad has a strong antipathy for the poets whom he accused of being inspired by the *jinn;* the Arabic term for poet *"shāᶜir"* stands for "he who senses," by extrasensory means.

5. Some of the finest Arab poetry dates to this period. For a collection of the *Muᶜallaqāt* (the suspended ones) see A. Arberry, *The Seven Odes,* Cambridge, University Press, 1957.

6. W. R. Smith, *Religion of the Semites* (New York: Meridian Library, 1959), p. 2.

7. Technically, "[the period of] ignorance" or barbarism, which is in reference to Arabia and its inhabitants in the era when they were not guided by Allah, the Qurᵓān and His Messenger Muḥammad.

8. Al-ᶜUzzah was one of the most venerated pagan female deities; even Muḥammad made her an offering when he was a boy. She is the Arab equivalent of the Greek Aphrodite or Venus.

9. Al-Lāt or *al-Ilāhah* (the goddess) was the popular object of worship in the environs of al-Ṭāᵓif, about sixty miles east of Mecca.

10. "Manāh" derives her name from *manīyah:* allotted fate; she was the goddess of destiny, and her sanctuary was situated mainly between Mecca and Medina.

11. Exodus 3:1, 18:10-12.

12. For details consult Henri Lammens, *Les chrétiens à la Mecque à la veille de l'hégire: l'Arabie occidentale avant l'hégire* (Beyrouth: Imprimerie Catholique, 1928), pp. 12 *seq.*

13. Such traditions were preserved by ibn-Rustah, *al-Aᶜlāq al-*

Nafīsah, ed. De Goeje (Leyden, 1892), pp. 192 and 217.

14. Cf. *Sūrahs* 2:140, 5:14, 15.

15. "The wandering Arabs are more hard in disbelief and hypocrisy, and were likely to be ignorant of the limits which Allah hath revealed unto His messenger." (Qur'ān 9:97).

16. These convictions were shaped mostly by animistic practices. C. Snouck Hurgronje, *Mohammedanism* (New York: G. P. Putnam's Sons, 1916), p. 36.

17. Eric R. Wolf, "The Social Organization of Mecca and the Origins of Islam," *Southwestern Journal of Anthropology,* Vol. 7, No. 4 (Winter, 1951), p. 338.

18. J. Wellhausen, *Reste arabischen Heidentums* (2nd ed.; Berlin, 1897), pp. 218 *seq.*

19. Same as Mandeans, or the so-called Christians of St. John, to whom the Qur'ān refers as peoples possessing scriptures.

20. Known also as *Majūs* or Zoroastrians. They too were treated as "Scripturaries" by Muḥammad and thus spared the ill-fate of the pagans.

21. Julius Wellhausen, *Skizzen und Vorarbeiten* (6 vols.; Berlin: Reimer, 1884-99), Vol. III, p. 88.

22. Leone Caetani, *Annali dell' Islam,* Vol. I (Milan: Hoepli, 1905), p. 148.

23. Frants Buhl, *Das Leben Muhammeds,* trans. H. H. Schaeder (Leipzig: Quelle and Meyer, 1930), pp. 36 *seq.*

3. Muḥammad the Prophet

1. Frants Buhl, *op. cit.*

2. For a detailed account based on original sources of the known facts of his life consult Sir Wm. Muir, *The Life of Mohammad* (Edinburgh: John Grant, 1923), pp. 13 *seq.*

3. Qur'ān 96:1-5.

4. The term by which pre-Islamic monotheists were known.

5. Qur'ān 10:95.

6. Qur'ān 74:1-5.

7. Qur'ān 94:1.

8. Literally "he who senses," i.e. the unknown, by some extra-sensory power ordinarily attributed to the person who is in "league" with the *Jinn.*

9. Qur'ān 17:22.

10. Qur'ān 17:18.

11. Qur'ān 49:11.

12. Qur'ān 49:13.

13. Ibn-Hishām, *op. cit.,* p. 119.

14. Qur'ān 41:4.

15. Qur'ān 41:6.

16. Qur'ān 22:52.

17. The three female deities were regarded by pagan Arabs, who deplored female offspring, as the daughters of Allah; hence the reference to "unjust division."

18. Qur'ān 53:21-23.

19. There are 17 references in the Qur'ān to demands made by the Qurayshites for a sign or a miracle.

20. Qur'ān 22:42-44.

21. It was officially established by the caliph ʿUmar in the year 639, as beginning with July (Rabīʿ I) of the year 622.

22. Arabic *"Hijrah"* does not mean "flight," as the misconception seems to prevail, but rather "a series of migrations."

23. Ibn-Hishām, *op. cit.,* p. 342; R. A. Nicholson, *A Literary History of the Arabs* (Cambridge University Press, 1956), p. 158.

24. For details, see Ibn-Hishām, *op. cit.,* pp. 231-34.

25. L. Caetani, *op. cit.,* Vol. I, p. 389.

26. Qur'ān 22:38-40.

27. Qur'ān 2:190-91.
28. Qur'ān 3:13.
29. Qur'ān 8:17.
30. Qur'ān 9:12.
31. Qur'ān 9:18.
32. Qur'ān 49:10.
33. Qur'ān 110:1-3.
34. Qur'ān 9:29.
35. Qur'ān 9:30-32.
36. Ibn-Hishām, *op. cit.*, p. 651 (translation modified).
37. Notably, al-Aswad, a Yemenite chief, a man of great wealth and sagacity who won over his tribesmen, forced himself on a number of neighboring towns killing Shahr, Muḥammad's governor at Ṣanʿā' who had gained the conversion to Islam of the Persian colony there and was killed by them in retaliation. The other two pretenders, Tulayḥah and Hārūn, or Musaylimah as he is better known, were not suppressed until after the Prophet's death, during the caliphate of Abu-Bakr (632-34).

4. Muḥammad the Man

1. Qur'ān 2:136.
2. Qur'ān 5:3.
3. M. J. DeGoeje, "Die Berufung Mohammed's," in *Nöldeke-Festschrift* (Giessen, 1906), Vol. I, p. 5.
4. Wm. Muir, *op. cit.*, pp. 329 *seq.*
5. Qur'ān 3:102-105.
6. Sam. v. 13; 1 Chron. iii, 1-9, XIV, 3.
7. Kings 11:3.
8. 2 Chron. 11:21.
9. In the Battle of Badr, Khumays was killed and his wife, Ḥafsa, daughter of his loyal supporter and the future caliph ʿUmar, was widowed. At first she was offered to ʿUthmān, another future caliph, but he declined, then to Abu-Bakr, Muḥammad's father-in-law, but he refused also. She settled for Muḥammad.
10. *Sūrah* 33:37.
11. De Goeje, *op. cit.*, p. 5.
12. These insinuations resulted from the 19th-century infatuation with scientifically superficial theories of medical psychology and the theories of those who applied them in their search for some scientific explanation based on such admissions as Muḥammad being in a semi-conscious and trance-like state with occasional loss of consciousness when he received revelations.
13. Tor Andrae, *Mohammed: The Man and his Faith,* trans. Theophil Menzel (New York: Harper Torch Book Series, 1960), p. 51.
14. Guillaume, *Islam* (Pelican, 1961 reprint), p. 28.
15. Qur'ān 2:136.
16. Qur'ān 3:144.
17. Qur'ān 33:40.
18. Qur'ān 2:113.
19. Qur'ān 2:120.
20. Qur'ān 2:121.
21. Qur'ān 5:57.
22. Qur'ān 5:59.
23. Qur'ān 5:51.
24. Qur'ān 22:35-36.
25. R. Bosworth Smith, *Mohammed and Mohammedanism* (London, 1889), p. 341.
26. Preserved by Ibn-Hishām, *op. cit.*, p. 151; trans. and cit. P. K. Hitti, *History of the Arabs* (7th ed.; London, 1960), p. 121.
27. *Sūrah* 17:22-37.
28. From *"Sūrat al-Nisā',"* Qur'ān 4:2 *seq.*
29. Qur'ān 17:38.
30. Qur'ān 17:39.
31. J. H. Hottinger, *Historia Orientalis,* 2nd ed., Zürich, 1651.
32. Published in London in

1730; cit. Tor Andrae, *op. cit.*, p. 173.

33. *Le Coran traduit de l'arabe précédé d'un abregé de la vie de Mahomet* (Paris, 1752), Vol. I, p. 221.

34. Hurgronje, *op. cit.*, pp. 23-24.

35. Tor Andrae, *op. cit.*, p. 175.

5. Foundation of Islam: The Qur'ān

1. *Sūrah* 43:4-5.
2. *Sūrah* 56:95; 69:1.
3. *Sūrah* 2:164, 255.
4. It is only in the 9th *Sūrah* that it does not occur.
5. *Sūrah* 69:40-41.
6. Qur'ān 26:224-226.
7. R. A. Nicholson, *op. cit.*, p. 159.
8. Qur'ān 113:1-3, 5.
9. Qur'ān 114:1, 4-6.
10. Nicholson, *op. cit.*, p. 166 (with minor alterations).
11. H. A. R. Gibb, *Mohammedanism* (2nd ed.; Oxford University Press, 1953), p. 41.
12. Qur'an 112:1-4.
13. Qur'ān 5:74.
14. Qur'ān 82:1 5.
15. Theodor Noldeke, *Geschichte des Qorāns*, ed. Fr. Schwally (Wiesbaden, 1961 reprint), Vol. I, pp. 53 *seq.*
16. Theodor Nöldeke "Koran," *Encyclopaedia Britannica*, 11th ed., Vol. XV (New York, 1911), p. 903.
17. See Julian Obermann's "Islamic Origins" in *The Arab Heritage*, ed. N. A. Faris (Princeton, 1946), pp. 58-120.
18. The alphabet lacked vowel symbols and even symbols to express emphasis. It also expressed several consonants by the same character. Were it not for dots, which did not exist at the time the Qur'ān was codified but added later according to a fixed order, in reference to the present form of these symbols the same symbol could mean B, T, Th, N, or Y at the beginning and in the middle of words, where F, Q and W could also be readily confused for each other.
19. Published in Cairo, 1321 A.H. (1903).
20. Ed. Nassau-Lees, Calcutta, 1859.
21. Ed. H. G. Fleicher, Leipzig, 1846-48.
22. Hitti, *op. cit.*, p. 126.
23. Published for the first time in 1930, reprinted by Mentor ten times 1953-63. It is the version utilized mostly in this work.

6. The Fundamentals of Islam: Beliefs

1. R. A. ʿAzzām, *The Eternal Message of Muḥammad,* trans. Caesar E. Farah (New York: The Devin-Adair Co., 1964), p. 35.
2. Qur'ān 3:19.
3. Qur'ān 22:78.
4. Qur'ān 3:3.
5. Qur'ān 6:84-90.
6. Qur'ān 3:64.
7. Arabic *"Umm al-qurah,"* title by which Mecca became known.
8. Qur'ān 6:91-93.
9. Qur'ān 5:3.
10. Qur'ān 25:2.
11. A. A. Galwash, *The Religion of Islam* (2nd ed.; Cairo: Iʿtimād Press, 1945), Vol. I, p. 139.
12. Qur'ān 112:1-4.
13. Qur'ān 7:54.
14. Qur'ān 16:3-12.
15. Qur'ān 13:9.
16. Qur'ān 6:59.
17. Qur'ān 3:26-27.

18. Qur'ān 7:180.
19. *al-Maqṣad al-Asna* (2nd ed.; Cairo, 1324 A.H.), pp. 12 *seq.*; al-Baghawi, *Maṣābīḥ al-Sunna* (Cairo: Khayrīyah, 1900), Vol. I, pp. 96-97.
20. Qur'ān 59:23-24.
21. Qur'ān 4:124.
22. Qur'ān 11:52.
23. ʿAzzām, *op. cit.*, p. 60.
24. Qur'ān 85:22.
25. Whence the English "genii."
26. Qur'ān 17:23-39.
27. Qur'ān 82:19.
28. Qur'ān 20:102.
29. Qur'ān 69:13-18.
30. Qur'ān 20:109.
31. Qur'ān 3:10.
32. Qur'ān 18:50.
33. Qur'ān 42:22.
34. Qur'ān 76:12-15, 19, 21-22.
35. Qur'ān 78:23-26, 30.
36. Qur'ān 10:27-38.
37. Qur'ān 4:48.
38. Qur'ān 4:56.
39. Qur'ān 42:40.
40. Qur'ān 10:108.
41. Qur'ān 54:49.
42. Qur'ān 3:145.
43. Qur'ān 87:2-3.
44. Qur'ān 9:51.
45. Qur'ān 15:21.
46. Qur'ān 25:2.
47. Reprinted from the official magazine of al-Azhar; Galwash, *op. cit.*, p. 221.
48. Reproduced from al-Azhar's official publication; Galwash, *op. cit.*, p. 222.
49. Qur'ān 16:90.
50. Qur'ān 6:163-164.
51. Qur'ān 2:155-157.
52. Qur'ān 18:30.

7. The Fundamentals of Islam: Obligations

1. Qur'ān 2:277.
2. Qur'ān 76:8-9.
3. Qur'ān 3:31.
4. Qur'ān 3:32.
5. Qur'ān 46:15.
6. Qur'ān 17:23-24.
7. Qur'ān 25:63.
8. Qur'ān 4:36-37.
9. Qur'ān 107:1-3.
10. Qur'ān 2:177.
11. Qur'ān 4:36.
12. Qur'ān 4:2.
13. Qur'ān 4:8.
14. Qur'ān 4:10.
15. Qur'ān 4:135.
16. The fundamental law of Islam.
17. Qur'ān 5:8.
18. Qur'ān 5:8.
19. Qur'ān 4:58.
20. Qur'ān 6:153.
21. Qur'ān 51:19.
22. ʿAzzām, *op. cit.*, p. 91.
23. Qur'ān 9:34-35.
24. Qur'ān 2:275-276.
25. Qur'ān 59:8-9.
26. Qur'ān 49:10.
27. Qur'ān 9:71.
28. ʿAzzām, *op. cit.*, p. 80.
29. Qur'ān 6:33.
30. ʿAzzām, *op. cit.*, p. 75.
31. *Ibid.*, p. 77.
32. Qur'ān 49:13.
33. Qur'ān 9:71.
34. Qur'ān 3:104.
35. ʿAzzām, *op. cit.*, p. 54.
36. L. V. Vaglieri, *An Interpretation of Islam,* trans. from Italian A. Caselli (Washington, D.C., 1957), p. 38.
37. Qur'ān 3:31.
38. Qur'ān 7:156.
39. Qur'ān 17:82.
40. Qur'ān 3:159.
41. Qur'ān 9:128.
42. Qur'ān 36:46.
43. Qur'ān 17:26-27.
44. Tor Andrae, *op. cit.*, p. 80.
45. From Arabic *masjid* or

"place of prostration," transcribing in a literal sense an essential component of the prayer ritual.

46. The day is called *"al-Jumʿah"* (the "congregation"), named for this particular ceremony.

47. *Sūrah* 62:9-10.

48. Qurʾān 17:78.

49. Mecca.

50. Jerusalem.

51. Qurʾān 4:43.

52. Vaglieri, *op. cit.*, p. 46.

53. At the beginning of his stay in Medina Muḥammad had chosen Jerusalem as the *qibla* of Islam but with the submission of Mecca he made it the center instead.

54. Fully illustrated by E. W. Lane, *Manners and Customs of the Modern Egyptians* (London, 1895), pp. 89-93.

55. Ameer ʿAli, *The Spirit of Islam* (London, 1952), p. 165.

56. Lane, *op. cit.*, p. 90.

57. Vaglieri, *op. cit.*, p. 45.

58. *Ibid.*, p. 46.

59. Qurʾān 29:45.

60. Qurʾān 24:56.

61. Qurʾān 57:18.

62. Qurʾān 9:60.

63. Qurʾān 2:183.

64. Qurʾān 2:184.

65. It is probable that the fast was formally instituted during Muḥammad's second year at Medina (624) when the corrected lunar year was in use and Ramaḍān, the ninth month, always fell in the winter when days were shorter. Then Muḥammad a few years later decreed the use of the uncorrected lunar year, which system has prevailed ever since.

66. Qurʾān 2:187.

67. Qurʾān 2:184.

68. Qurʾān 2:187.

69. Qurʾān 3:97.

70. M. Gaudefroy-Demombynes, *Muslim Institutions* (London, 1954), p. 99.

71. Refers to Muḥammad's nocturnal ascent to the Seventh Heaven.

8. Solidarity Through Institutional Unity

1. Developed out of Qurʾānic and Traditionalistic legislation. See below, pp. 160-61.

2. Their caliphate was centered on Damascus and lasted from 661 to 750.

3. Ruled from Baghdad, 750–1258.

4. Literally "someone who comes between."

5. At one time, in the tenth century, there were three independent caliphs, at Cairo, Cordova, and Baghdad.

6. A variety of what may be termed "ethnic nationalism."

7. During the caliphates of the ʿAbbāsid al-Mutawakkil (847–61) and the Fāṭimid al-Ḥakam (996–1020) certain extra-legal discriminations occurred.

8. Sanctioned by the Ḥanafite, one of the four principal schools of jurisprudence in orthodox Islam.

9. Principally sanctioned by the Mālikite school of jurisprudence.

10. A sort of dowry paid to the bride's father or guardian.

11. The formal "demand" in marriage or "engagement" after preliminary investigations and negotiations had taken place.

12. Literally when the "appointment for consummation" is to be held, or wedding day.

13. A specific type of school called *maktab, kuttāb* where the Qurʾān and related subjects are taught.

14. Someone who has committed the text to memory.

15. The other three are: Māliki, Ḥanafi and Ḥanbali.

16. Their centers of study were invariably their meeting places

known as *ribāṭ, khanaqāh, takīyah* (tekke) and *zāwiyah.*

17. Known in Turkey as Büyük Bayram, and in certain parts of the Arab World as al-ʿĪd al-Kabīr or ʿĪd al-Qurbān. See above, p. 149.

18. Known also as al-ʿĪd al-Ṣaghīr (the little feast) and Küçük Bayram.

19. Muḥarram, Ṣafar, Rabīʿ al-Awwal, Rabīʿ al-Thāni, Jumāda al-Awwal, Jumāda al-Thāni, Rajab, Shaʿbān, Ramadān, Shawwal, Dhu'l-Qaʿdah and Dhu'l-Ḥijjah.

20. *Sūrah* 2:276.

9. Heterodoxy and Orthodoxy

1. For the line of descent in order of their Imāmate: ʿAli (d. 661), al-Ḥasan (d. 669), al-Ḥusayn (d. 680), ʿAli Zayn al-ʿĀbidīn (d. ca. 712), Muḥammad al-Bāqir (d. 731), Jaʿfar al-Ṣādiq (d. 765), Mūsa al-Kāẓim (d. 799), ʿAli al-Riḍa (d. 818), Muḥammad al-Jawād (d. 835), ʿAli al-Hādi (d. 868), al-Ḥasan al-ʿAskari (d. 874), Muḥammad al-Muntaẓar (al-Mahdi) (d. 878).

2. Adam, Noah, Abraham, Moses, Jesus, Muḥammad, and Muḥammad al-Tāmm, son of Ismāʿīl.

3. Included among others Ishmael, Aaron, Peter and ʿAli.

4. For details consult M. A. al-Shahrastāni, *Kitāb al-Milal wa-'l-Niḥal,* ed. Rev. W. Cureton (*Book of Religious and Philosophysical Sects, Parts I and II*) (London, 1842), pp. 145 *seq.* and W. Ivanow, *A Guide to Ismaili Literature,* London, 1933.

5. Hitti, *op. cit.,* pp. 443-444.

6. See L. Massignon, "Karmatians," *Encyclopedia of Islam,* Vol. II (Leyden and London, 1927), pp. 767-772.

7. We have an interesting description of them by Marco Polo, who passed through the region shortly after its destruction in his *The Book of Ser Marco Polo, the Venetian,* trans. Henry Yule (2nd ed.; London, 1875), Vol. I, pp. 46-49.

8. P. K. Hitti, *The Lebanon in History* (New York: St. Martin Press, 1956), pp. 261-262.

9. In reference to the fez-like cap they wear.

10. H. A. R. Gibb, *op. cit.,* p. 99.

11. Full Title: *Kitāb al-Jāmiʿ al-Ṣaḥīḥ* (The book of the verified compendium), ed. for the first time by L. Krehl and T. W. Juynboll (Leyden, 1862). It actually lists 7275, of which 3275 are repetitions.

12. *Kitāb al-Sunan* of Abu-Dāʾūd (817-888) (ed. Cairo, 1863; Lucknow, 1888; Delhi, 1890); *al-Jāmiʿ al-Ṣaḥīḥ* of al-Tirmidhi (d. ca. 892); *Kitāb al-Sunan* of Nasaʾi (830-915) (ed. Cairo, 1894), and the *Kitāb al-Sunan* of ibn-Māja (824-866) (ed. Delhi, 1865 and 1889).

13. It includes an introduction to the "Science of Tradition," edited for the first time in Calcutta, 1894.

14. Based on the Sharīʿah.

15. Guillaume, *op. cit.,* pp. 97-98.

16. G. Bergstrasser, *Gründzüge des Islamischen Rechts,* ed. Joseph Schacht, cited by H. A. R. Gibb, *op. cit.,* p. 106.

10. Formalism and Free Expression

1. For details consult A. de Vlieger's *Kitāb al-Qadr,* materiaux pour servir a l'étude de la doctrine de la predestination dans la theologie musulmane, Leyde: E. J. Brill, 1903.

2. Known also as the "Imām of al-Ḥaramayn."

3. Gibb, *op. cit.*, p. 135.

4. Louis Massignon, *La Passion d'al-Ḥallaj: martyr mystique de l'Islam* (Paris, 1922), Vol. II, p. 518.

5. Al-Ḥujwīri, *Kashf al-Maḥjūb*, new ed. R. A. Nicholson (London: Luzac, 1959), p. 363.

6. *Ibid.*

7. D. B. MacDonald, *Development of Muslim Theology* (New York, 1903), pp. 238 *seq.*

8. R. A. Nicholson, "Mysticism," in *Legacy of Islam*, ed. Sir Thomas Arnold and Alfred Guillaume (Oxford University Press, 1960), p. 222.

9. Guillaume, *op. cit.*, p. 149.

10. Hitti, *op. cit.*, p. 587.

11. See J. P. Brown, *The Darwishes or Oriental Spiritualism* (Oxford, 1927) for further details.

12. Founded by Aḥmad al-Badawi (d. 1276), and known sometimes as Aḥmadīyah, with two other offshoots in Egypt: Bayyūni and Dasūqi orders, popular in the lower confines of the Nile Valley.

13. From an unpublished manuscript, Madeleine F. Habib, "A Nakshbandi Session," p. 3.

11. "Medievalism" and the Dawn of "Renaissance"

1. Translated into French by B. Michel and M. Abdel Razik, Paris, 1925.

2. First published in London, 1922.

3. Guillaume, *op. cit.*, p. 160.

4. Published for the first time in London, 1934.

5. H. A. R. Gibb, *Modern Trends in Islam* (Chicago, 1950), p. 60.

6. *The Reconstruction of Religious Thought in Islam* (London, 1934), p. 54.

7. Maḥmūd Aḥmad, *Ahmadiyyat or the True Islam* (Calcutta, 1924), p. 32.

8. M. Aḥmad in *Review of Religions* (Feb. 1952), p. 8. Cited by H. J. Fischer, *Aḥmadiyyah* (Oxford, 1963), p. 45.

9. C. C. Adams, *Islam and Modernism in Egypt* (London, 1933), p. 129.

10. M. Aḥmad, *Ahmadiyya Movement* (London, 1924), p. 46.

11. *Review of Religions* (expresses the Qādiyāni view) (March, 1952), p. 40, cited by Fisher, op. cit., p. 59.

12. Charles M. Remey, *A Series of Twelve Articles Introductory to the Bahá'i Teachings* (Florence, 1925), p. 29.

13. *Ibid.*, p. 145.

14. *Ibid.*, p. 146.

12. Resilience and Dynamism

1. Justus M. Van Kroef, "Some Social and Political Aspects of Islam in Indonesia," *The Islamic Review* (Woking, July 1957), p. 33.

2. Ruled China from the seventh to the eleventh centuries.

3. Yang I-fan, *Islam in China* (Hong Kong, 1957), p. 15.

4. *The Agrarian Reform Law of the People's Republic of China* (Peking: Foreign Languages Press, 1953), pp. 2, 6.

5. Such as his *On the People's Democratic Dictatorship, on New Democracy, the Chinese Revolution and the Chinese Communist Party.* Yang I-fan, *op. cit.*, p. 54.

6. *Jen Min Jih Pao,* August 5, 1952 and *Kwangming Jih Pao,* September 24, 1952.

7. *Kwangming Jih Pao,* May 25, 1955.

8. Ma Chien, translator, *Ku-lan Ching* (Shanghai: Commercial Press, 1952), Vol. I, p. 1.

9. *Sūrah* 16:78.

10. *Ku-lan Ching*, pp. 11-12.

11. *Sūrah* 10:37.

12. *Ku-lan Ching*, p. 30.

13. *Sūrah* 58:22.

14. *Hong Kong Ta Kung Pao*, November 22, 1944.

15. Asa Bā Faqih, an Indonesian Muslim who visited Muslim places in China and reported his findings in his *A Muslim Visits China*, Singapore, 1955.

16. For details see Jean-Paul Roux, *L'Islam en Asie* (Paris: Payot, 1958), pp. 237 *seq*.

17. European Russia and Siberia; Central Asia, Trans-Caucasia, Daghestan and the Northern Caucasus.

18. Roux, *op. cit.*, p. 246.

19. Pierre Rondot, *L'Islam et les Musulmans d'Aujourd'hui* (Paris, 1960), Vol. II, pp. 37-38.

20. P. Azam. "Les limites de l'Islam africain," *L'Afrique et l'Asie* (January, 1948), p. 45.

21. J. N. D. Anderson, *Islamic Law in Africa* (London, 1954), p. 219.

22. J. Richard-Molard, *Afrique Occidentale Française* (Paris, 1949), pp. 87 *seq*.

23. P. Alexandre, "L'Islam Noir," *Marchés tropicaux du Monde* (October 12 and 19, 1957), pp. 2386-2387.

24. E. Psichari, *Terres de soleil et de Sommeil* (Paris, 1923), pp. 262 *seq*.

25. The practice is especially evident among the Lebou. See Rondot, *op. cit.*, p. 43.

26. M. Chailley, *Aperçu sur l'Islam en A.O.F.*, unedited papers of a conference held at Dakar in 1959, cit. Rondot, *op. cit.*, p. 45.

27. E. D. Morel, *Nigeria, Its People and Its Problems* (London, 1911), pp. 216-17.

28. G. Haines, ed. *Africa Today* (Baltimore, 1955), p. 95.

29. Malcolm X speech to Harvard University Law School Forum in 1960.

30. Louis E. Lomax, *When the Word Is Given . . .* (Cleveland and New York, 1963), p. 87.

Glossary

A

ʿabd—servant, term applies to worshiper of God.

adab—the science of proper upbringing; in literature it relates to "belles lettres".

ʿādah (*ʿadāt*)—customary practices usually local (see ʿĀdāt) having sanctity of law.

ʿĀdāt—corpus of law deriving from custom and usage, legislation of secular heads.

"afkhar al-umam"—"noblest of nations"—Arab conception of his ancestry.

"ahl al-dhimmah"—peoples, i.e. Christians and Jews, whose protection was enjoined by the Qurʾān.

"ahl al-Sunnah wa-'l-Ḥadīth"—literally "the people of Sunnah and Ḥadīth," official title of those adhering to orthodox Islam.

"ahl al-tawḥīd wa-'l-ʿadl"—literally "the people of unitarianism and justice," title applied to the rationalists Muʿtazilites.

ajāwīd—title given to the most pious members of the Druze sect.

al-Amīn—"the trustworthy," name by which Muḥammad was known.

al-asmāʾ al-ḥusna—"the nicest names," ninety-nine, attributes of God.

"al-Baqarah"—"the Cow," second chapter of the Qurʾān.

al-ʿĪd al-Kabīr—see *ʿĪd al-Aḍḥa* (below).

al-ʿĪd al-Ṣaghīr—*see ʿĪd al-Fiṭr* (below).

al-Ikhwān al-Muslimūn—The Muslim Brethren, militant lay society applying the strict tenets of Islam to present living.

al-Ilāh—"the deity," a variant of "Allah."

"al-ʿImrān"—"the Family of ʿImrān," third chapter of the Qurʾān.

al-Islām—see *Islām.*

al-Jamʿīyah al-Islāmīyah—"The Islamic Society."

al-Jazīrah—"the Island," i.e. the Arabian peninsula.

"al-Kawthar"—"the Abundance," Chapter CVIII of the Qurʾān.

al-Kitāb—"the Book," i.e. the Qurʾān.

al-Khulafāʾ al-Rāshidūn—"The Orthodox Caliphs": first four successors of Muḥammad.

Allah—God.

Allāhu akbar—"God is great"—begins ritual prayer

al-Mukarramah—"The Highly Honored," appellation reserved to Mecca.

al-Murābiṭūn—a dynastic power heavily tinged by Ṣūfism that ruled North Africa and Spain ca. 1061-1147.

al-Muwaṭṭaʾ—the corpus of Tradition compiled by Mālik ibn-Anas.

"al-Naṣr"—"The Succor," Chapter CX of the Qurʾān.

"al-Nisāʾ"—"The Women," fourth chapter of the Qurʾān.

al-Raḥīm—"The Most Merciful," a quality of God.

al-Raḥmān—"The Merciful," a quality of God.

al-Sāʿah—"The Hour," a term applied to the "hour of reckoning" with God.

"al-salāmu ʿalaykum wa raḥmatu ʾl-Lāh"—terminal point in the ritual prayer, recited by the worshiper, literally: "[May] peace [be] with you and the mercy of God [also]."

al-shahādah—see *Shahādah* (below).

al-Shayṭān al-Kabīr—"the Great Satan," also stele at Mina where a pilgrim casts his seven stones.

al-Tābiʿūn—plural of al-Tābiʿ, term applied to a follower of the Prophet's companions.

al-ʿUrwah al-Wuthqa—title of al-Afghāni's important work on a revitalized political Islam.

ʿamalah—plural of *ʿāmil.*

amān—safety of person and possession decreed by the Muslim community for foreign residents.

ʿāmil—an official who supervised the collection and distribution of tithe.

amīr al-muʾminīn—"commander of the believers," title by which caliph was also known.

amīr al-umarāʾ—literally "prince of princes," title first given to Seljuk Sultans by ʿAbbāsid caliph.

amr—"decree," i.e. command of Allah.

"ana al-Ḥaqq"—literally "I am the truth," famous utterance of al-Ḥallāj that cost him his life.

Anṣār—"Companions" of Muḥammad, his followers among the Medinans.

Anṣār Allah—formal title whence *"Naṣārah,"* or Christians derive.

ʿaqaba—steep slope, such as at beginning of road to Muzdalifa from Mina.

ʿaqd al-nikāḥ—formalization of the marriage vows.

ʿāqil—someone in full control of mental faculties; also singular of *ʿUqqāl* (see below).

ʿaql—mind, intelligence; the "universal mind" to the Ismāʿīlis.

ʿaṣabīyah—strong "clannish spirit" popular in pre-Islamic Arabia.

"ashhadu anna la ilāha illa ʾl-Lāh"—formula by the proper utterance of which one becomes a Muslim.

ʿaṣr—period of sunset, time of one of the ritual prayers.

"Ayyām al-ʿArab"—period in pre-Islamic Arabia characterized by strong internecine wars.

B

bāligh—see *ʿāqil.*

bāṭini—esoteric, hidden or inner meaning of Allah's word in the Qurʾān.

bayān—rhetoric as a discipline of study.

Bayān (The)—*Expositor,* principal source of doctrine of the Bahāʾi sect.

Bayt al-Lāh—"House of God."

bidʿa—"innovation," heresy, extra legal interpretations of Sharʿī law when *ijtihād* technically ceased.

birr—"beneficence".

"Bism ʾl-Lāhi allahu akbar"—"In the name of God; God is great."

Büyük Bayram—Turkish term for *ʿĪd al-Aḍḥa.*

D

dāʿi—a missionary of the esoteric sects of Islam—Assassins, Druze, Ismāʿīli.

dā'i al-du'āt—grand master of the order of Assassins, literally "missionary-in-chief."

Dā'i al-Kabīr—title granted the head of the order of Assassins.

Dār al-Ḥadīth—Seminary for the study of the corpus of Traditions.

dār al-harb—territory outside the boundaries of Islam where wars of jihād were permissible.

dār al-Islām—lands of Islam where technically no war was permissible.

Dār al-'Ilm—school for the study of the "religious sciences."

darwīsh (dervish)—initiate of a Ṣūfi order.

dhimmis—see *ahl al-dhimmah* (above).

dhu-'l-Ḥijjah—Muslim month when the formal pilgrimage to Mecca is staged.

dīn—term applied to the sum total of a Muslim's faith.

dīyah—"blood money," compensation for spilled blood to avoid retaliation in kind.

du'ā'—"invocation," or supplication.

E

El—head of the pantheon among early Semites, particularly Canaanites and Hebrews.

F

fanā'—Ṣūfi "passing away in God," the mystical union of the soul with God.

faqīh—Islamic jurist.

faqīr (fakir)—a poor man, one in need; also a member of a Ṣūfi order, a dervish.

farḍ—canonically imposed duty or obligation of faith.

"Fātiḥah"—opening chapter of the Qur'ān.

fatwa—an opinion of a mufti on an issue of canonical law.

fidā'i—"self-sacrificer," he who did the killing for the Assassins.

fidya—expiatory alm rendered in compensation for a missed canonical obligation.

fi sabīl-'l-Lāh—"for the sake of Allah": a good deed to be counted on Judgment Day.

Fiqh—the corpus of Islamic jurisprudence.

fuqahā'—plural of *faqīh* (above).

fuqarā'—singular of *faqīr*.

fuṭūr—the meal which breaks the period of the fast, usually at sunset. Cf. *suḥūr*.

G

Ghulāh—extremist Shī'ite who believes Allah mistakenly chosen Muḥammad for the prophetic role which He intended for 'Ali.

Ghusl—full ablution ceremony involving the entire body.

H

ḥadath—a type of defilement which would invalidate the ritual prayer.

ḥadīth—"sayings" of Muḥammad.

Ḥadīth—corpus of the sayings of Muḥammad, the man.

ḥāfiẓ—he who has committed to memory the verses of the Qur'ān.

ḥājib—term applied to the chamberlain; official position under 'Abbāsids.

Ḥājj—one who has performed the pilgrimage to Mecca.

ḥajj—formal pilgrimage, usually in dhu-'l-Ḥijjah between the 7th and 10th of the month.

ḥalaqah—a "circle" of students or disciples of a given teacher or "master."

ḥanīf—title by which pre-Islamic monotheists were known.
ḥarām—canonically forbidden.
ḥaram—hallowed area, especially around the monuments of Mecca.
Ḥashīsh—Arabic for opium; term from which "assassin" derives.
ḥuffāẓ—plural of *ḥāfiẓ*.
ḥujjah—those who propagandize for the Ismāʿīli doctrines.
ḥulūl—Ṣūfi term for the stage of "indwelling with God" after *fanāʾ* takes place.

I

ʿibādāt—acts of worship necessary for the discharge of the devotional rites of Islam.
Ibāḍis—sect of Islam, stemmed from moderate elements among the *Khawārij*.
Iblīs—the Devil.
ʿĪd al-Aḍḥa—feast of sacrifice on the 10th of dhu-'l-Ḥijjah commemorating the ritual started by Abraham.
ʿĪd al-Fiṭr—major feast heralding the end of the month of Fast (Ramaḍān).
ʿĪd al-Qurbān—same as *ʿĪd al-Aḍḥa*.
ifāḍah—quick march to Mina after the *wuqūf* at Muzdalifah on the ninth day of pilgrimage.
iḥsān—"right-doing" or proper conduct, a moral duty enjoined by Islam.
ijāzah—permission granted by the master to the disciple to repeat his discourses elsewhere.
iʿjāz al-Qurʾān—"miraculousness of the Qurʾān," argument for it not being created in time.
Ijmāʿ—principle in jurisprudence of legislating by consensus of those in the community who knew Islamic dogma.
Ijtihād—individual interpretation of the tenets of the faith, a principal of jurisprudence.
Ikhwān al-Ṣafāʾ—Brethren of Purity, Ismāʿīli society that flourished in Medieval Islam.
Il—pre-Islamic title of head of pagan pantheism.
Ilāh—see *al-Ilāh*.
Imām—spiritual guide of the Shīʿite sect.
imām—head of the community and/or leader in the congregational prayer among Sunnis.
imām khaṭīb—the person who delivers the *khuṭbah* (see below) at the Friday noon prayer.
īmān—beliefs, i.e. of the religion, or faith.
Injīl—Gospel.
in shāʾ-al-Lāh—"God willing."
iqāma—call to prayer repeated at the beginning of the prayer ritual.
ʿirḍ—"honor."
ʿishāʾ—"evening meal," time of the fourth ritual prayer of the day.
Islam—literally "submission," i.e. to Allah.
isnād—the chain of transmitting *ḥadīth*.
istiḥsān—deducing a legalistic principle on the basis of prudence.
istiṣlāḥ—principle of jurisprudence whereby a legal principle may result from considering the welfare of the Islamic community at large.
iʿtazala—"to secede"; see *Muʿtazilah*.
Ithna ʿAsharīyah—"Twelvers," title of the principal Shīʿite sect who believe in the twelve Imāms.
iʿtidāl—"erect posture," first and third steps in the ritual prayer.
izār—seamless white cloth wrapped around loins to knee level by the pilgrim performing the ḥajj.

J

Jahannam—Hell.
Jāhilīyah—"Times of Ignorance,"

Arabia before it received the revelations of Allah.

jāʾiz—canonically permissible deed.

jāmiʿ—"mosque," Muslim house of worship.

Jamʿīyat al-Daʿwa wa'l-Irshād—"Society for Propagation and Guidance."

janābah—great defilement necessitating the *ghusl* before the ritual prayer is to be rendered.

jihād—striving on behalf of the faith, known also as the "holy war."

jinn—"spirits," two types: evil and helpful.

jiwār—protection granted an outsider in pre-Islamic Arabia usually the result of dwelling in the ḥaram of a sanctuary.

Jizyah—tribute tax paid by non-Muslims enjoying the protection of the Muslims.

julūs—"sitting on base of heels," sixth and eighth steps in the ritual prayer.

K

kabīrah—major unpardonable sin.

kāfir—term for infidel, non-believer.

kalām—Muslim dialectics.

khalīfah—"caliph," successor to Muḥammad's secular authority.

khalwah—secluded place where the Druze sect holds its religious meetings.

khātimah—the seal, end or last, i.e. Muḥammad's prophethood.

Khawārij—first puritanical albeit militant sect of Islam.

khīrqah—special robe of investiture for an initiate of a Ṣūfi order.

khiṭbah—declaration of intent on marriage.

khuṭbah—sermon delivered by the imām in the mosque to the congregation, usually at the Friday congregation.

khuṭbat al-naʿt—an eulogy sermon following a fixed formula.

khuṭbat al-waʿẓ—sermon oriented towards pious exhortations.

kiswa—vesture covering the Kaʿbah, draped annually, presented in recent times by the sovereign of Egypt.

kuttāb (*kātib*) *al-sirr*—scribe-confidents, official positions in the Islamic administration under the ʿAbbāsids.

kuffār—plural of *kāfir*.

kursi—chair, in reference also to Allah's throne in Heaven.

L

"la ilāha illa al-Lāh"—"there is no god but God," first part of *Shahādah*.

lawḥ maḥfūz—tablet upon which the Qurʾān is preserved in the Seventh Heaven.

lughah— language.

M

madhāhib—plural of *madhhab*.

madhhab—juridical rite to which a Sunni Muslim may adhere.

Madīnah—Medina, second holiest city in Islam.

Madīnat al-Rasūl—"City of the Prophet" or Medina.

madrasah—originally school of canon law.

maghrib—"sunset."

Maghrib—West North Africa.

maḥmal—planquin, used to bear the kiswa annually at pilgrimage time to the Kaʿbah.

mahr—form of dowry, a normal condition involved in a contract of marriage.

makrūh—canonically frowned upon deed.

malāʾikah—"angels."

Manār—*Lighthouse,* official publication of the Salafīyah.
manāsik al-ḥajj—full ceremony of performing the pilgrimage.
mandūb—recommended not imposed act of faith.
Maqām Ibrāhīm—A monument in Mecca consisting of a sacred stone on which Abraham allegedly stood while building the Kaᶜbah.
maqṣūrah—enclosure inside the mosque for prayer out of sight.
maᶜrifah—Ṣūfi "knowledge of the Creator": gnosis.
Masjid al-Ḥarām—sacred mosque inside the ḥaram near the Kaᶜbah in Mecca.
maṣlaḥah—concept of "public good" or "general welfare."
maṭāf—ellipsoidal roadway surrounding the Kaᶜbah on which the pilgrim circumambulates the Kaᶜbah.
Matāwilah—title by which the Shīᶜites of Lebanon are known.
mathal—"example," theologically: parable.
Mathnawī—also *Masnavi,* title of al-Rūmi's classical composition of Ṣūfi poetry.
mawāli—"clients": converts to Islam dependents of Muslim Arab aristocracy under Umayyads.
mawāqit—see *mīqāt* (below).
Mawlid—Muḥammad's birthday, occasion of feasting.
maẓālims—legal category of "wrongs."
Miḥna—inquisition set up by the caliph al-Maᶜmūn to enforce Muᶜtazilite views on doctrine.
miḥrāb—niche in the mosque pointing to the direction of Mecca.
mīqāt—prescribed station on the approach to Mecca for performing preliminary rites in preparation for rendering the pilgrimage.
Miᶜrāj—Muḥammad's nocturnal journey to the Seventh Heaven.
mubāḥ—see *jā'iz* (above).
mufti—juriconsult, interpreter of Islamic law among Sunnis.
Muhājirūn—"Emigrants," i.e. those who went to Medina from Mecca with Muḥammad.
mujāhid—he who exerts himself on behalf of the faith, particularly in a jihād.
mujāhidūn—plural of *mujāhid.*
mujtahid—religious spokesman and interpreter of dogma of the Shīᶜite sect.
mujtahīdun—plural of *mujtahid.*
mulk—dominion, territorial possession, symbol of secular power.
Munāfiqūn—Hypocrites, a Medinan party tolerated by Muḥammad.
Muntaẓar—awaited Imām of the Shīᶜites.
murū'ah—pre-Islamic Arab concept of "manliness."
musaḥḥir—determiner of the time to begin the fast at dawn. Cf. *muwaqqit.*
muslim—"one who submits."
Muslim—He who officially adheres to the faith of Islam.
mustaḥabb—see *mandūb* (above).
mutᶜah—contracting temporary marriages, sanctioned by the Shīᶜites.
Muᶜtazilah—Important school of rationalists of the ninth century championing "free will."
Muwaḥḥidūn—plural of *Muwaḥḥid:* a Unitarian.
muwaqqit—"time setter," reminds the faithful in Ramaḍān when to start the fast.

N

nabi—"prophet."
nadhīr—"warner."
nafs—ego, soul, the "universal soul" to the Ismāᶜīlis.
naḥw—science of grammar, specifically syntax.

*na*ʿ*l*—piece of leather sole strapped to bottom of feet by the pilgrim performing the ḥajj.

Naṣārah—Christians.

niṣāb—minimum value set on products of the soil for determining the amount of the poor-due.

niyah—declared number of "bowings" in prayer by which validity is determined.

Q

*qara*ʾ—"to read," "to recite" verbal root of Qurʾān.

qibla—direction of prayer in Islam, i.e. Mecca.

Qiyās—principle of jurisprudence, derived by use of analogical deduction.

*Qur*ʾ*ān*—the "Bible" of Islam.

Quṭb—"Pole of the World" to the Ṣūfis, or the top-ranking saint of the hierarchy.

*qu*ʿ*ūd*—same as *julūs*.

R

raḥmah—"mercy."

Raḥmān—"Most Merciful," an attribute of God.

*rak*ʿ*āt*—plural of *rak*ʿ*ah,* each stands for a full prayer cycle.

rasūl—"messenger."

ra'y—personal opinion or judgment exercised by the jurist in deriving a principle enjoying legal sanctity.

razzia—term for "foray" or "raid" from Arabic *ghaza.*

ribāṭ—Ṣūfi monastery.

*ridā*ʾ—seamless white cloth draped around the shoulder by the pilgrim performing the ḥajj.

Risālat al-Tawḥīd—"The Epistle on the Unity of God," title of ʿAbduh's important work.

rūḥ—"spirit."

rūḥ al-qudus—"holy spirit."

*rukū*ʿ—kneeling in obeisance during ritual prayer.

S

sabbiḥ—"praise!" i.e. the Lord, God!

ṣadaqah—voluntary non-statutory alm rendered for the sake of acquiring merit with Allah.

sadd bāb al-ijtihād "closing the gate of ijtihād" or ending personal exertion in the interpretation of doctrine.

*ṣaghā*ʾ*ir*—minor sins which can be expiated.

Ṣaḥīḥ—"Verified," i.e. *ḥadīth;* title of Bukhāri's compilation of traditions.

ṣaḥn—great open space or courtyard of the mosque.

*saj*ʿ—rhymed prose.

sakīnah—calm, tranquillity: result of the mystic beholding the Creator.

Salafīyah—"Reformed Traditionists," a "modernist" movement started in Egypt in this century.

ṣalla-'l-Lāhu ʿ*ala Sayyidina Muḥammad*—"May Allah cause His prayers [to descend] on our lord Muḥammad," intercession for him in the ritual prayer.

ṣalāh—ritual prayer, ordained five times a day.

*Ṣalāt al-*ʿ*Īd*—formal prayer at termination of the month of fasting.

*ṣalat al-jum*ʿ*ah*—Friday noon prayer performed usually in congregation.

Sanat al-Wufūd—"Year of the Delegations" in 631 when representatives from all of Arabia came to Mecca and pledged allegiance to Islam and Muḥammad.

Ṣawm—legal fast, basic prerequisite of the faith.

Shahādah—the process of reciting

the testimonial which initiates one into Islam.

shahīd—someone killed fighting for the faith.

shāʿir—literally "he who senses," term applied to "poet."

Sharʿī—pertaining to *Sharīʿah.*

Sharīʿah—Fundamental Law of Islam: its "constitution."

Shawwāl—tenth month of the Muslim calendar, follows Ramaḍān.

shaykh—same as "sheik," or chief, head, leader of a tribe or Ṣūfi order.

Shaykh al-Islām—chief official spokesman for Islam, formal office in the administration of the Ottoman Turks.

Shayṭān—"Satan."

Shīʿat ʿAli—"partisans of ʿAli," fourth caliph, who formed a distinct sect (Shīʿite).

shiʿr—"poetry."

shirk—associating other deities or "partners" with the worship of Allah.

shuhadāʾ—plural of *shahīd.*

shuʿūbīyah—form of "ethnic nationalism."

ṣubḥ—morning time.

Ṣūfism—title by which Islamic mysticism is known.

suḥūr—meal at dawn at start of period of fast. Cf. *fuṭūr.*

ṣujūd—"prostration," high point of ritual prayer.

sulṭān—literally: "possessor of ultimate authority," official title of Turkic heads of dynasties.

sunnah—conduct of Muḥammad as a man.

Sunnah—corpus of the Traditions.

sūq—market place, center of trading and social gatherings.

Sūrah—chapter heading of the Qurʾān.

T

Tābiʿ—see *al-Tābiʿūn.*

tafsīr—exegesis, i.e. of Qurʾān.

taḥallul al-ṣaghīr—state of partial desanctification begun by pilgrim after ʿĪd al-Aḍḥa.

ṭahārah—state of ritualistic purity.

takbīr—"magnification," i.e., of Allah, in prayer.

takbīr al-iḥrām—stage in the ritual prayer when its highest point of sanctity is achieved.

tanzīl—process of "sending down" the revelations of the Qurʾān from heaven.

taqīyah—"dissimulation," formally sanctioned by Shīʿism.

tāqlīd—"imitation" of precedents established by the ulema.

ṭarīqah—path followed by the Ṣūfis to achieve gnosis.

tāslīm—reciting the formula "May peace and the mercy of God be with you!"

ṭawāf—process of circumambulating the Kaʿbah during pilgrimage time.

ṭawāf al-ifāḍah—circumambulation of the Kaʿbah, last act heralding the end of the pilgrimage.

tawḥīd—in mystical terms: unity with God; in orthodox terms: proclaiming the unity of God.

Tawrāt—Torah.

tazakka—purifying the self spiritually, absolving oneself in the eyes of God.

taʿziyah—"consolation" procession, staged annually by Shīʿites in commemoration of the death of Ḥusayn, the Prophet's grandson.

tekke—place where Ṣūfi orders, like the Bektāshis, held their *dhikr.*

U

ʿUlamāʾ—English "ulema" plural of *ʿālim;* refers to collective body of those knowledgeable in Islamic beliefs and dogma.

ʿUmra—lesser pilgrimage.

ʿUqqāl—collective body of Druze leaders having access to the sect's secrets, i.e. doctrines.

ʿushr—the fixed amount of the legal tithe (*zakāh*), literally "one-tenth."

W

"wa anna Muḥammadan rasūlu 'l-Lāh"—"and that Muhammad is the messenger of God"—second part of the *Shahādah.*

wājib—see *farḍ* (above).

waqf—"mortmain."

wuḍūʾ—limited ablution in preparation for prayer.

wuqūf—"station before Allah," most important phase of the pilgrimage ceremony, held on the ninth day.

Y

Yawm al-Dīn—"Day of Judgment."

Yawm al-Qiyāmah—"Day of Resurrection."

Yhwh—Semitic prototype for "Jehovah," God of Kenite tribe of Sinai adopted by Moses.

Z

ẓāhir—apparent or literal meaning of Qurʾān as opposed to the *bāṭini.*

ẓuhr—noon, time for the third ritual prayer of the day.

zakāh—statutory alms of a portion of worldly possessions in expiation of what a Muslim retains.

zakāt al-fiṭr—statutory alms offered on the day ending the month of fasting.

Recommended Reading

The following is a useful list of important titles dealing with the various subjects treated available in the English and other Western languages:

1. Jāhilīyah Arabia

Lammens, Henri. *Le Berceau de l'Islam, L'Arabie occidentale à la veille de l'Hegire*. Rome, 1914. Classical study of Arabia on eve of Islam.

———. *La Mecque à la veille de l'Hegire*. Beyrouth, 1924. Valuable reference for knowledge of Mecca and society at birth of Islam.

O'Leary, D. L. *Arabia before Muḥammad*. London, 1927. Compact but scholarly study of the peninsula and its pre-Islamic values.

Philby, H. St. J. B. *The Background of Islam*. Alexandria, 1947. Useful study by an expert on Arabia.

Smith, W. R. *The Religion of the Semites*. 3rd ed. London, 1927; Meridian, 1956, 1957, 1959. Classical study of the religious beliefs of the Semites in and out of Arabia.

2. The Range of Islam

Ali, Syed Ameer. *The Spirit of Islam*. London, 1922, 1923, 1935, 1946, 1949, 1952, . . . A penetrating Muslim modernist's treatment of Islam as a socio-religious force.

Arnold, Sir Thomas. *The Preaching of Islam*. London, 1896, 1913, 1930; Lahore, n.d. A classical study on the spread of Islam.

———, and Guillaume, Alfred (ed.). *The Legacy of Islam*. Oxford University Press, 1942, 1944, 1945, 1947, 1949, 1952, 1960. A series of authoritative articles on Islam as a socio-religious and cultural force.

ʿAzzām, A. R. *The Eternal Message of Muḥammad*. Translated by Caesar E. Farah. New York, 1964. A Muslim's view of Islam in the modern world, challenging and illuminating.

Gibb, Sir H. A. R. *Mohammedanism*. Oxford University Press, 1949. 1950; 2nd ed. 1953; Galaxy Book, 1962. Penetrating study of Islam.

Guillaume, Alfred. *Islam*. 2nd ed. reprint. Pelican Book, 1961. A useful general study of Islam.

Hodgson, Marshall, *The Venture of Islam*. 3 vols. Chicago: University Press, 1974. Sweeping integral treatment of historical Islam.

Jeffery, Arthur. *Islam: Muḥammad and His Religion*. New York,

1958. A study of Islam from original sources translated and cited.

Williams, John A. (ed.). *Islam*. New York, 1961; paper ed. 1963. A handy compact study based on translations from original sources.

3. Life of Muḥammad

Andrae, Tor. *Mohammed the man and his Faith*. Translated by Theoophil Menzel. Harper Torchbook, 1960. A brilliant exposé of Muḥammad's life and doctrine.

Buhl, Frants. *Das Leben Mohammeds*. Translated by H. H. Schaeder. Berlin, 1930. Standard Western study of Muḥammad's life and work.

Ibn-Hishām. *The Life of Muḥammad*. Translated by Alfred Guillaume. Oxford University Press, 1955. The standard original account with useful notes.

Muir, Sir William. *The Life of Mohammad*. Rev. ed. Edinburgh, 1923. Detailed and thorough, from original sources.

Watt, W. Montgomery. *Muḥammad Prophet and Statesman*. Oxford University Press Paperbacks, 1964. Short useful account of life and career of Muḥammad.

4. The Qur'ān

Arberry, A. J. *The Holy Koran*. London, 1953. Contains helpful introductory material.

Bell, Richard. *Introduction to the Qur'ān*. Edinburgh University Press, 1963. Useful reference on study of Qur'ān as a literary work.

———. *The Qur'ān*. 2 vols. Edinburgh, 1937-39. One of the best translations, attempts a critical arrangement.

Blachère, R. *Introduction au Coran*. Paris, 1947. Standard on history of Qur'ān.

Jeffery, Arthur. *Materials for the History of the Text of the Koran*. Leyden, 1937. Handy for a critical study of the Qur'ān.

Nöldeke, Th. *Geschichte des Qorāns*. 2nd ed., 3 vols., 1961 reprint. Leipzig, 1909-38. Classical study of Qur'ān.

———. *Remarques critiques sur le style et la syntaxe du Coran*. Translated by G. H. Bousquet. Paris, 1953. Excellent study on composition and style of the Qur'ān.

Pickthall, M. M. *The Meaning of the Glorious Koran*. Mentor Religious Classic, 10th printing 1963. Eloquent, true to spirit and meaning of the Arabic.

Sell, Edward. *The Historical Development of the Qur'ān*. London, 1909. Old but still useful for understanding the background.

Stanton, H. U. W. *The Teaching of the Qur'ān*. London, 1919. Summarizes the essence of Qur'ānic doctrine.

Tisdall, W. St. Clair. *The Original Sources of the Qur'ān*. London, 1911. Opinionated but helpful for understanding Qur'ānic derivations.

5. Islamic Doctrine

Ali, M. Muḥammad. *A Manual of Ḥadīth*. Lahore, n.d. A selection of Traditions translated from the Arabic of al-Bukhāri annotated.

Bokhari. *Les Traditions Islamiques*. Translated by O. Houdas and W. Marçais. 4 vols. Paris, 1903-14. Ultimate recourse for the verified *Ḥadīth*.

Gardet, Louis and Anawati, M. M. *Introduction à la théologie musul-*

mane. Paris, 1948. Discusses the evolution of theology from a Thomiste point of view.

Goldziher, Ignaz. *Le dogme et la loi de l'Islam*. Paris, 1958. Classical treatment of doctrine, law and theology in Islam.

———. *Muhammedanische Studien*. Vol. II. Halle, 1890, 1961. Excellent source of study on Ḥadīth.

Guillaume, Alfred. *The Traditions of Islam*. Oxford, 1924. Useful study based in part on Goldziher's work.

Macdonald, Duncan B. *Development of Muslim Theology, Jurisprudence and Constitutional Theory*. 1903 reprint. New York. Standard work in English on the subject.

Margoliouth, D. S. *The Early Development of Mohammedanism*. London, 1914. Helpful study of the formulation of Islamic doctrine.

Tritton, A. S. *Muslim Theology*. London, 1947. Useful reference to various aspects of doctrinal development.

Wensinck, A. J. *The Muslim Creed*. Cambridge, 1932. Critical study of the rise of the orthodox view.

6. Institutions and Practices

Arnold, Sir T. W. *The Caliphate*. Oxford, 1924. Still the best on relating the development of the caliphate.

Calverley, E. E. *Worship in Islam*. Madras, 1925. Excellent exposé of the articles of faith.

Fyzee, A. A. A. *Outlines of Muhammadan Law*. London, 1949. Useful introduction to the development of canonical law.

Gaudefroy-Demombynes, Maurcie. *Muslim Institutions*. Translated by J. P. Macgregor. London, 1954. Relates principal institutions of Islam from original sources.

Gautier, Émile F. *Moeurs et coutumes des musulmans*. Paris, 1955. Useful study of Muslim customs.

Jeffery, Arthur (ed.). *A Reader on Islam*. The Hague, 1962. Substantial study from original sources illustrating beliefs and practices.

Lammens, Henri. *Islam: Beliefs and Institutions*. Translated by Sir E. Denison Ross. London, 1929. Indispensable source of reference.

Lane, E. W. *The Manners and Customs of the Modern Egyptians*. London, Everyman's, 1954. Illustrated first-hand observation of Muslim institutions in practice.

Levy, Ruben. *An Introduction to the Sociology of Islam*. 2 vols. London, 1933. Standard for sociological development of Muslim institutions.

Schacht, Joseph. *An Introduction to Islamic Law*. Oxford, 1964. The standard reference.

Tritton, A. S. *Islam: Belief and Practices*. London, New York, 1951, 1957. Practical and helpful.

von Grunebaum, Gustav. *Muhammadan Festivals*. New York, 1951. Comprehensive on the subject.

7. Formalism and Intellectualism

Abdouh, Mohammed. *Rissalat al tawhid, Exposé de la religion musulmane*. Translated by B. Michel and M. Abdel Razik. Paris, 1952. Classical treatise on true Islam by an outstanding modernist.

de Boer, T. J. *The History of Phi-*

losophy in Islam. London, 1933. Valuable brief account.

de Vaux, B. Carra. *Les Penseurs de l'Islam.* 5 vols. Paris, 1921-26. Invaluable source of reference for Muslim thinkers of different schools.

Donaldson, D. M. *Studies in Muslim Ethics.* London, 1950. Standard work on the subject.

Makdisi, George, "Ashʿari and the Ashʿarites in Islamic Religious History," in *Studia Islamica,* Vols. XVII (1962), pp. 37–80 and XVIII (1963), pp. 19–40.

Watt, W. M. *Free Will and Predestination in Early Islam.* London 1948. Excellent study, valuable reference.

———. *Islamic Philosophy and Theology.* Edinburgh University Press, 1962. Comprehensive, useful.

———. *Muslim Intellectual: A Study of Al-Ghazali.* Edinburgh 1963. Most informative and intriguing study of the man and his environment.

8. The Sects and Religious Life

Abd-el-Jalil, J. M. *Aspects interieurs de l'Islam.* 2nd ed. Paris, 1952. Valuable insight by one who knows Islam.

Bousquet, G. H. *Les grandes pratiques rituelles de l'Islam.* Paris, 1949. Cultic practices, including the mystical approach.

Donaldson, D. M. *The Shīʿite Religion.* London, 1942. Thorough but not critical.

Hitti, P. K. *The Origins of the Druze People and Religion.* Columbia University Press, 1928. Beirut, 1964. Authoritative and revealing.

Hodgson, Marshall G. (Translator). *The Order of the Assassins.* The Hague, 1955. Collection of translations of various authors; most complete on the subject.

Lewis, B. *The Origins of Ismāʿīlism.* Cambridge, 1940. A basic work on this important sect.

Macdonald, D. B. *The Religious Attitude and Life in Islam.* Chicago, 1912. Excellent insight into Islam at work.

al-Tabataba'i, M. Husayn, *Shīʿite Islam.* Trsl. Seyyed Hossein Nasr. State University of New York Press, 1977.

9. Mysticism

Affifi, A. E. *The Mystical Philosophy of Muhyid Din ibnul-Arabi.* Cambridge, 1939, 1964. Courageous attempt to reduce a difficult subject to order.

Arberry, A. J. *Sufism.* London, 1950. Recommended reading for a brief account with translated samples.

Birge, J. K. *The Bektashi Order of Dervishes.* London, 1937. Detailed full treatment of the order, history and doctrine.

Brown, J. P. *The Darwishes or Oriental Spiritualism.* Ed. H. A. Rose. Oxford, 1927. Useful reference for Ṣūfi organization and observances.

Dermenghem, Émile. *Vies des saints musulmans.* Paris, 1942. Special study of beatified leaders of the Ṣūfi orders.

Massignon, Louis. *Al-Hallaj, Martyr mystique de l'Islam.* 2 vols. Paris, 1922. Definitive work on the founder of Ṣūfi theology.

———. *Essai sur les origines de lexique technique de la mystique musulmane.* Paris, 1922, 1954. Ultimate recourse for Study of Ṣūfi origins.

Nicholson, R. A. *The Mystics of Islam.* London, 1914, 1963 reprint. Best single study on the subject.

Smith, Margaret. *Readings from the Mystics of Islam.* London, 1950. Excellent selections fully illustrative of the subject.

Watt, W. M. *The Faith and Practice of al-Ghazali.* Oxford, 1952. Insight into a leading theologian's attitude towards his faith.

10. Relation to Christianity and Judaism

Andrae, Tor. *Der Ursprung des Islams und das Christentum.* Uppsala, 1926. Authoritative study on common origins of Islam and Christianity.

Bell, R. *The Origin of Islam in Its Christian Environment.* London, 1926. Relates the impact of Syrian Christianity on Muḥammad.

Cragg, Kenneth. *The Call of the Minaret.* New York, Oxford, 1956. Interesting study in contrast between Christianity and Islam.

Katsh, Abraham I. *Judaism in Islam.* New York, 1954. Biblical and Talmudic backgrounds in Sūrahas 2 and 3 of the Qurʾān.

Rosenthal, Erwin I. J. *Judaism and Islam.* London, New York, 1961. Attempt to show Islam's dependence on Judaism.

Sweetman, J. W. *Islam and Christian Theology.* 3 vols. London, 1945-55. Useful but necessitates caution, contains much information on the sects.

Weil, Gustav. *The Bible, the Koran and the Talmud.* New York, 1863. Dated but still valuable as a study in comparison.

11. Islam in the Modern World

Adams, C. C. *Islam and Modernism in Egypt.* London, 1933. Authoritative study of Afghāni, ʿAbduh and the Salafīyah.

Allen, H. E. *The Turkish Transformation.* Chicago, 1935. Impact of modernism on Islamic tradition in Turkey.

Amīn, ʿUthmān. *Muḥammad ʿAbduh.* Translated by Charles Wendell. Washington, D.C., 1953. Important work on a significant element in Islamic modernism.

Anderson, J. N. D. "Recent Developments in Sharīʿa Law." Nine articles in *The Muslim World.* October 1950 to 1952. Standard reference for transformations in Sharīʿah laws.

Arberry, A. J. and Landau, R. (eds.). *Islam Today.* London, 1943. Series of articles on Islam in recent times.

Bousquet, G. H. *L'Islam maghrebien.* Paris, 1943, 1955. Revealing study of Islam in West North Africa.

Fisher, Humphrey J. *Aḥmadiyyah.* Oxford, 1963. Most comprehensive to date, slanted to the movement in Africa.

Gibb, H. A. R. *Modern Trends in Islam.* Chicago, 1947. Penetrating speculative study, critical and valuable.

———. *Whither Islam?* London, 1932. Treats Islamic trends in North Africa, Egypt, India and Indonesia.

Gouilly, Alphonse. *L'Islam dans l'Afrique occidentale française.* Paris, 1952. Commendable source of reference for Islam in West Africa.

Hartmann, R. *Die Krisis des Islam.* Leipzig, 1928. Critical study of Islam's confrontations in the modern world.

Hitti, P. K. *Islam and the West.* Princeton, Anvil, 1962. Fascinating expertly presented study of foci of contact.

Hurgronje, C. Snouck. *The Achehnese*. 2 vols. Leyden, 1906. Definitive study of Islam as a socio-religious force in Indonesia.

I-fan, Yang. *Islam in China*. Hong Kong, 1957. Brief but most revealing.

Iqbal, Muḥammad. *The Reconstruction of Religious Thought in Islam*. 2nd ed. London, 1934. Penetrating attempt at a modern rethinking of Islam.

Lincoln, C. Eric. *The Black Muslims in America*. Boston, 1962. Attempt at objective study of a movement in flux.

Lomax, Louis E. *When the Word Is Given . . .* New York, 1963. Emotional, penetrating and revealing study of the "Black Muslims."

Miller, W. M. *Bahaism, Its Origin, History, Teachings*. New York, 1931. Useful one volume reference.

Monteil, Vincent. *Essai sur l'Islam en U.R.S.S.*, volume for 1952, *Revue des Études Islamiques*. Paris, 1953. Factual, objective and commendable.

Rondot, Pierre. *L'Islam et les musulmans d'aujourd'hui*. 2 vols. Paris, 1958-60. Critical and penetrating.

Roux, Jean-Paul. *L'Islam en Asie*. Paris, 1958. Compact useful study of Islam in most countries of Asia.

Smith, Wilfred Cantwell. *Islam in Modern History*. Princeton, 1957; Mentor, 1959, 1961, 1963. Challenging controversial study of Islam in the state of flux.

le Tourneau, R. *L'Islam contemporain*. Paris, 1950. Lucid exposé of Islam today.

Trimingham, J. S. *A History of Islam in West Africa*. Oxford, 1962. Valuable source of data, an updated study.

Wilson, S. G. *Modern Movements among Moslems*. New York, 1916. Outdated but valuable to the historian.

12. References

The Encyclopaedia of Islam. 4 vols. Leyden, 1913-1938; new edition in preparation. A must for those interested in all aspects of Islam.

The Shorter Encyclopaedia of Islam. Leyden, 1953, Cornell reprint. Emphasis on religion and canonical law.

Hitti, Philip K. *History of the Arabs*. 7th ed. London, 1960. The best reference on the historical development of Islam.

Hodgson, Marshall, *The Venture of Islam*. 3 vols. Chicago: University Press, 1974. Sweeping integral treatment of historical Islam.

Hughes, T. P. *A Dictionary of Islam*. London, 1885, 1935. Useful reference though somewhat outdated.

INDEX